MW01052058

Line Screw

Line Screw

My Twelve Riotous Years Working Behind Bars
In Some of Canada's Toughest Jails

An Unrepentant Memoir
by
J. Michael Yates

M&S

Canadian Cataloguing in Publication Data

Yates, J. Michael, 1938-
Line Screw: my twelve riotous years working behind bars in some of Canada's toughest jails

ISBN 0-7710-9082-X

1. Yates, J. Michael, 1938-   . 2. Prisons – British Columbia. 3. Prisons – British Columbia – Officials and employees – Biography. I. Title.

HV9509.B7Y38 1993   365′.92   C93-094186-1

Parts of this book have appeared previously in *Books in Canada* and *The Cacanadadada Review*.

The publishers acknowledge the support of the Canada Council, the Ontario Arts Council, and the Ontario Ministry of Culture, Tourism and Recreation for their publishing program.

Typesetting by M&S, Toronto.

Printed and bound in Canada.
The paper used in this book is acid-free.

McClelland & Stewart Inc.
The Canadian Publishers
481 University Avenue
Toronto, Ontario
M5G 2E9

1 2 3 4 5   97 96 95 94 93

To the guards and inmates who gave me my most entertaining decade, and to the memory of two who knew when an inmate is a fellow human being and when a jail is a jail: John Chapman and Ted Colley. They died young.

Contents

The Line is an idea . . . one needs a special kind of vision to perceive The Line. . . . Death is hardly a "spice". It is the ultimate experience and common destiny of all living beings. To be in the shadow of death is to come as close as anyone alive can to the absolute unknown of the Beginning and the End. Death, whatever it may be, is the closing chord, the perfect balance, the quiescence of all scales, the final equilibrium of nature. Between it and life there is a short gap. . . . This is where The Line runs, at the edge of this final mystery. . . . The object is never death; it is only the price of admission. For those who would dice with God the stakes are high. The feeling doesn't come except in the presence of mortal danger.

– George Jonas, *A Passion Observed*

Preface

——————— • ———————

*The Line is comprised of those members of a system
who contiguate most directly with the **end user** of the
service which that system offers. Thus: **Line Police,
Line Nurses, Line Teachers, Line Corrections staff,
Line Firefighters.** These people are comparable
to the dogface, the soldier in the trench at the
front lines of a war.*
– Itzik Currach, *The Architecture of Management
Styles*

PRISON. There are numberless academic theories about why
people break the law and wind up in prison. Only one reality of
being there.

This book is about being there. It's written from the viewpoint of
one line officer – prison guard, *line screw* – whose perception of the
criminal justice system goes something like this: It is the business of
the courts to try, find, and sentence law-breakers. It is not the business of a prison or a prison guard consciously to inconvenience further those in custody. Like any institution, a prison has rules that
must be observed or, quite simply, the numerous people in this relatively confined space couldn't be fed and accommodated.

Let's get the hot questions out of the way at the outset. Whom
does a peace officer, a line screw, serve? He or she works more directly
for the law than the citizen upholder of the law.

The most powerful tool we have with which to enforce the law is

9

the law-abiding public. It is they on whom others model their behaviour and it is they who do not hesitate to report a breach of the law, or "raise the hue and cry," according to our British common law tradition. They keep the peace but are not formal "peace officers."

Under certain circumstances, in the event that someone declared to be dangerous to society is escaping custody, I am empowered to shoot the escapee. Can I find it within myself to shoot the escapee? Absolutely.

To maintain systems of management, operations, discipline, and security, would I use "as much force as necessary" to execute my duty? Let there be no doubt in your mind. The government hired me to do a job whose duties were clearly specified.

Would I obey a manifestly unlawful order from a superior officer to inflict corporal or other punishment on an inmate? No way. I like many cons, both those presently in tenure and those emeritus, but not so much that I want to wear their numbers and uniform. It is a very short trip from one side of the bars to the other via following a stupid order.

Once an inmate knows the parameters of my job and I have explained to him the parameters of his job, I wear one uniform and he wears another; I have an employee number and he has a correctional-services number. But we're both locked behind the same bars. All human beings together. We are the line.

You should immediately get rid of the notion that the line in a prison is part of a larger thing called prison, and that the prison is part of a larger thing called Corrections, and that Corrections is part of a larger thing called the Ministry, and that God is in Heaven and all's right with the world.

Anywhere there are walls full of files and computers everywhere you look, communication is bad to nil. Depend on it.

There is the line, and then there is the rest of the mess. Parts of the rest of the mess disagree with other parts, but there is nothing anyone on the line can do about it. They've tried since the beginning of the whole system of *doing time*. To no avail. Thus the elements of the line stick together – guards and inmates – more or less back-to-back against the rest of the mess.

This book is about the line. If the rest of the mess takes a few salvos along the way, that's a bonus.

Prison is tragic. But not serious. This, it seems, is not the popular view. However, it is mine, and its foundation is more than a decade of thinking, seeing, hearing, smelling, saying, and being prison. Also, I am a poet, and a significant part of a poet's job is to look at what passes for reality and point out fraud. It's been this way since the beginning of poetry.

I'm certainly not serious. I ceased teaching at universities because they were such serious places, and when I moved to broadcasting I found that it takes itself terribly seriously. I've also been a logger. Logging takes itself much too seriously.

To me, teaching in a university and being a line screw have the same value and status: no more or less than a way to pay the bills while a world turns in which poetry pays less than crime – and crime, supposedly, doesn't pay at all.

I went to work in prison because I was looking for a job that would engage my imagination while at work; that would pay the damn bills; and, very important, that did not cause me to take work home and interfere with my time for writing poetry.

I found that job in prison.

I remained because, as one who reveres the silly, I had found my comic context.

But aren't there violence and blood and non-God-fearing language in prisons? Certainly, and things even more unpleasant. But this in no way distinguishes life in prisons from what we see in daily life outside prisons, much less on television. Much less in war, in which state we have been for the entirety of my lifetime.

There is violence across the board in the human experience, which we seem to deny when viewing violence in our institutions. I don't expect to see violence vanish from the face of evolution. At the end of language, force waits – regardless of setting.

We forget much too easily that media people, corrections brass, and, quite simply, people have the same social problems as guards and inmates. Usually it is a matter of degree and of who gets caught. And, these days, how the information is packaged for the rest of society. Corrections has proved itself inept at informing the public, and yet it despises the impression the public has of what goes on in prisons.

What's tragic about being human is that we must make laws and then strive to observe them. And fail. Hence the birth of the prison where one *serves time*. It could be said that we all serve time anyway. It passes and it damn well doesn't serve us. Nonetheless, *doing time* is man's most humane antidote to man's "inhumanity to man." Having invoked Wordsworth, I now defer to an earlier and perhaps more potent authority: Dante.

Dante wrote not *The Divine Tragedy* but *The Divine Comedy*. It takes some life experience to understand the reasoning behind Dante's choice of title.

And, it takes considerable life experience to join the line in prison and emerge twelve years later having had a wonderful time.

ACKNOWLEDGEMENTS

For years, George Jonas has prodded me to write this book.

Officer Geordie Craig must wear the responsibility for the appearance of this book at this time and it does indeed look good on him, to use one of his favourite phrases. Others who should be "centred out," as we say in the trade, are the very Dutch Deformed Henk Van Staalduinen, Officer Laurel Wade, lately of the Laurel and Hardly show, Cracked Frank Boshard, and Machmellow Ouellette.

Ian Murdoch and Pat and Eileen Kernaghan gave me very important assistance and encouragement. In the home-stretch department, I must acknowledge the extremely effective Denise Bukowski, Diane Bergeron, who gave this project industrial-strength CPR, Dinah Forbes, my patient and good-humoured editor at M&S, and Sandra Payne, possibly the best organizational mind in the Squamolean empire.

Finally, I should like to thank Jack McClelland. In 1967, you were the only honest mind in the Windsor Hotel. If we "young turks" did anything of significance, it was because of your grounding us in literary/commerical reality.

If I have praised faintly such as Big Little Man, Lumpy, Swede with Swagger Stick, or Howdy Doody, I'm sure they will let me know.

DISCLAIMER

In order to avoid
Having my aging but still quite beautiful
Ass sued off,
I have falsified certain people, times, and places

1

What's a Nice Guard Like Me Doing in a Dirty Business Like Poetry?

———————————— • ————————————

All time to write is stolen time. There is nothing
in the landscape of living that does not
contravene time to write.
— Cesare Pavese

I BECAME a prison guard through a fluke: by simply driving
through Vancouver's Kitsilano district at three in the afternoon
and getting rear-ended. The woman responsible had never had a
ticket, was not drying her nails, and was not blinded by the sun, but
she hit me so hard that I was knocked unconscious and into an old
Mercedes ahead of me.

Following this little reminder that the random exists came intermittent blindness, migraines (I'd never believed in them before then),
severe pain to the whole left side of my body (a shrink told me not to
worry about the left side of my head since it is the rational side and of
no use to an artist anyway), extreme sound and light sensitivity, and
worst of all, loss of memory. Before the accident I could (and now
again can) describe the picture-frame hat, the pumps, and the colour
and pattern of my mother's dress the first time she took me fishing
with bacon-rind, string, a stick and safety-pin when I was three. After
the accident, I could tell you the year when *John the Baptist* was
painted but I couldn't tell you that the painter was Caravaggio. I had
to resign my position as British Columbia Head of Public Relations
and Promotion for the Canadian Broadcasting Corporation where I

had a huge office, two secretaries, an outrageous salary, and did little day after day.

Attempting to access my memory for purposes of writing was analogous to setting up to paint a landscape and then, at a critical moment, when the light is perfect, turning to find that all the most essential paints and brushes have vanished.

I had never been very fond of Hemingway, despite that his being a fisherman may have had something to do with my winding up a writer. As a kid, I kept seeing him in all the major magazines with fish he had caught and reasoned that anything you could do while fishing must be a good idea. I wasn't proud to be a writer the day the news remarked that he had fellated the business end of a 12-gauge. They had given him electro-shock for depression. It hammered his memory. He said: "I'm a novelist. Without my memory, I don't exist." And thus exited time. *Now* I was learning whereof Papa Ernie spoke.

I tried amazing schemes: I bought a huge drafting table, which I could tilt radically, and an odious orange recliner. Then using a C-clamp I suspended a blue IBM Selectric typewriter like a rat hanging by its tail, reclined the recliner, then eased into the cockpit. It was the only angle at which I could work without excruciating pain. When I rolled the paper into the platen, the page fell down over the keyboard. I never did come up with a way to solve that problem, and when I touched the keys they instantly forgot English. What appeared on the page was a hash of German and French with granules of Anglo-Saxon, Old Norse, and Old Irish. It was intelligible only to me. I tried to navigate in German only. It wasn't dreadful, but I couldn't translate it and haven't to this day – it was sufficiently bad not to bother.

Terrified to toss the monkey-wrench of suicide into the delicate machinery of family, I spent a large part of each day attempting to dream up a way to extinguish myself so that it would appear to be an accident.

Eventually acupuncture whacked the migraines and I've never had one since. This made me considerably more functional, but the other symptoms dogged me.

By 1981, my wife, Hortense, had had enough and said she just couldn't cope any longer with two pre-school girls and "a wounded animal." And that was that. She helped me find an apartment a couple of miles away and we translated me from nuclear father to apostate.

Gone the job. Gone the poetry. Between 1978 and 1984 I published nothing and wrote about the same amount. The writing community didn't know what the hell to do about me. It was easiest just to treat me as if dead. Only George Jonas and Rosalind MacPhee didn't give me up for dead. And one or two officers at Canada Council.

By 1981 I was sufficiently beyond the migraines to live without drugs. I had little more than a low-grade headache to deal with and complete mistrust of my memory and cognitive faculties. I lived in a fourth-floor apartment in North Vancouver with a balcony and a stupendous view of famed Dog Shit Park.

Togged out in white tennis shorts and shoes, and expensive V-necked sweater, Bob Yamamoto knocked on my door to inform me that Oakalla was hiring. I'd met Yamamoto and an ex-spy by the name of Kiley Lark years earlier. Lark had written a spy book while working graveyard shifts at Oakalla and they both swore it was the perfect job for a writer.

My only experience with the criminal justice system was in Colorado as a kid where the local bulls bum-rapped me and a friend and decided to keep us in jail overnight to scare the hell out of us. It turned me into a cop-hater for most of my youth, but the hatred had worn off. I was neutral toward the cops, and my notion of prison was the same as anyone else's who watches television: guards beat the hell out of people for a living, and inmates take guards hostage and riot and retaliate at every opportunity.

I had just applied for my permits in North and West Vancouver to drive a cab. I knew I could drive. But I feared that my brain wouldn't handle much more. Even the idea of a job as a guard was terrifying. There would be procedures to be remembered.

Yamamoto set me straight. It was a job, he said, which had a lot of satisfaction, paid decently, and offered time to write. He pointed out that my brain worked well enough to read and pay my rent and buy groceries.

I applied for the job.

By and by, they called me for an interview.

As I ran the possibility that I might get the job through my thoughts, I wondered whether there was something that might disqualify me. Bob had assured me I had all the prerequisites: self-defence (military, boxing, or martial arts), grade 12, and to be breathing. For self-defence, I had Reserve Officers Training Corps training, San Antonio Golden Gloves weight-class champ (needed one, had two. *Two outa three ain't bad*). I was big. I was demonstrably metabolic.

The idea of having time to write while getting paid for it had a very powerful appeal (never mind that I wasn't writing and rather suspected I never would again, certain habits of mind persist: being a writer is mostly a quest for time to write). On the other hand, I have never been an aficionado of pain, much less death. Getting smacked around wouldn't be nice. Getting dead wouldn't be nice. But, then again, Bob and the other guards I had met never seemed to be beaten up or especially tough.

What the hell did I know about prisons? What would I say in an interview? In a panic, I called Bob, who came right over. Bob mentioned that he had told Williams, the personnel officer, that I was a college graduate, which may have been a mistake. Williams had gone to work at Oakalla as an auxiliary security officer and couldn't hack it, so he went back to school, picked up a degree in one of the social sciences, and came back as an administrator. Bob said a senior correctional officer (S.C.O.) or higher and the personnel man would be conducting the interview. I was to tell them, in answer to why I sought to be a prison guard, that I was looking for work and felt myself suited to the position. He said they would begin throwing scenarios at me. What if I have an inmate running down toward Deer Lake and I am armed with a 12-gauge shotgun? Answer: First, I yell, "Stop!" Second, I fire a warning shot in the air. Third, I shoot at six o'clock low and pepper his legs. The birdshot hurts more being plucked out by the nurse than it does going in. If I'm armed with a .38 pistol, same deal, except that I bead in on one of his legs. Guards use bullets called wadcutters which go right through and come out the same size, if not stopped by bone. If they asked me what I would do if the con is a nickel-and-dimer running toward Royal Oak Street and I'm armed with a .38, I would not perform the fourth step, shooting at the leg, because it might carry and hit a passing automobile or a house on the other side of the street.

I drove the 1100 Yamaha up Royal Oak and punched in at the gate with the guard wearing a pistol and a radio, to go down to the Main Gaol (yes, spelled that way – and there were guys who had been there for eons who pronounced it "goal" when giving directions). Past the gate there was a fork in the asphalt. The left went toward Westgate A and B.

The Main Gaol, with its classic Auburn architecture sailing there on the crest of the ridge, gave off august, even heroic vibes to the eye. The Westgate complex exemplified in form how far the human spirit could fall. It bermed down the ridge like an accordion spilling when one hand has drunkenly let go.

"A-side" was the segregation unit – the digger, the hole, isolation, iso, and a dozen other monikers of prison lore – where those who had breached the *Correctional Centre Rules and Regulations* and had been found guilty in Warden's Court did time in isolation while they did their time. Here the protective-custody inmates were housed separate from the population inmates, in a kind of double social ostracism.

"B-side" was a sentenced unit (provincial: "deuce-less" – two years less a day). It had a maintenance area, a Tier Nine (where meals were served, movies were shown, and the "weight-pit" was located – recreation tier), and eleven tiers of cells.

The right-hand spur of pavement went, according to the sign, to the Main Gaol. Along the right fork, a shotgun tower. With the profile of a man in the window. In a uniform. With a shotgun. Could have been a movie set but there were no cameras, lights, façades, or action.

There was a button at the front gate and a uniform let me in and made me sign in a big ledger – like the guest-book at a historic site – then pointed me upstairs toward the personnel office.

It was late afternoon and the two men inside were obviously bagged from interviewing people like me all day. I knew from Bob's description the one in uniform was Mike Adler, a deputy director, by his blond curly hair. The other guy, Williams, was a little bristly, per-haps from not being the only university graduate in the room.

I handed him the application. The interrogation began. I gave them a stream of idiocy about why I wanted to be a guard. None of the three of us was listening.

Then came the scenarios.

"Mr. Yates, you have an inmate running across the grounds toward the fence. The fence which parallels Royal Oak. You are armed with a .38 revolver and you have a radio. What do you do?"

"I would call for the inmate to stop at the top of my voice. If he stopped, I would arrest him and take him into custody. If he didn't, I would fire a warning shot into the air. If he still refused to stop, I would not fire."

"Why?"

"Royal Oak is a busy street. There would be danger to passing cars. A .38 has a long trajectory; there are houses on the other side of the street." (I grew up with gunsmiths and have always known firearms, although I don't own so much as a .22 rifle and wouldn't have one in my house.) "I would radio the whereabouts of the person escaping."

"What if this person is charged with violent crime and escaping from a maximum unit?"

"I'm not prepared to risk missing."

"Good thinking, Mr. Yates."

"Thank you."

The interview was a breeze. And, yes, when Adler left, Williams did give me the homily about people too educated to be guards. His final nail was that no one with a degree had ever survived the West Wing. I knew that Bob worked in that wing, but I had no idea yet what the term "remand" meant or the difference between maximum and medium. I was asked to wait in the hall. Williams went down-stairs and talked to Mike Adler. He came back and said I was hired. He said to go home and wait till he called me and stay close to the phone. I would then come in to stores, pick up my uniform, and be sworn in.

Right.

I sat by the phone for a month.

There was a minor glitch. Bob had let it out that I was a writer.

Moonlighting and the Public Service Act of B.C. were big issues back then; the no-moonlighting part of the act was struck down following the proclamation of The Charter of Rights. Williams insisted that I write the minister and confess that I was a poet, pointing out that it was a rare year when I made enough revenue to cover postage and paper. I was tempted to add that poetry, as any Aristotelian critic could prove, ceased to be relevant to the human experience somewhere between *The Iliad* and *The Odyssey*. They evidently already knew that. On ministry letterhead I received a special dispensation to persist with my poetry.

On September 15, 1981, I reported to Central Control at the main desk and told them I was new and supposed to report to Mr. Adler. Mike greeted me with a big smile and invited me into his office as if I were visiting royalty. Politely, he oriented me: I was to come to the administration building each day to sign in and find out to which wing or building I'd been assigned. For the next ten days I would be assigned a training officer and be doing O.J.T. (on-the-job training) at Westgate B.

"You'll be working four-on and two-off until you complete your ten-day training period with a training officer. Then you'll be on call. Right now, we're very short of call-board. You should get a lot of work. And there is a seniority list for auxiliaries. As you rise up, you'll get more work. You could even be assigned permanently to one of the units.

"If you have any problems, come to me or Mr. Brent. We run the call-board. If you get a permanent assignment, let us know. Some of the units aren't very good at communicating with administration except for counts.

"It's almost three. You need to go upstairs to have the warden swear you and the other twenty we've just hired in as peace officers.

"I think you have an edge on the younger fellows, Mr. Yates, and that is life experience. This is a human place on both sides of the bars and we need all the wisdom we can get. You cannot learn what we call jail-wisdom in any classroom or book. Stay close to the ones who have been here a long time and don't let their gruffness put you off. Common sense is the chief tool of corrections." He rose, cuing me to get my ass upstairs. "Just one thing I can give you which may be of value . . ."

"Sir?"

"Be a distant presence or be a nice guy or a definable mix of the two, but be *consistent.* Consistency of staff in an institution will prevent a lot of trouble and save a lot of lives."

"Thank you."

"Welcome aboard."

All twenty-one of us headed off to Westgate B to be assigned a training officer.

Within four years, of the twenty-one sworn in that day, only I was left in service.

Thus began my picaresque journey through three very different corrections institutions and twelve very educational years. The structures varied from ancient and classic (Oakalla, now demolished, was a classic piece of prison architecture) to state-of-the-art high-tech ultra-max (Vancouver Pretrial Services Centre is the highest-security custodial unit in North America) to the heritage vernacular architecture of the administration building (Samuel McLure, who with Rattenbury is one of the two fathers – no, mothers – of B.C. architecture, would have been beaming) which presides over sixty-eight fertile and productive acres of New Haven Correctional Centre.

Entering corrections and going back to school to study criminal law was a great gift. I owe corrections for getting my body into shape and proving to me that my memory, my mind, was intact after all.

In the books I wrote during the years I worked in corrections, you will not find the word "prison." No prison metaphors. I didn't enter service as a peace officer to write about or expose the prison system. I had planned to write a memoir in my dotage, and my prison years would necessarily have been a part of the chronicle.

What changed my mind about the *timing* of my writing this book was a corrections friend, Craig Orson, who took me for a four-hour coffee. He pointed out that if I didn't write, no one would. No one ever had. Or worse, it would come out as a vapid doctoral dissertation with all the humanity footnoted out of it. And most importantly, the old-timers, cons and guards, wouldn't be around as resource people. He listed off those who had already died and were about to die. The life expectancy of those who work in law enforcement (as it is in ambulance services, firefighting, and so on) is very short post-retirement.

Whenever a corrections peace officer addresses a group of other peace officers – say, when he has been seconded for a tour of duty as a teacher at the Justice Institute of British Columbia – he must first establish his credentials. Which jails did he work as a line screw? In 1981, if you had worked Oakalla's West Wing you had the attention of all.

Actually, all you had to say was, "I was a West Winger." In those days it was deemed that anyone who worked Oakalla would work there forever – on the assumption that these people were much too heavy to transfer to Prince George Regional Correctional Centre, Vancouver Island, or Kamloops. Inmates and guards of the West Wing were mythologized as the heaviest of the heavy, big as sasquatches, with the temperament of wolverines. Oakalla was to Canadians what Alcatraz was to the Americans.

A load of nonsense, but it's the same process as amplifying Captain Steele (or Sergeant Preston) of the North West Mounted Police, Almighty Voice, Paul Bunyan, or Dan'l Boone. It's a part of human nature that we just have to put up with. Humans have always dipped people and groups of people in folklore, and the process is not likely to change.

PART ONE

Oakalla

2

The Warehouse:
On-the-Job Training

Welcome to Hotel Oakallafornia . . .
– Line by the Eagles,
retooled by Oakalla staff and inmates

O AKALLA was the Victorian-era provincial maximum-security dungeon just outside Vancouver that was shut down in 1991. It was once a rust-coloured jewel crowning the steep ridge that oversaw berms of wheat and other crops below. In its early days it was called Oakalla Prison Farms. Work-shops hummed, and its fields were full of gangs doing genuine work. Inmates produced the food they ate and the uniforms they wore, they turned wrenches on the equipment they used, and they built the barns and stables in which the farm animals were housed.

The view of the Coast Mountain massif was magnificent. The grounds – over a mile – between the Main Gaol and Deer Lake were full of pheasant, fox, and rodents of all sorts. The lake was full of trout and carp.

I'm told by the old-time cons and guards that doing time was easy when Oakalla was a prison farm, which it was from 1913 until the early seventies, because there was so much to do. Sentenced time at Oakalla (which was a maximum of two years less a day, as in all provincial institutions) you could do "standing on your head" – although in the old days, they still had corporal punishment. Until the sixties, death row and the gallows were in active service.

Bit by bit, the vast productive organism that was Oakalla was whittled away by the Socred and NDP governments. By the time I arrived in 1981, the lands between Oakalla's grounds and Deer Lake had been handed over to the Municipality of Burnaby, the city in which the prison resided, on the condition that the city convert them to a park; but the real point was to hand over the supply of food and services to the institution to the Burnaby business community – Burnaby was too poor to create the park. So the berms became wild wheat and marsh-grass to run through and hide in while making the great escape.

By and by, there was nothing left of the work crews but the landscape gang, the kitchen gang, and hit-and-miss clean-up crews. Then Vander Zalm privatized the kitchen. The cons didn't appreciate the new small portions and powdered eggs, and so there was a riot in 1983 over that one. What had once been a virtually self-supporting institution was by that time costing the taxpayer roughly $85,000 per year per con.

Incarcerated people are no more or less lazy than other people. They prefer at least the option to busy themselves at something. But by the time the politicians finished their spoils-of-office number, handing out pieces of corrections to their election backers, we had little left. Oakalla was just a warehouse for cons. We did nothing by way of keeping them busy while in stir. We did nothing by way of programs to assist them in making re-entry.

In the units of Oakalla that housed sentenced prisoners, East Wing and Westgate B, there were no libraries. What few books inmates had to read were dusters and other formula commercial stuff, and porn mags. And we had a deal with Air Canada: once a week, if anyone remembered, the staff go-fer drove out to Vancouver International Airport and picked up magazines. Week-old current events (*Time, Der Spiegel, Business Week*) were better than nothing.

I once ducked into the basement with my work gang because of a cloudburst. After radioing in position, I began to poke around and found a gigantic library. There must have been ten thousand volumes: dictionaries, anthologies of stories, poetry, classic novels, law dictionaries. It was a couple of decades out of date, but there was enough air down there so that nothing had been destroyed by mildew.

I reported my find and suggested that the books could be distributed to the units. It would be a great work project. I was even cooking up some ideas about a central resource centre, and carts like little book-mobiles going around from tier to tier. And on I dreamt. The proposal was rejected by the local director, who said that if the cons wanted to read, their visitors could bring in reading material. He said that what we really needed was a truck to come in and haul all that stuff away. And by the way, if there were any books I wanted down there, I could go after shift and take them home. I would be doing the joint a favour.

It all added up to long, empty days in which cons had nothing to do but cook up mischief and go stir-crazy, which led to half-baked escapes, sit-ins and riots. Oakalla became a pressure-cooker that cranked up the collective blood-pressure of the jail until it blew. Then things would be quiet for a while, and then it would blow again in another wing or unit.

The number of suicide attempts rose. The number of successful suicides rose. The number of days of absenteeism rose among line staff. There were more heart attacks, more by-pass surgeries. There were more guards who did a shift at Oakie, a shift drinking at the Legion or Police Athletic Club, a few hours sleeping, then got up in time to reel back on shift and pray for tower duty, where they could sleep it off, or a good work-gang, where everyone could hide. One con acted as a six-man (look-out) to watch for brass while the cons dicked around and the guard slept off the hangover.

The design of the red brick building was based on the classic Auburn model – cruciform: West Wing (remand – for those awaiting trial or sentencing); East Wing (provincial sentenced – two years less a day); South Wing (segregation – for inmates of any ilk who could not pull time in population; also access to gallows); North Wing (administration).

Still, the grounds of Oakalla were beautiful. There was lots of parking, and lots of kidding in the parking lot and camaraderie as uniformed people ducked in the gate and strolled down the hill to their units. We descended a hill from the gate to get to the Main Gaol. There were many geese on the well-kept lawns, and the hill was fairly steep. If the geese had strayed off the grassy areas onto the driveway, you could take a goose-poop route to Workers' Compensation, as many a guard has done in fact and in fraud. No one was allowed to harass the geese. The geese were holy to both inmates and guards.

It took five or six minutes walking fast down the hill to get to the Main Gaol. First you slipped past Tower Two, a shotgun tower set on the outside of the driveway. And past Tower One, which was the command position for the West Wing yard. The guard in Tower One was locked in by the man in patrol position. Tower One contained the alarm system and telephone, and its guard kept constant radio contact with other positions and Central Control. The tower was built of concrete and leaned out over the yard itself. Any place in the yard could be seen from the Tower One position, except for the area immediately beneath it, which was covered by Tower Two and the count position.

Directly across from Tower One was the entrance into the West Wing: the count position. Here the cons were allowed out to the yard and back in for phone calls. It was not a great idea to respond to a scuffle in the middle of the yard from the count position. If it turned into a mess, the shooting would begin from the towers and the life of the count man wouldn't be worth much.

The thing I always loved about coming on morning shift or coming off graveyard was the spectacular view down the ridge and over what is known as the flats. And Deer Lake, which at this time of the morning always had a mysterious saucer of mist suspended over it, was absolutely breathtaking in its colours; the long marsh-grass down the hill was either winter-brown or spring-green. Out over the fields, which once had been tilled but now lay fallow, you could see wildlife of all kinds ambling around.

For both staff and inmates in the West Wing, where I worked most of the time I was at Oakalla, this postcard view had a calming effect. You could look out at it from any tier that faced north; you could see all of the Deer Lake area and the entire massif to the north, including Seymour and Grouse mountains, and the Lions that guard Vancouver.

Inside Oakalla, once you got used to it, the sound of gates far and near, opening and closing, also had a lulling effect. The bars and walls had been painted with a god-awful off-yellow lead-base paint in layers and layers. When I was first hired at Oakalla, a fire marshal came in and estimated that, should we have a major fire, all life on the top three landings would be lost to smoke inhalation thanks to the paint. A few years afterwards fire-doors were installed at the exit of each tier outside to the yard.

When you first entered Oakalla it smelled institutional: it smelled of food, of wax, of wax-stripper, of disinfectant and human fluids. Then it passed from being an alien smell to being the smell of home, and then the smell was not noticed at all. It became the familiar olfactory landscape, like the smell of your mother's purse when you were a child.

The Main Gaol (the front of North Wing, called Administration) housed the warden's office, officers' mess, and manual records upstairs; the deputy warden, accounting, Central Control, and chaplain's offices on the main floor; electronic records, change-room, book-in/book-out on the ground floor downstairs. Up the stairs of the Main Gaol brought you to Front Hall, which serviced all the departments listed above on the main floor and led to the locked visitors' cage (for visits by telephone through a glass barrier). The Front Hall man keyed you in the North door, the Centre Hall man keyed you into Centre Hall. The Centre Hall man's desk was dead centre to the visitors' cage doors (doors for visitors and for inmates on either side), South Wing was behind him, East Wing to his right, and West Wing to his left. Also located in Centre Hall were conference rooms for lawyer consultations.

East (provincial sentenced) and West (remand) wings were essentially identical. East differed only in that the kitchen was located on One Landing Left. West was unique only in that all new inmates and those returning from courts were frisked in through the West door to Centre Hall.

Both East and West were of normal capacity, holding 150 to 200 drums (cells are called drums or houses, never cells). There were five landings of two tiers, that is, each landing had one tier of twenty cells on the left and one on the right. One guard per tier (two per landing) with some exceptions, such as the "cleaner" or trustee tier. This tier was relatively self-policing. The range was the area on each tier directly in front of the cells. The catwalk ran behind each row of cells (along the outside edges of the building) and provided precarious access to the televisions cons could watch from their drums. Beyond the catwalk were the windows.

On every landing, adjacent to the endgate, there were two boxes, each about three feet wide by six feet tall and a couple of feet deep. These tier-boxes were made of heavy-guage steel and painted with the inescapable Oakie yellow lead-base paint. When closed, each had a Master-brand padlock securing it, which was threaded right to left through the hasp ("right hand on"). Every guard in the jail carried a key that fit all of these locks so that, if called during an emergency, he could rush in, jam the key in with his right hand, twist fingers and hand clockwise and have the key off in a single motion, and fling open the door of the tier-box with his left hand.

Inside the box was a fire extinguisher and the locking system. Two long brass levers hung down. Except at night, the longest of the two was pulled toward the door of the tier-box. It was the night-bar and doubled the security of the locking system. The other bar was the tier- or day-bar. At head level was a beautifully tooled brass dial, about ten inches in diameter, surrounded with cell numbers 1 to 20. It had a pointer and a knob. We cranked the pointer around to the desired cell number and then lifted the day-bar. Tumblers rolled and thunked much like those in a bank vault (or as one imagines them), and that cell door unlocked. The dial also had the letter A. When you turned the pointer to A and lifted the day-bar, it unlocked all the cells in the tier. It took more muscle to lift the bar when cracking the entire tier, but there was a wonderful sound of craftsmanship and good materials. Like the sound of a Rolls Royce door shutting. No one ever commented, but I think everyone liked the sound of the tiers cracking open. The sound of locking down was tinny and unpleasant as the tumblers moved the opposite way. I don't mean anything symbolic by this; it's simply an impression. In prison one can review the parts of sight and sound. It passes the time.

The South Wing was called "the bug wing." It housed – separately – those inmates who for one reason or another could not "make it" in the general population. Instead of twenty, the tiers were only ten cells deep and staffing was doubled. The entrance to the gallows was from South Wing. Such celebrities as Clifford Olson and the Butler Brothers of the Montana Uprising were kept in South Wing Observation where one or two officers stared at them around the clock, seven days a week, to ascertain they did not escape or do injury to themselves or one another. Below South Obs, there was another door which was heavily chained and locked. In case of a riot in the wing, those upstairs, like Olson, in "triple protective custody" would be safe, with staff, from the mob. Actually, given that implements could be made from broken bunk-frames, those upstairs were not safe at all. But prisons, like handcuffs and leg-irons, are only restraints; anyone who would tout them as escape-proof is an idiot. There are such idiots in the ranks of corrections. They do not make life easy for serious line staff who have to cope with escape artistry.

I began my tour of every unit on every shift. The situation of an auxiliary (also known as "scrot," "rookie nookie," and "impersonator of a prison guard") is not pleasant. You sit by the telephone an hour or two before the beginning of each shift – 0500, 1300, 2100 – quivering like a dog attempting to poop a peach seed, hoping it will ring and you will be posted for a shift.

However, ring it did. And I was luckier than most. Some work a few shifts and then sit at home for a month waiting. Once started, I don't think I missed my four-on/two-off rotation even once until I was permanently posted to the West Wing.

ON-THE-JOB TRAINING, LESSON ONE:
BOMB SQUAD DUTY

It was graveyard shift in the West Wing and I was, contrary to regulations, poring over the endless mind-numbing pages of required reading necessary for a promotion. I'd only been on the job three months, but my principal officer had insisted that I compete in the first promotion competition that came up. He said I wouldn't get promoted the first time I tried (it was traditional not to get promoted the first time), but possibly the second or third, and he handed me the huge *Standards* and *Operations* manuals to take home and study (which was against regulations; it was also against regulations to read or study while on duty).

I was on shift with Ian Blocker, who looked like Ichabod Crane. The wing was in the hands of two guards who didn't have six months of experience between them. As senior officer on shift, I was commander of the wing.

I had had the misfortune to work a landing with Blocker one afternoon shift when he almost started a riot over Aspirin. A con had asked for three Aspirins. Blocker insisted that it was reasonable to have two or four but not three, and the temperature of the argument rose alarmingly. I took four Aspirins from my medication box and showed them to Blocker, then indicated for the con to open his hand. He did. I dropped three tablets into his hand and the fourth one into my mouth and walked back to my seat. Blocker couldn't figure out what had happened but decided to let it pass for the moment. Later, he concluded that I had fucked him over and cooked up a grudge. I didn't mind. We were both auxiliaries, but I was senior officer by about a week. It became routine that he mouthed off to me at every opportunity and I pulled rank in return.

During this graveyard shift, Blocker was doing everything he could to botch my studying, including observing that he could "write me up" for studying on shift. I responded by making him do the nominal roll. In those pre-electronic-records days, once a month, a lined composition book had to be cleaned up manually, by deleting the names of released or sentenced prisoners. Each name had to be copied from the board inside the desk cage on legal-size stationery with the number of the con beside it. The list was then sent via the Centre Hall man out to Central Control to be matched against the master count of the entire Oakalla complex.

I figured that hand-printing 180 to 200 names would keep Blocker busy for a while. I repaired to the office to get away from him until hourly check time. I knew he would come up with something new to spin me when he finished and so, as I studied, my mind was also making a list of rat-shit errands and duties to dump on Blocker.

The phone rang. It was Control. Deputy Director Ollie Brent, the night-jailer (acting warden during graveyard shifts). "We have a bomb threat at Westgate," he said. "Back-up is being called in, but meantime we need one man from each unit to report to the armoury, then to Westgate."

"Right, sir," I replied. Blocker was listening on the desk phone. He figured I'd send him down and that he was home-free on the nominal roll. He was wrong. I decided to send myself.

Blocker began to protest, insisting that the senior officer had to stay in the wing.

"Call Control and get the warden's number. Wake him up and complain," I told him on my way downstairs to the staff-room to get a parka and hat.

"What about hourly counts?" he argued.

"You can't do 'em without back-up."

"I think this is against procedure."

"There's a bomb out there. Now, if you want to draw heat by calling Control every five minutes while they're running a command post, go to it. They'll fire your ass and good riddance. Centre Hall, crack this gate!"

The three of us from East, West, and South hit the gate at the same time. At the armoury, the Control officer tossed each of us a shotgun, ammo, and a radio. The Front Hall kid had opened the front gate and we filed into the night air on the double, cramming shells into the shotguns and radio-checking with Control one by one.

It was December, and the ground was frosty and slick under our leather-soled shoes. The screw from East fell on his ass at the bottom of the Main Gaol stairs and his shotgun clattered across the pavement. We picked him up and told him graphically what we'd do to him if he dropped a loaded weapon near us again.

At Westgate Ollie Brent was waiting for us.

"The caller has been on the phone twice. He knows the Westgate area. Probably did some time down here. The bomb could be any-where." Counting the segregation unit at the top of the Westgate complex, the lives of between two and three hundred cons were on the line.

A couple of squad cars arrived from the Burnaby RCMP, and a few minutes later our own prowl truck, DB107, drove up.

The Mounties told us that their SWAT was being mustered. Ollie Brent didn't wait. Like the other thirty-year corrections veterans, he was unsurprised by anything; he instantly formed a plan and imple-mented it. He handed flashlights to the three of us from the Main Gaol and to the three Westgate staff and sent a couple of people around the perimeter of the complex with instructions what to look for.

"Get me a tall ladder," he ordered. Someone scurried to get it. When it arrived, Brent turned to me. "Mr. Yates, I want you on the roof. Good place to plant a bomb."

When I was a floating auxiliary during my first weeks on the job, Ollie had been my boss and had patiently answered all my stupid questions. We had become friends. I put my hand on a rung of the ladder. My flashlight was a heavy monster that could blind people in Alberta. I didn't have enough hands. I started to hand him my shotgun.

"Take it up."

"Is this a skeet-shoot?"

"You might surprise a perpetrator up there."

I have no idea how I made it to the roof on that slick aluminum ladder holding a shotgun and radio and flashlight all in two hands. The Westgate building covered the better part of an acre, tiered down the slope. Its flat-top roofs were punctuated by mossed-over sky-lights. I could see myself falling through one on top of a sleeping con. So far, they had no idea what was going on while they slept. I strolled around and climbed from one level to the next and then moved back down, examining every likely place a bomb might have been planted. It was getting boring. When I ran out of nooks to check I sneaked up to the edge of the roof and flattened myself and looked over. When I found a cop or guard stalking a garbage can or a Smithrite or a shed, pistol or shotgun at the ready, I'd sight the megalight carefully and fire it on and off so quickly that he couldn't be sure where the momentary daylight came from. Then I'd roll back beyond the edge of the roof and find another victim.

It was cold. Dawn was trying to make up its mind.

Next, I tried peeling the moss off one of the skylights. Some of the moss came off, but the plastic underneath was so brown no light could be seen from below. The building was as ugly from the roof as it was inside.

As dawn broke through the clear winter air, the view of misted-in Deer Lake was magical.

Then, finally, I got called on the radio. "Mr. Yates, we have to conclude this is a hoax. Come on down."

I hastened across the roof toward the ladder. It was worse going down. Ollie had that get-your-ass-back-to-your-unit expression, but one of the Westgaters handed me a cup of hot coffee. Then over the radio came the news that they'd had another call. The threat had changed. The bombers were going to lob the bomb from Royal Oak Street, which ran past the jail. I was warming my hands on the Styrofoam cup.

"Mr. Yates." Ollie was looking at the ladder.

"Again?"

He nodded.

I handed him the coffee and the light and started up. Half-way up, I stopped. "Mr. Brent?"

He looked up.

"Is there a catcher's mitt in the armoury?"

"Up."

It was wake-up time. I spent the remainder of the shift on the roof of Westgate, amusing myself by rapping on the skylights and waking the cons who, having never been awakened in such a manner, assumed they were under siege from on high and refrained from their usual good-morning greetings like "Dummy it, you fucking assholes."

The O.J.T. Lesson: It is holier to be the officer ordering the rookie up the ladder than the rookie obeying the order. And even holier to be somewhere in between with neither supreme responsibility nor naked bomb-fodder jeopardy.

ON-THE-JOB TRAINING, LESSON TWO:
VIOLENCE CONTROL

It is traditional that in winter the prison counts are far higher than in warmer weather, and in November we were nearing the critical stage. Staff were being borrowed from one unit to the next for mere escort duty. Regular staff who had been assigned to maximum units for years were being shanghaied to minimum units to cover graveyard shifts. Central Control had a man on the telephone around the clock attempting to coax people back from days of rest or annual leave, or to hasten the healing of the sick. The screws were burned out from overtime, and the overcrowded cons were jittery. With phones going crazy with pleas for staff, everyone was shooting from unit to unit to give the appearance of coverage. Sometimes it was only to cover the line for a meal, sometimes for inside yard, sometimes full shifts for a week. Principal officers (P.O.s) and senior correctional officers (S.C.O.s) were key-jockeying as needed. The people in records were logging all kinds of overtime booking in new bodies. They were haggard and bitchy. I was posted to Westgate B.

In times like these the riot hazard is high. The staff are too tired to be patient with inmates, to joke with them, to take an inmate aside and listen for an hour while he tells you his father has died in India and he should have been there. Daily, staff morale slumps and the inmates pick up the drift. This is very much a two-way street, because a jail has a pulse.

Prison fights are sometimes very deadly affairs, sometimes mostly for show. This one could have been scripted by Mark Twain. First I heard the usual male tones of physical threat rising above the hellish white noise of twelve tiers full of activity. I checked it out at the endgate. Sure enough, there on the range (the area between cells and walls – quite spacious at B-side), just like boys on the playground, two men were standing with their dukes up, shouting at the top of their voices, while the rest of the tier gathered around, watching intently.

But no punches. I yelled "Staff up!" and called Centre Hall to key the door. When the key was heard in the gate the first punch was thrown. One grabbed the other around the head, they clinched and fell to the floor. I trotted in with back-up and grabbed the guy on top. My back-up grabbed the other guy. It was truly amazing how easily they broke apart. We took them out separately. When I reached back to my belt where the cuffs were tucked, the con noticed the move. "I'm cool, boss. No problem."

"You sure?"

"No shit."

On the way down to the staff-room, where the con and I and the P.O. (if available) will have a coffee and a T.M. (tailor-made smoke) and discuss the cause and long-term implications of the altercation, the con said, "Good thing you pulled me off when you did, boss, or I'da killed the cocksucker."

"Right. Lucky thing."

Over coffee, my con decided that his beef with the other guy was not that serious and maybe he overreacted. There is provision in the *Correctional Centre Rules and Regulations* for apology and amends-making, thus diverting the perpetrators from the internal justice system. I offered it to him.

"If I Section 29 you and you apologize and shake hands, how do I know this is not dress-rehearsal for a real performance?"

"You have my word." I knew this guy, and anyway he owed me, so his word was solid currency. Had I not known him, he would have had my word that the next time he mixed it up, I'd buy him serious hole-time and put a bug in the ear of the line screws who work the segregation unit.

"Done. Wait here. I should make you fill out the incident report, you dildo. If you had to do all the paperwork, it would take the fight out of you for the rest of your life."

The other officer was waiting in the hall. We compared notes. Seems his con allowed that maybe he was overreacting, too. The erstwhile fighters shook hands and we explained that circumstances in the jail just then were hard on everyone and the last thing we needed was two ninnies smacking one another around. I started on the paperwork. The other screw cuffed them together and took them down to the hospital to get them certified as undamaged. The P.O. sent along a shotgun man to tail the procession. When they returned, we plunked them back on the unit.

The fight was definitely bullshit. It could have been a release of the frustration over the restriction of privileges. It could have been subterfuge to reduce the number of roving or available staff while the tier laid a beating on someone on the tier who had offended the tier in some manner. It could have been staged to buy someone else time to smoke a joint in a back tier and disperse the green smoke, or to get rid of watchful eyes, then get Centre Hall to crack someone out who owed a guy up on Tier Two a deck of weeds (when, in fact, he was muleing a load of narcotic in the deck to the other tier).

It is understood that the guards get conned a time or two during a shift. It is understood that the rule-breakers screw up from time to time and get nabbed. The understanding between guards and inmates in a prison is wide and deep. And unwritten. When things go wrong, the con takes his hole-time without snivelling. A guard takes his verbal or written reprimand or few days of suspension without snivelling – unless he can grieve the suspension, spend a week or two drinking at the Legion Hall or the Police Athletic Club, and then collect a fat cheque for back-pay.

ON-THE-JOB TRAINING, LESSON THREE: SUICIDE

Shortly after the pseudo-fight, Tier Eleven in Westgate B was mine for the afternoon shift. I had been called off the tier countless times for back-up and escort duties. The place was absolutely nuts. There was no ventilation. It was difficult, because of the tobacco smoke, to see from one end of the tier to the other – even harder to see the length of Centre Hall from the endgate. I had been on the same tier for two days, long enough to go through the file of each inmate and make a mental note of those with any psychiatric history, those who had been charged internally, and especially those who had been charged in outside court with assaulting a peace officer (some people just can't relate to people in uniform, whether a gas attendant, cop, or guard). If the guy whose record suggests he doesn't like uniforms was getting "short" (nearing end of sentence; this term is also used in guard lingo – a guard is getting short when he nears retirement), you discounted him as a problem.

In a provincial sentenced unit like B-side, the population are younger and not terribly sophisticated in the grammar of violence, but they are full of energy. Baby-sitting them for an afternoon shift can be more exhausting than loading boxcars.

Five or six of them were reading or writing letters on their bunks in their drums. One was in the can – I could see his feet. One was down the hall on the phone. The rest were playing poker. They are not supposed to play poker on the tier. But, as it keeps them absorbed, the game has my blessings. I flipped through the files. A kid by the name of Singh drifted away from the poker game and strolled over to see what I was doing.

"What's in my file, Mr. Yates?"

"Near as I can tell, you can find out exactly what is in your file, but not at the line-screw level."

"What does that mean?"

"It means that you can make out a request form to see the P.O. and read your file in his presence, but I'm not allowed to let you read it in my presence." I flipped it open, but held it up so that he couldn't read upside-down. "Nobody says that I can't summarize the contents. What do you want to know about yourself? Height? Weight? The name of your mama?"

"Anything bad about me in there that might affect my parole?"

"Nary a thing. Says you're sound of mind and limb, have grade 12, and have been working for your brother apprenticing as a carpenter. You haven't pissed anybody off in Westgate. In fact, your gang boss says you have been working your ass off and recommends that you be bumped up to a classier gang. You could get carpentry shop. In fact, if you'd like that, remind me to make a note in your progress-log to that effect."

"Thanks, Mr. Yates." He started to walk back to the poker table. He was in for getting drunk and boosting a Lotus. God knows where he found it. The car chase involved many North Shore squad cars, a roadblock, and some cowboy-cop gunfire. Cops wound up shooting cops by accident.

"Hey, Singh." He strode back. "Says in your file that you're Moslem."

"Yeah."

"Nice Moslem boys don't drink, do they?"

"They don't steal expensive cars, either. I'm not real religious and I do like to go drinking, but I don't want to come back to this place." He grinned.

"Watch it, Allah will bite you."

"Sure."

The P.O. appeared at the endgate. The noise and smoke were atrocious. "I need you to double back in the morning," he said. "Church escort." I brightened up at hearing this. I had never been to a prison church service. There were two services, Catholic and Protestant. For prison purposes, Moslems and Hindus and Jews were Protestants. No one ever seemed to know or care which service would be on which Sunday. It was the number-one marketplace where major drug shipments passed from one wing or unit to another. The place was absolutely nuts. There was no ventilation. Catholic or Protestant, the problems were the same.

"Fine," I said.

"Tier's quiet. Are they all high?"

"Not according to my nose."

"What are they playing?"

"Canasta."

"What are you guys playing in there?"

"Canasta, Mr. Moreland," they chimed.

Moreland vanished.

Earlier in the evening I had had to tell them what canasta was, and they had another deck ready to double the number of cards if heat came down. The tier was mellow. Most were first-time adult offenders. The game was quiet. No arguments. I was grateful for the smooth shift on Eleven, even though the calm had been broken fairly frequently by my having to rush off and deal with ruckuses on other tiers.

Ten o'clock. Lock-down. When the cons have appreciated the evening, they scurry about and assist the tier cleaner with his duties without being ordered to do so, and they jump into their cells and roll the heavy doors closed themselves. Such was the case this evening. If they don't like you, they'll drag ass until the P.O. arrives to chew your head off because you're not ready for inspection. You'll have to close every cell door yourself, then just as you're about the drop the night-bar, two or three inmates will have to get out on the range to find something.

That night the tier was clean. I put the night chain on the tier gate. "Night, guys. Good shift. Thanks."

"You doublin' back?"

"Yeah."

"See you in the morning, Mr. Yates."

I was running late in the morning. You can't really see the entrance to B-side until you round the gymnasium. What I saw slowed me for a moment. There were Mounties' squad cars, plain-clothes cars betrayed by too many aerials, two ambulances, and a trauma-team truck all clustered around the entrance of Westgate B at crazy angles in the crisp, clear, blue tinge of 6:30 light. I sped up my pace and skidded on the frost. Goddamn driveway was always slick, from frost in the winter and goose poop in the summer.

I ran through the door of Westgate. The desk man behind the bars looked up.

"Riot?" I asked, nodding toward the rolling stock parked outside.

"Stringer," he replied. Suicide.

I looked through the bars and through the murk down the long hall. Coming toward the two barred doors was a gurney bearing a zipped-up body-bag. A cop, a nurse, and a few staff were still in a clump at Centre Hall desk, talking. The P.O. and two guards were behind the desk filling out forms, with files open before them. I went to the staff-room to grab a coffee.

Klaus Friesen, the P.O. on graveyard shift, came in, grabbed a coffee and sat down across from me. "Sonofabitch was getting short. He was smart, a good worker. I met his family at visits, good people. Nothing in his file to fuck up his parole."

Joe Grewal came in just then. Joe was a big jolly East Indian who was a favourite with the cons. "Grewal, you had that kid on a gang, didn't you?"

"Yes. His people are from the Punjab in India. I rag him all time, he speaks no Punjabi. His people are ragheads and he don't know no Punjabi. Born over here and all Canadian. Good kid. Hard worker."

"Any idea why he strung?"

"Nah."

I wasn't really twigging to any of this.

"Who was on Eleven last night? I haven't checked the roster," Friesen asked.

This woke me up. "Eleven?"

"Yeah." Friesen was patting his shirt pockets for a cigarette. Grewal flipped him a weed.

"I was on Eleven last night. It was the only mellow tier in the unit."

"Notice anything about this Singh kid?"

"Which one? There are two Singhs on the tier."

"Rajinder." Friesen had brought the kid's file in with him and now he flipped it open to the face-sheet and handed it to me. The nice kid I had been talking to was staring at me from the shitty black-and-white Polaroid on his face-sheet. He was smiling. Usually, they try to look tough or make faces at the camera. This kid was too green: if it's a camera, you smile. I looked around on the page. His mama's name was still the same. The pieces of the jigsaw of reality before me were floating, not interlocking into a graspable picture. Someone asked me something. A voice sounding approximately like mine answered.

"No . . . I talked with him . . . for a while. He was fine, in a good mood."

"Anyone crowding him on the tier?"

"No, he was playing cards with a whole tableful and getting along with everyone."

"What's your name?"

"Yates."

"Yates, you better do up a report."

"What kind?"

"Anything. A page on con stationery. Just a summary of the evening and the mood of the tier."

"I have to crack the tier pretty soon, then breakfast line, and I think I'm on church escort."

"Do it after church and give it to the morning P.O."

"Yessir."

Of the next couple of hours I don't remember very much. I cracked the tier. I do remember that the inmates were very subdued. Breakfast passed. Then came the call for church. We went outside and John Chapman and I lined up the cons in twos to march up the hill to the Main Gaol. Church was in a room I didn't know existed in the centre of the jail, upstairs above the gallows, the entrance to which was through South Wing.

The cons were sectioned off according to unit in chairs turned toward the pulpit, if it could be called that. The service was given by a group of born-agains who had been playing country music in some barn or honky-tonk pub the night before and were hungover as hell. Every now and then between gospel songs the lead idiot would step up and testify a sentence or two. I glanced over at Chapman. He tried dozing. No go. He looked toward the ceiling. An angry expression kept returning to his face.

The surrounding room was growing vague and distant. The music was distant. What I could see was rapidly growing distant. I felt nauseated. I realized I was about to faint. If I fell off my chair onto the floor and staff rushed over to check me out, the year's crop from the Golden Triangle would change hands. Possibly, I had picked up the flu. With my last grain of consciousness, I bent forward. It helped. I untied my left shoe slowly, then messed around with the laces. I felt less faint. Slowly and deliberately I retied the shoe.

I sat up again. Good. Chappie and I made eye contact and he didn't seem to suspect anything. Good. I was okay. Then I flashed on Raj Singh's picture in the file and my mind rocketed from that image to the conversation with him the previous evening. I folded up again.

This time I went after my right shoe. I pulled out the whole lace and relaced the shoe, then tied it. I had to keep the film of Singh from re-running in my mind. I couldn't. It was one of the longest hours of my life. Again and again I dove for my shoes. I think Chappie had some notion of what was going on but he never mentioned it.

Surely I had missed something in the kid's conversation. Helplessly I dredged my mind, gathering in every word, every gesture of body language that I could recall. I knew his file almost by heart, but I knew I would go over it several more times when I got back to the unit. There had to have been a clue I had missed. Some indication.

By the end of the church service I was seriously considering packing it in as a line screw. Surely a man who nearly faints in a work setting hasn't the right stuff for corrections. I wasn't seeing the right things. I wasn't hearing the right things. The kid had probably spoken to me clearly between his words and I had blown it.

Between church and return to the Main Gaol, something like self-exoneration occurred. I simply couldn't find anything to hang my guilt on.

I went to the P.O.'s desk and demanded Singh's file. I took it up to Eleven and relieved the man who had been covering for me. Again and again I read the file. I wrote the report, which stated that nothing had happened the previous evening. The piece of paper subsequently vanished into the empyrean of prison papers.

That day, the inmates on the tier spent most of their time in their drums. Three played a sullen, virtually silent game of cards. The shift ended. I went home. The suicide was a mystery.

But only for about a year. One of the cons who had been on Eleven that night showed up again in remand. I hadn't thought about Singh for a while, perhaps not until I saw this kid. One evening I brought up the subject, and he had a story to tell. It went something like this:

Toward the end of the evening of card-playing, Singh had said something. It was not received with good humour. After lock-up and lights-out, the offended party decided to get back at Singh by labelling him a skinner (rapist) who was in population with the cover-story of the car theft. No one really believed the guy who was attempting to label Singh as a skinner. However, the whole tier, in whispers, pretended to go along with it and began to plot out loud what they were going to do to Singh when the cells were cracked in the morning. They taunted the kid for a couple of hours, then everyone dropped off to sleep.

Except Raj Singh. He remained awake tearing his sheet into strips and braiding those strips into rope. Between the next-to-the-last hourly check and the last one before shift change, he tested the quality of his night's work.

3

Weapons Training in
Black and White

—————————— • ——————————

I consider myself an average man, except in the fact
that I consider myself an average man.
— Michel de Montaigne

ONE HEARS the term "back-up" on television cop shows year in
and year out with no real sense of what they are talking about.
The term does refer to sending more manpower. But, most importantly, it has to do with one's demeanour toward another officer – any
other officer, not just one's partner. Firefighters and police share this
understanding of "back-up." To be labelled "bad back-up" as a guard
is equivalent to being labelled a rapist as an inmate. If your partner
gets into a tough spot, you back him up. Even if the situation is something he brought on himself? Yes. If you fold under pressure, you
might as well fold your uniform and take it back to stores. The life of
the back-up officer is as much on the line as that of the officer being
backed up.

I felt pretty good the day I saved Jonathan Marshall's life (and
reminded him of it almost daily thereafter). So I shouldn't have been
surprised when he let me make an idiot of myself a couple of weeks
later at weapons training.

Jonathan Marshall had a twenty-two-inch neck. He was a down-
home Canadian black (of which there are comparatively few), a B.C.
boy, ex-military. His shoulders were so broad that if you pushed him
over sideways, he would be the same height. Nothing bothered him.

He was about as laid-back as they come. He was by no means the only black on the staff of the West Wing, but he was the only home-grown one.

He was so strong and so big that he usually ended any scuffle on his landing by one of two methods. He either grabbed the closest perpetrator and held him at arm's length above his head and threatened to drop him unless the nonsense ceased immediately, or if there was a pile of people punching and kicking one another, he ran across the landing and jumped on the topmost combatant. This usually knocked the wind out of all of them and had the desired result.

Very early in my career as a guard, before I had been posted to the West Wing and was still drifting a shift at a time from wing to wing, I was put on my first day shift in the West. That day on Two Landing one con bit off the ear of another. After the blood was staunched, Jonathan was on the desk and overseeing handcuffed inmates, who were told to stand against the wall and wait to be taken down to hospital and segregation. I'd assisted in settling the ruckus, then had been ordered down to One Landing to assist with the breakfast line. The floors at Oakalla were old reinforced cement and picked up every vibration. I could hear thumping upstairs and raced back up.

I could scarcely believe my eyes. Cuffed-up inmates, and a couple who were not, were in a huge pile, punching and kicking one another. Jonathan had done his famous dive into the middle of them.

A con who had been standing over by the south window had walked over – he was cuffed behind – and was standing on Jonathan's blind side on one leg, with the other drawn back to kick Jonathan in the head. I dove across the floor like someone sliding into home plate and dumped him forward on his mush.

Jonathan looked around and said, "Thanks, honky." The principal officer was now out of the office and tossing us cuffs and leg-irons. As we were jerking and whacking bodies around and fastening restraints, I pointed out to Jonathan (as I do to this day) that he owed me his life.

One day after I had been posted permanently to the West Wing, Jack Cornelius, the desk man, told me I was on patrol during yard (the inmates' outdoor playtime). I explained to him in a whisper that

I had never done that particular job and had no idea what equipment I was supposed to draw or what duties the job entailed.

"How do you think you'll ever learn anything if you don't get your ass out there and do it?" Cornelius howled at me. "You afraid of a little water?" It had been raining on and off.

"Rookie Yates, Campbell is Tower One and Windfors is Tower Two. They'll show you what to get from the armoury. Go to your locker and get your jacket and don't forget to put the plastic bag thing on your hat."

Campbell, Windfors, and I entered the armoury. Campbell grabbed a shotgun. Windfors grabbed a shotgun. Campbell opened a drawer and drew five green and brass shells. Windfors grabbed five shells. I reached for a shotgun. Windfors called me an asshole.

"Anyone knows the patrol carries a .38. Get one."

"Where?"

"Over there." The .38-calibre pistols were around the corner from the shotguns. I picked one up and wondered where I should carry it. In my hand?

"Yates, you'll probably want to off yourself with that in front of the visits coming down the hill, but you'll need some ammo to do it," said Campbell. I hadn't thought of that and hadn't seen any bullets in the drawer with the 12-gauge shells. I pushed the catch forward on the Smith and Wesson and rolled the pistol left until the empty cylinder dropped out on its hinge. I stared at the empty cylinder ports, then reached for the other drawer and found it full of wad-cutter bullets. I picked up six of the silver, waxy, smooth bullets.

"Five, you brain-dead moron."

"Six holes."

"The hammer sits on an empty chamber. Procedure."

"Right." I began dropping the bullets into the voluptuously machined bluish holes.

"Hey, Derek!" Campbell yelled so loud that Derek Van Hendrik, the administration desk man and the brass behind the bars in Control, could hear. "This jerk is loading a weapon in your armoury."

"Shoot the cocksucker," Derek replied.

"Can't. No shells in my shotgun," Campbell yawned. "Doesn't that rookie turd know it's against procedure to load a weapon inside the jail?"

"You idiot, take those bullets out of there and put them in your pocket," Derek yelled from the other room. I took those bullets out of there and put them in my pocket.

Windfors called me back. "You gonna walk around for two and a half hours with that fucking gun in your hand? Get a belt and a holster."

Belt and holster on, gun in holster, I headed for the door again. Derek was into the game now and caught me at the doorway. "What's your radio number?"

"What radio?"

"Exactly. How do you expect to communicate with the universe?"

"I have no idea what I'm doing."

"And probably haven't known for, what, sixty years?"

Windfors and Campbell have cracked up in the armoury. They had a radio and case, which they handed me, showing me how to fasten it to the belt. Then they moved toward the door. I was standing in front of it. "If there is one more thing I'm supposed to have and don't, I'm gonna trash both of you with the radio in one hand and an empty weapon in the other."

"You got it all." Campbell handed me the flat, the key, and the two of them walked past me. I slammed the steel door and locked it with the flat and started down the hall where the Front Hall man was waiting to key us out the front gate of the jail.

"Hey, gimme the flat." Derek was laughing so hard, he was wiping his eyes behind his glasses. The big brass behind him in the cage were trying to maintain supervisory mien as though they hadn't been pissing down their legs while I was being given the treatment.

Windfors walked down the stairs loading his shotgun, then on ahead around the curve of the yard. It was enclosed by thick corrugated tin and surrounded by a heavy and high hurricane fence. The top of the posts were bent inward forty-five degrees and linked by three strands of barbed wire topped by coils of concertina (razor) wire. We came to a door in the corrugated tin wall. The door to the tower. It had a heavy Master padlock on it. Campbell ordered me to open it.

"What, shoot the lock off?"

"Your tier-box key fits it." Each guard had a heavy chain with a single key on it. It fit every padlock securing every tier in the prison. I tried it on the outside lock. Surprisingly, it worked. "You better load the .38," Campbell said. "When I get in, lock the door."

"Lock you in the tower?"

"Yup."

"Why?"

"Procedure." He turned and climbed up into the tower. I could see him pick up the telephone to call I knew not whom. I locked him in and switched on my radio. I could hear one radio after another calling in. My turn.

"Mainland Base, this is portable 2068, radio-check, please."

Base (it was Derek): "Portable 2068, I read you loud and clear."

"Roger."

"Portable 2068, what is your twenty?"

"What?"

"Where are you?"

"Oakalla."

"I know what institution you work for. Just tell me your position." I could hear him sniggering as he went through this number. He knew which wing's yard security had just gone out the door. And checking on my "twenty" was not a mandatory part of procedure.

"Yard."

"No. I can see the West Wing yard from here and it is empty. It will remain empty until I call the wing and tell them to let the inmates out. Try again."

"I'm outside the tin fence where I just locked a man in a tower and don't know why."

I must explain that every correctional institution from Oakalla to Stave Lake Camp (near Mission, which is nearly fifty miles away) was on the same frequency. Not counting cops and reporters and every other nerd with a scanner, a minimum of one hundred people were tuned in to this clown show.

"You are the West Wing patrol position. Did you read that?"

"Yeah."

"Roger."

"Roger."

I put the radio back in its holster and turned the volume down to a low yammer and looked off toward the North Shore massif at the Lions, Grouse Mountain, Seymour, and east toward the Golden Ears. Campbell slid open the tower window.

"You heard the man. You're patrol. Don't just stand there. Patrol, you asshole, patrol!"

I started to walk back toward the door to the Main Gaol.

"No, fuckhead, the other way. You're not going back to the wing. Patrol!"

So I pivoted and strolled west instead. I walked past Tower Two and on up the hill toward the main gate. I had no idea what I was looking for, or where I was going, or what might happen, or what procedure might be should it come to pass. I strolled and looked left and right as if I knew exactly what I was doing in my mix-and-match uniform.

Visitors were streaming down the hill, and so were miscellaneous vehicles of various colours with alphanumeric strings painted on their sides. I fleetingly wondered whether I should challenge those walking down the hill and demand identification and whether I should be stopping vehicles. I was looking guardly and patrolish and making it up as I strolled along. The visitors didn't look as though they expected to be stopped. Neither did the vehicles, which whipped around the blind corner at three times the speed limit. Some of the visitors (who were a hell of a lot more at home on Oakie turf than I was at that point) smiled. Some said hello. I gave them my most guard-like nod and carried on patrolling.

Step by measured step I sank further into feeling quite smug. I had the walk down, I had the nod, I had the patent bill of my hat pulled down low, and behind my glasses I had an inscrutable look in my eyes. I passed the base of Tower Two in a trance, forgetting that any-one was up there, and walked fifty yards beyond it. Streams of mostly women and a few men passed to the left and right of me. I was the symbolic island and they gave me a foot or two of berth.

Then, with fifteen or twenty people strung out around me on the drive, a voice boomed, "Hey, fuckhead, are you patrolling all of Burnaby or what?"

I turned around, of course, and looked for the source of the voice. Twenty other people did the same thing. It was Windfors. "Come back here, you fucking jerk."

Quickly, purposefully, I strolled back down the road and looked up to receive instruction from on high. My audience of twenty waited expectantly.

"Yates, you patrol between Tower One and Tower Two."

"Right. Why?"

"Look to your left." I looked to my left. "You can see everything from here to the main gate."

"Right."

"You patrol from here back to Tower One. From Tower One you can see everything from there to the front door of the Main Gaol."

All twenty-one of us were nodding in perfect and submissive understanding.

Pretty soon I became an old hand at patrol and at the other yard posi-tions. I even had occasion to train new auxiliaries in the duties of each position. I liked Tower Two and the count positions the best. One could see more of Oakalla from West Wing's Tower Two than from any other position. The count position gave one maximum contact with the cons.

As the junior in the wing, I was frequently stuck with the patrol position. Within a few months, I had been there long enough to do all the positions, including Tower One (which procedure strictly limits to regular staff no lower than the rank of correctional officer, as it was the command position). I was heading out one day when Principal Officer Horatio MacKay, a.k.a. "Plankface," asked to see my gun certificate. Each guard was obliged to carry, at all times, a card stating his peace officer identification and his scores with pistol and shotgun.

"What does it look like?"

"It's the card that the staff training officer gives you after your gun qualification. Henry Abbot usually signs them personally."

"Who's he?" I asked.

This made Plankface pause. He figured I was having him on. Day after day, he had watched me go out to yard, knowing full well that as junior jerk I was getting stuck with the .38, the radio, and the walking up and down in the rain.

"Give me your fucking card."

"Haven't got one."

"Haven't you been to gun training?"

"No."

"Who's been sending you out to the tower and patrol position?"

"Everybody."

Plankface rushed out the door of the P.O.'s office to the desk man. Lloyd was on the desk.

"Are you sending this man, who has never had gun training, out to draw a weapon and take one of the outside yard positions?" he screamed.

"Not a chance. I'd never send a man without gun training outside."

Nonsense. Lloyd had sent me outside a dozen times. Plankface looked at me. It was guard-solidarity time. Silence. No expression. "I just assumed I was on patrol," I lied.

"Who the fuck has been sending untrained personnel out to handle weapons?"

More silence. Even more lack of expression. The other two outside guys were at the gate waiting for the tirade to subside. One of them, Cornelius, asked, "Are we having yard today, MacKay, or not?"

"Shut up." Plankface jumped back in the office and picked up the phone. "Hello. Henry, I need a man scheduled in for gun training right away. Right." And right then and there I was given a time and a date. "Yates, you're on count," he ordered.

I grinned. This meant some other asshole got to shuffle around in the rain. The count man could stand in the doorway and stay dry.

It was at least a month before I could be spared for a couple of hours for gun training – in the meantime, I was on patrol several times when Plankface wasn't on shift.

When I finally made it to training, there were about ten of us on the range trying to qualify. All officers were supposed to qualify annually, but I knew several who hadn't been near the firing range for at least ten years. Some had never qualified at all. Those who were qualifying for the first time, like me, were new staff. They were not necessarily new to guns. Some of the rookies were ex-Mounties and ex-military, for whom this training was just a formality.

One guard showed up in special yellow target-shooting glasses, and probably would have worn an ammo vest if he thought he could get away with it. He was very serious about guns. He belonged to gun clubs and lived for the next issue of *Soldier of Fortune.* He had a house full of weapons, few of them legal.

About two-thirds of us were qualifying for the first time. The other third were staff in to requalify. The day I went in, Jonathan Marshall had been assigned something he didn't want to do and so came along because he was "way past due" requalifying "and it is very important – in the military this was proved again and again – to qualify regularly."

We all arrived after lunch. Henry Abbot was not there, so we stood around in the twilight of the windowless barn-converted-to-firing-range smoking and gossiping. I have to say I was a little worried about this exercise, because I hadn't held a hand-gun in my mitt in fifteen years, let alone fired one.

Suddenly Abbot loomed over us. He called us in a tight circle to hand out ear-muffs and tell us that we would do shotguns first, then hand-guns. Abbot was almost haemorrhaging from the eyes. Between his grizzled mop and grizzled moustache, his face was red as a tail-light. He scared the hell out of the rookies, and I decided that if Abbot jacked me around, I would remind Jonathan he owed me his life and demand that he pick Abbot up over his head and stow him somewhere. Only the gun fanatic was hanging on Abbot's every word and asking questions.

A 12-gauge with number-8 shot was our first lesson. It couldn't do serious damage beyond twenty-five yards, but was deadly up close. Abbot mostly – and rightly – wanted to give those who had never fired a 12-gauge – or who hadn't for some time – a feel for the weapon, its recoil, nomenclature, and pattern. We got the "six o'clock low" lecture: just pepper their asses and the backs of their legs. In the parking lot, you could just fire into the gravel behind them. The gravel would spatter up and they would think they had been hit when they hadn't and stop.

The critical part was the hand-gun training. Pistol rounds carry a long way. Unlike shotguns, pistols required that decisions made under pressure be good decisions. The wad-cutter bullets did minimal destruction to tissue. If you hit a bone in the leg, you stopped the escapee. If the round passes through the fleshy part of the leg, chances are he wouldn't miss a stride. I've had cons tell me that there was a brief burning sensation, but no real pain.

We lined up and at Abbot's signal fired first from this position, then that. Standing. Crouching. From behind a post. With one hand. With two hands, like the guys on TV, facing the target frontally. The targets were human profiles: heads in the bull's-eye areas, with other circles radiating from this centre. They were drawn in black ink on crude white paper, and they stood fifty feet away.

It surprised me how familiar the pistol felt in my hand. We were told to cut the blade of the front sight in half with the crotched back sight and put the centre of the bull on the alignment and to squeeze, not pull, the trigger. The standard police .38 is a good all-around instrument. It does the job without too much recoil. Not much shocking power, but enough for law-enforcement purposes.

I finished one set of five shots and looked to my right, where Jonathan and the gun fanatic were still firing. I thought I was hallucinating. Jonathan was known throughout the jail as a hell of a shot. Had won a bunch of competitions in the army as a marksman. While I was firing, I thought I had heard ricocheting noises through the muffs. Jonathan stood there with a big grin on his face, firing one shot up into the ceiling and the next at an angle into the cement far under the target. I ducked behind my post and continued to reload.

Abbot noticed Jonathan's wild waving of the arm and ran up and whacked him on the shoulder. Others were still firing. Jonathan stopped firing, still grinning. I pulled my muffs down around my neck and walked over.

Abbot shouted, "Marshall, are you out of your African mind?"

"No, I'm fine."

"Can't you see the target?"

Jonathan looked at the target. "Yeah, I can see it just swell."

"What's the problem?"

"Nothin'." Jonathan pointed at the target. "See that target?"

"Of course I see the target," Henry exploded.

"What colour is it?"

"Black."

"I don't shoot at black people. For obvious reasons."

I thought Abbot was going to grab one of the shotguns and brain him. Instead, without another word, he stomped off down the runway toward the target, with the others still firing away until they finally saw him and stopped. Not even Jonathan suspected what Abbot was up to. When he got to the target, he unclipped it, flipped it around and clipped it up again. A shadowy outline showed a negative image on the other side. Abbot stomped back to Jonathan.

"Now, asshole, shoot the white guy."

Jonathan promptly reloaded and blew the head to shreds.

After we finished the final exercises, each of us collected his stack of targets and we filed off to Abbot's office to have our scores tabulated.

Abbot looked up at me from his desk and said, "Very good, Yates, very good. This is the highest score I've seen in a few years. Ninety-three per cent." I couldn't believe it. My hat size increased on the spot.

"Thank you, sir." I was a hero.

Abbot turned to Jonathan, who had shot very well. Before Abbot could say anything, Jonathan said, "Write down sixty-two per cent."

You had to make sixty per cent or you couldn't carry a hand-gun. Shotgun only.

Outside, Jonathan noticed me strutting like John Wayne. "You ignorant honky dickhead."

"Hmmm?"

"Nobody ever tell you about standard of care?"

"Nope." I was busy staring at the numbers on my card and considering which lady-friend I should show it to first.

"Okay, white-ass, listen up. Suppose there's a guy going over the fence, and you draw down on his leg."

"Right."

"You get the shot off. But just as you shoot, he trips, and you put the bullet through his head, instead of his leg."

Jonathan had my attention now. "Whoever shoots him is going to a hearing and maybe to trial. Now, if the shooter is a guy with a low score – like below sixty-five per cent – no problem. He obviously can't hit shit. He just barely qualified to carry a sidearm in the first place. He couldn't be expected to shoot very accurately." I wasn't sure I knew where this was going, but I was beginning to dislike the whiff of it. "Now, same scenario, but the guy who wasted the inmate is carrying a card with ninety-three per cent. This guy is a sharpshooter. He's going down on Murder Two or manslaughter or criminal negligence."

"I'm going back and get Abbot –"

"You? A rookie? You got no chance of getting Abbot to fake your card."

"Why didn't you warn me?"

"Hell, everybody knows white people can't shoot. Black-asses have to know how."

4

Taking Direct and Paying Back

•

*There are two kinds of men who never amount to
much: those who cannot do what they are told, and
those who can do nothing else.*
– Cyrus H. Curtis

THE *Correctional Centre Rules and Regulations* (a shirt-pocket
compendium of gibberish concentrated from many huge manuals of procedure and standards written in altitudinous *Hansardese*)
states that a correctional officer shall obey the *direct* order of the
director or his agent (anybody of higher rank or anybody who has
been in service longer) unless the order is "manifestly unlawful."

In the course of a day, an officer may receive the better part of a
hundred orders. In a prison context the adjective "direct" possesses
awesome magic and terror when it precedes the noun "order." No one
knows why. Like many prison traditions, it is simply so.

Obviously, all staff-to-staff (superior-to-inferior) orders are direct
orders. If not, what the hell is an *indirect* order? Suggestion? Advice?

There is one use of the word "direct" which carries clear meaning
if uttered with very formal inflection.

An example: I have a work-gang of perhaps five men. We have
been given some stupid task such as sweeping the driveway which, for
once, is clean enough to eat on. We put brooms and shovel in the
wheelbarrow and amble along telling jokes and talking sports until
the coffee-truck comes along. Eventually we saunter to within view of

the windows of the Women's Unit (it was renamed Lakeside Women's Correctional Centre, but was always the Women's Unit to anyone jail-wise). If their guards aren't watching, the women may give us a few bumps and grinds and peekaboo mammaries. Harmless enough.

My deal with each man in my group is don't draw heat on the gang. No shouting. Just shut up and watch the show. But one of the cons, Woodward, let's say, can't resist shouting and gesticulating. Soon staff and inmates of both the Men's and the Women's Unit are gawking at us from the windows. Now I have to do something.

First I say, "Woodward, cut it out."

Then, "Woodward, I want silence and I want it now."

Then, "Woodward, I am giving you an order." When a guard says the word "order," it is time to take him seriously.

Then the penultimate, "Woodward, I am giving you a *direct* order to cease your noise and gestures, grab the handles of the wheelbarrow, and get on up the road."

The word "direct" commits what follows. If Woodward still refuses to comply, I will explain the section and article of the *C.C.R.R.* (which I have whipped out of my pocket and glance at from time to time) under which he is being charged, then call for the prowl truck to take him back to the unit where he will await internal trial.

That scenario is exceptional. Bear in mind that the rest of the cons on the gang put their own self-interest first. When they have an easy-going guard running the gang, the last thing they want to do is ruin a good thing. Before I used the word "order" the first time, they would have been nudging him and telling him he was being an asshole and a heat-bag.

There is one overriding vulnerability to all correctional systems. No matter how high you elevate the standards for staff, at a whim of the provincial caucus or federal cabinet, the best programs of the best institutions go with the winds. If they target corrections as a place to hit the public-sector budget, the best commissioner of corrections with the best intentions has no choice but to pass it down to his insti-tutional directors.

Just prior to my entering service, they were still double-bunking at

Oakalla, with counts as high as fourteen and fifteen hundred. The
place would be virtually splitting at the seams with counts of seven
hundred when single-bunking. Comparatively, Vancouver Pretrial
has an emergency (absolutely maximum) gazetted count of one hundred and fifty. New Haven's is forty. Logic would suggest that when
the counts go up, you increase staff to cover; the reverse when the
counts drop. Never so.

The politicians pass it down from Victoria that corrections is to
cut fat or they'll start closing institutions, which they have often done.

This vulnerability produces serious morale problems, stress problems, in the line staff and inmates. With staff cuts, each remaining
guard is at greater personal risk on the job. This has bred a deep-
running resentment, however irrational, among line staff. The
"brass" should figure out a way to stand up to the politicians (who
know nothing about the parts of the criminal justice system except
as they appear as ciphers in the total budget). For the most part, of
course, they don't.

Hence there is an ongoing resentment and pay-back in the form of
"dirty tricks" for anyone who enters middle management. It is a practice rife with mixed signals because most of the brass were once line
staff who pranked their superiors. And this has been going on for
more than a hundred and fifty years. Thus there is a high wall
between line screws and all corrections personnel above them. It
becomes a situation of guards and cons against the system. The
inmate code of silence and the guard culture are distorted mirror
images of one another.

As a rule, the cons organize and run their own operations very effi-
ciently. When they hit something that they need help with, they let
the line staff know.

Whenever a staff-member receives a promotion, screws and cons
declare open season on him – a well-deserved antidote to various
diseases like principal-officer-itis or senior-correctional-officer-itis.

New P.O.s haven't a clue what to do other than hand out keys to the oncoming shifts. So they attempt to reinvent the wheel. They suck in their guts, throw out their chests and drive everyone nuts for a couple of months, telling staff to do jobs which they are already doing at the time they're being told by the greenhorn to do them.

The old-time P.O.s sit in their offices, read magazines, monitor calls if they're bored, and keep an eye out for pranks directed at them. As soon as the whole shift is accounted for, they give the desk man a look that says, "The shift is yours," and disappear. But not the new guys. They practically beg for abuse.

The movie *Brubaker* was popular with both guards and cons, as was *The Last Yard*. In fact, any movie to do with prison was popular. But especially those which showed the inmates in a favourable light and, better yet, the system to be god-awful.

The weather was mild but it had been raining lightly. The pulse of the jail was not good. It was yard time, but there could be no yard because the urinal in the yard was gefritzed. Nothing but crap on television. The wing was antsy.

The time was about 1530 and the shift was under way. I was desk man. What a boring afternoon.

I was searching my imagination for mischief when it was delivered to me.

Ollie Brent (Shift Emperor of all the republics of Oakalla) called to say that we should double-check security on doors to the yard because they were going to open the massive secure gates and allow in a couple of plumbing contractors to fix the pisser.

I reported to Falkland, the acting principal officer. He didn't look up from his book. So I checked the three doors. Secure. Called Brent back and told him to send them through.

It took about ten minutes to get the gate open to the yard. By looking out the window to my left, I had a vista of most of the yard. The plumbers wheeled in a one-ton truck with a zillion doors for tools. The gate closed behind them and two little farts in hardhats and bright yellow rainsuits warily got out of the truck and stared at the locked gate. There are few things emptier and more forlorn than an empty enclosed prison yard.

I could feel my face breaking into a grin. *Brubaker* had been on only a few nights before and I had been moved by some of the issues that the film treated.

On the left side of the desk before me was a wonky old intercom with two long lines of toggle-switches. It was so sensitive that, on graveyard shift, you could hit the switch for a landing and hear how many guys were snoring, or pick up a whispered conversation or someone farting in his sleep. During the day you could only speak to the staff because there was too much white noise.

The plan was coming together in my brain. Meanwhile, the two obviously terrified plumbers out in the rain had fetched pry-bars from the truck and were driving them into the asphalt to expose the drainpipe of the pisserino. *Brubaker* . . . pry-bars . . . digging . . .

Yesssssssss! I had it.

The intercom had speakers, well-hidden up under the eaves of the roof on the five-storey building, to call people at yard in for phone calls, converse with them during riots and sit-ins and – when you could get away with it – insult the staff in the towers.

I stared at the toggle labelled "Outside Yard." Then I looked out the window at the plumbers, who obviously had serious doubts that even government money was worth the rain and all the ten-feet-tall criminals just a wall away from them. I prayed they had seen *Brubaker* too.

I had to do it. I hit the toggle and grabbed the microphone. "That's it, right there, dig right there. That's where the bodies are buried." It was wonderful. One of them dropped his thirty-pound pry-bar on the spot. I could hear the clank inside. Both stopped dead and looked at one another for a reality check.

The cons on the right side of the wing instantly knew what I was up to and lined up on the range to watch. I could hear them roaring with laughter.

Falkland couldn't make out what I had said, but he knew the sound of the speaker outside. He beetled out to have a look.

"What the fuck are you up to?" he demanded.

"Updating the log, acting sir."

"Bullshit." I pointed out the window. Falkland grinned. "Oh, fuck, that's beautiful. What did you say?" I told him what I had said. Falkland's mind was whizzing. The two plumbers were still looking around, and then looking at one another. I hoped administration, whose windows also border on the West Wing yard, hadn't heard me. But then the loudspeaker at this time of day – yard time – was quite common. Finally, the worried workmen went back at it. Falkland wanted in. I pushed back in the creaky old chair and handed him the mike. He hit the toggle and roared at the top of his voice: "Take the fucking truck hostage and don't negotiate!" There's no way Brent could have missed that blast. The plumbers were spinning around like dervishes looking for the source of the commands. The cons on Two Landing had tears streaming down their faces from laughter. Falkland dashed out of the desk cage and hid in the P.O. office at the first ring of the telephone.

"West. Yates," I answered.

"Mr. Yates, this is Ollie Brent. Is everything all right in the West."

"Certainly, sir. The inmates are napping or watching TV."

"You on desk?"

"Yessir."

"Who's P.O.?"

"Falkland, acting."

"Good God. Well, the girls in the office thought they heard the word 'hostage' from the yard."

"We're not even running yard. The urinal is down. There are only a couple of workmen and a truck outside."

"Oh, that's right. Well, I think I'll take a stroll back anyway."

"Come right ahead, sir, we have a fresh pot of brew in the staff-room."

I could hear the various doors keying and clanking as he came through from Front Hall. Meanwhile, the two plumbers had put their tools back in the truck and were honking desperately. Staff came out from admin and spoke to them over the fence. The plumbers said they had some other emergency and needed to be let out of the yard. They would return to finish the job. The job was finished by other plumbers. The two little yellow guys never returned.

When Brent entered the wing, to my delight he interrogated

Falkland for half an hour and got nowhere. Then he strode up from landing to landing and asked cons and guards if they had heard anything. Not a thing.

Solid, baby, solid.

When Ed Blandish was made director of the mighty West Wing, he at last got to associate with the high and powerful.

For at least the last fifty years of Oakalla's life, politicians had been threatening to close the jail. One consequence was that there was never any new equipment for offices. Everything was old, had three legs, and initials carved into it: walls, desks, chairs, even the plexiglass in the towers. Everyone hated Tower Two. It had no toilet. If you had to take a leak, both cons in the yard and visitors coming down the hill could see quite clearly a thirty-foot arc of wee-wee arching out the door. It was drafty in the winter. Very exposed, and it wiggled on its frame as you climbed. And the goddamned chair was deadly. Hard wood, the back gone, and one loose leg so that it rocked and woke you up each time your weight shifted.

Tower One jutted out in a concrete turret over the yard itself and the chair was reasonably comfortable.

There was actually a Tower Three between the jail door and Tower One, but it was so rickety that it had been condemned by Workers' Compensation. Not removed. Nothing was ever removed. Someone had hung a crude sign on it in red which read: *Condemned.*

The furniture in the P.O.'s and director's offices was just as rickety. Blandish was having none of this shit. He was king of the wing and wanted a throne. The government wasn't going to buy him one.

He beefed up the locking system on the door between the P.O.'s office and the office occupied by the director and the S.C.O.

Now, a new and more complicated lock on a door in a prison wing inevitably kicks the collective imagination of the line staff and cons into overdrive. Think of the pool of lock-breaking talent you have in a prison wing.

Blandish shopped for days before he finally found an appropriately expensive high-backed office chair and forked out five hundred dollars for it. He even called administration and arranged for the furniture company to deliver it right to the front door of the Main Gaol, so that he could supervise its transport straight to the wing and his office.

He made the mistake of telling everyone that he was shopping for a chair. So, plans to "jap" it (fuck it up) in some manner were under way long before he announced that he had made the purchase.

There were thoughts of epoxying it to the wooden floor or deucing the springs in the back so that when he sat in it, the back would fall flat. But finally, someone thought of Tower Two. That way we could ping Blandish, drive him nuts, and the guards would have the benefit of a new chair for Tower Two.

Logistics. Likely a chair that expensive would be heavy. The only way into the tower was up a narrow ladder. What we needed was to temporarily anchor a winch on the roof of the tower, then block or double-block (if very heavy) the chair up, with guards pulling the rope from below. One guy in the tower could simply swing it in the door, release the chair and unhook the anchor and rigging.

The necessary equipment was gathered and stashed at the home of a guard who lived about a block from the jail, because neither Blandish nor we knew exactly what day or time of day the chair would arrive.

There were other matters to organize. Administration controlled the gate, the prowl truck, Centre Hall and Front Hall. It would be necessary to alert the gate man about the time it would be going down, to be sure that the night-jailer (graveyard was the obvious time) was kept busy or sent on some goose-chase to the hospital or got too drunk to notice, and to bring the prowl truck man in on the prank because the truck's headlights might be very useful.

With all in readiness, the chair arrived at about 1300 on a Friday. Blandish went out to supervise. The desk man instantly got on the phone to alert those on shift who formed the central part of the conspiracy, and to call at home those who were off shift and would be let in by the gate man to do the deed.

The acting S.C.O. in charge of the entire institution would likely be pissed as a newt by 0200, knowing him. We would have to keep him tied up with paper or some phony problem until the prank was pulled. Bad news to have him stagger into the middle of it while on rounds.

By the time the chair was uncrated and behind the desk, it was 1400. Shift was over at 1500. Blandish paid half a grand to sit in that chair for an hour. Then he was gone for the weekend.

A long line of lock-picking heroes had had a look at the three locks, which included an eighteen-inch dead-bolt. There were bets all over the jail about how long it would take to get in without forcing the door.

Seven minutes took the money. Not a mark on any of the locks. We could have gotten illegal picking tools from cops or the locksmith, but one con said they were a snap and he could make what he needed from crap lying around the wing.

Half an hour after Blandish had left the wing, the locks were unlocked and the door closed but waiting.

The desk man was alerted to let the wing know, after dark, when the S.C.O. wouldn't be watching Front Hall, so that we could get the chair outside and to the foot of the tower. When Lewis, the big boss, sat down to dinner in the staff-room of admin, the desk man called the wing, Centre Hall and Front Hall. Thus all the doors were opened wide so that the chair could be rushed straight out from the wing and down the front stairs. Half the problem was solved.

Under cover of dark, the guys with the winch rigging were let in by the gate officer, drove down, and dumped the rigging near the chair, then got the vehicle back to the upper parking lot.

While this was going on, there was a bit of a scare, because the S.C.O., who had had a few belts, decided to walk up and check out the Women's Unit (which is routine). The usual route would take him right by Tower Two. The desk man was fast on his feet and told the S.C.O. that the hospital had called to report a serious problem with a suicidal con on the secure ward. The S.C.O. could check that out and then walk up the other side of the Main Gaol. By the time the S.C.O. got to the hospital, the guards had set up a very unsuicidal con with a promise of a deck of tailor-made smokes, the brand of his choice, to act like he was going to off himself at first opportunity. Later we learned that the S.C.O. had almost knocked the con over with his breath and had given the poor bastard a long repetitive homily on why life was so profoundly worth living. This was truly cruel and unusual punishment so the guards gave the con three decks instead of one for his Oscar-winning performance and Job-like forbearance.

Meanwhile, the riggers had scampered up the ladder to the roof and anchored the blocks, trussed up the chair, hauled it up to the door, and swung it into the tower. The prowl truck gave them a ride to the upper lot and they left for a local bar to drink and howl the rest of the night, anticipating Blandish's expression on Monday morning.

Moments after the chair was out the office door, the con relocked the doors without putting so much as a scratch on the brass facings.

If all capers were as well-planned as this, there would be no cons in jail and guards would be out of jobs.

On Monday it took Blandish several minutes to open all the new locks. When he swung the door open, he looked thunderstruck. The chair was so big that you couldn't have hidden it behind the desk even if you had pushed it over sideways. Blandish was so disbelieving that he actually walked around the desk and looked under it. The P.O. in the outer office was stone-faced because he knew nothing about it. The S.C.O. was still in the staff-room brewing up.

Blandish began to bellow. The P.O. rushed in. The S.C.O. double-timed it up the stairs. The desk man, who knew all about it, charged in; he was looking for an excuse to see Blandish's reaction anyway. The cleaners (trustee cons) lined up outside the door in their white jackets to check out whatever the matter might be. There wasn't a con or a line screw in the entire institution (including the Women's Unit) who didn't know exactly where that chair was, how it got there, and who put it there. But not one person so much as blinked that he might know anything.

After shouting at everyone standing around him, Blandish screamed at the Centre Hall man to crack him through to admin. He stomped upstairs and straight into Charlie Bessasson's office and demanded that the warden call the horsemen, Inspection and

Standards, and, if necessary, God in the service of retrieving his chair and punishing by firing or corporal punishment those responsible for its disappearance.

Charlie asked whether the locks had been japped.

No, not visibly.

Was this provincial government property?

No.

Then Charlie couldn't possibly set a dangerous precedent by calling in the cops every time the personal property of staff disappeared. This was a place where people who steal live. It would be unusual if they didn't steal. Staff should know better than to tempt them.

A huge five-hundred-dollar chair? Where the fuck would they put a five-hundred-dollar chair in a wing?

Had he searched all the tiers?

No.

Charlie suggested he start there.

Blandish knew intuitively it wasn't in West Wing.

Charlie was having a terrible time keeping a straight face. He asked Blandish whether he was sure he had actually taken delivery of the chair.

That tore it. Blandish stomped back down to the wing and ordered a "roust" (a search of every cell including its occupant, whose personal property frequently gets damaged in the process. There are searches – lift up things carefully and put them back; frisks – go over everything including the high cross-members of the bars and mess things up, but don't break anything; then rousts).

Cons, for obvious reasons, dislike rousts. This one was expected, but never happened. The guards simply hung around on their landings and came down and reported the entire wing had been rousted. No chair.

Blandish interrogated every staff-person who had been on every shift between Friday afternoon and Monday morning.

The look in his eyes began to resemble something I couldn't place. Ahh . . . Wile E. Coyote in the "Roadrunner" cartoons. He then called the Burnaby detachment of the RCMP; they weren't sure about jurisdiction and kept asking whether the chair was government property.

By the end of the week, all the line staff and cons of the 154 provincial jails in British Columbia, and even those who had gone on to the federal system in B.C. and Kingston, Ontario, knew about the great Chair in the Tower caper. It could scarcely have been more widely known if Lloyd Robertson had reported it on CTV News.

Over the course of the next month or two, Blandish personally searched every tier and every cell of every active and abandoned unit, the dilapidated shops and barns left over from the days of Oakalla Prison Farms. He never found the chair.

He was obsessed with finding those responsible for his loss of chair until the moment he walked out the gate for the last time in 1991. I saw a friend recently who had seen Blandish not long before. Early in their conversation Blandish brought up the chair. He still didn't know any more than he did that Black Monday in September 1982 when he opened the door to his office.

One could argue that, like convicts, guards have too much time on their hands – to dream up pranks as cons dream up escapes.

After the West Wing was closed and all of us folk-heroes of the Old West were scattered on the winds of paper to other wings, B-side, hospital, admin, and segregation, I was transferred to B-side (Westgate B). B-side is the training unit where all the rookies are weeded out and, therefore, is never really out of prank gear.

A daft S.C.O. was transferred in and took one look at that dungeon and decided that order was in order.

If there was anything that Oakie could resist better than any institution on earth, it was systems analysis and streamlining. Self-appointed and formal efficiency experts were reduced to dingleberries by Oakiefenoakie Swamp staff and inmates. I was still in West Wing when the jail switched from manual to electronic records. The computer was japped several times a day by records personnel who resented having change thus thrust upon them. Oakie ran by tradition, what was comfortable, and what kept cons and line staff happy – not by any logic.

This didn't stop the new S.C.O., of course. He spent several days arranging and rearranging the furniture in his office and making brief sorties out to tell the P.O.s who had been there since the Pleistocene Age to hand out forms according to his new criteria. They ignored him.

Finally, he decided that the rest of the hell-hole could do what it wanted, but his office would be a model of efficiency. He had only one job: to put together work-gangs and assign security levels to the gangs, and designate staff to them. This he could do in half an hour at the top of the shift and have the rest of the day to turn his office into a paragon of efficiency.

A real guard would have organized gangs in the morning, and then closed his door and read or slept or carried on moonlight business by telephone for the rest of the day.

Not him. After he arranged his desk and chair and wastebasket in a configuration of supreme effectiveness, he commanded the carpentry gang to put up new fake-grained wall-board on the wall next to his desk. He then screwed a handful of brass cup-hooks into the board. From these hooks he hung clipboards labelled in the order that he sent out the gangs: metal-shop, tailor-shop, carpentry, brew (coffee) truck, landscape, and so forth. He arranged these clipboards, which hung on the walls like degrees in a doctor's office, so that each could be reached with an absolute economy of movement – without his having to push back his chair or stand up. Even the farthest clipboard could be reached without his having to do anything but reach back with his left arm and grab it. He checked the board, handed the gang boss officer his gang list with his right hand and the dude was outa there. Next. Our new S.C.O. was in his late thirties. This idea was his achievement of a lifetime.

The vibes of that office – this guy was more impersonal and mechanical than the mainframe computer up in records – were so bad that just going into the office could wreck your whole morning. Also he was very "professional" (this word would gain incredible meaning at Pretrial), extremely fastidious about his uniform and person, and entirely too clean.

One weekend we came up with the perfect prank. We would break into his office and saw the legs off his chair so that he couldn't reach any of his damned clipboards and thereby blow his brain.

Easy compared to the Chair in the Tower number.

Damn, were we wrong.

It was easy enough to send a rookie up to the carpentry shop with a key and a list of tools. We chose a guy who swore he was the same height and wore the same size clothes as our Kommandant. Now we could check out just how much we needed to take off the legs.

We wanted him out of the unit. We wanted him taken away to the rubber ranch. Nobody liked this non-smoking, non-drinking, non-swearing jerk.

The door to his office was a snap to open, and we thought fixing the legs of the chair would be easy. Just cut a few inches off, tap the metal sliders back onto the bottoms and rub some dirt on the leg ends to hide the fresh saw-cuts.

With the first cut we had the height approximately right, but when we sat our ersatz Kommandant in the chair we made two terrifying discoveries. The legs looked and measured the same length, but one or more was shorter and now the damned thing rocked. It had been solid before we began tampering. It would be an instant tip-off. And no one had calculated that when we lowered the height of the chair, its relationship with the desk-top would change, which would be another tip-off – and the desk was one of those ancient eight-legged wooden monsters.

Talk about hard work. It took three shifts of guards and cons filing and tapping and trying for size beginning late afternoon shift on Friday and ending Sunday graveyard (Monday morning) to get it right.

We could hardly wait. My gang was about mid-way through the line-up on Monday morning. Apparently, when the S.C.O. made his first grab for a clipboard and turned up about two inches short, he couldn't believe it. He jumped up and ran over to examine the wall for holes. Nothin' shakin' in that department. He sat down again and pulled his chair into the desk to the usual distance between his gut and the desk edge. He tried another grab. Missed again. Finally he stood, slid the chair into the nook where the knees go, and stood by the wall taking down each clipboard as needed. He then walked over to the desk and picked up the gang list and handed it to the gang boss. Then walked back and replaced that clipboard on its hook, called for the next gang, grabbed the wrong clipboard, and gave the gang boss the wrong list, which the gang boss was obliged to call to his attention.

By the time he had the gangs out on the grounds, our good Kommandant was really rattled. He headed for the staff-room. He wasn't a coffee drinker either, but he poured himself one and vanished back into his office when other staff entered to coffee-up.

All day the staff who remained in the unit made excuses to go to his office and ask questions about the gangs, which would occasion his checking his clipboards, just to keep him cooking. By lunchtime, he looked ready to lose it. By the end of the day he was standing at attention beside the clipboard wall attempting to look nonchalant.

The next day, he unscrewed all the hooks and reinserted them so that he could grab the clipboards as before. There was no way we were going to attempt to level all those legs again. But I guess we had altered his life forever. He requested transfer that day, claiming that he just couldn't handle the B-side experience. They found a corner for him in admin and there he remained until he transferred out.

It was a lot like swatting a fly with a sledgehammer.

The Oakalla Hospital was a thing of beauty and would annoy forever.

At Oakalla, any con who couldn't make it in population – because he was little or weak or pretty, or couldn't even make it on the protective-custody tier because he had ratted out someone on the tier, or because he was a dirty judge, lawyer, Mountie, guard, sheriff, or cop – did his time in the hospital.

The wars were between the medical brass and the security brass. The cons and line staff simply wanted entertainment.

Things were a little dull. I don't know who cooked up the scam, but a guard and a con were cast in the lead roles to put one over on

our security-hating Boss Docteur Sutherland. The con was legiti-
mately recovering from some injury or surgery and was due to be
released back to his unit.

This was the script: The con would mouth off to the screw. The
screw would order him upstairs to his drum. The two would continue
arguing up the stairwell, ascertaining that the doctor was watching.
Then the con would swing wide on the guard. The guard would
appear to deck the con, who would go down on the stairs. The guard
would then grab his collar and apparently whack the hell out of the
con while he was down. These two guys could have joined a stunt
team. Because the stairwell was narrow, no one would be able to see
any actual contact because the angle was wrong. The guard would
pull the punch and the con would slap his own chest, making it sound
as if the blow had landed. The guard would yell, "Staff up!" and security staff would rush up and escort the con to his cell where they
would all collapse laughing.

The plan was executed and the doctor freaked.

Ping. Did Sutherland ever ping (ping and spin are terms for flying
into a rage). He stood and stormed about the brutal slime in uniform.
The local director rushed out and almost collided with the doctor at
the door. They called one another everything in the book. The logical
thing would have been for the doctor to demand to examine the victim, but he was too busy screaming at the local director. The P.O.
rushed up and averred he had seen the whole thing and the con had
assaulted the guard. Not true, screeched the doctor, he had seen the
whole thing. All the brass in the hospital dashed out the door and up
the stairs of the terrace toward the Main Gaol and Charlie's office.

The plan depended on the understanding that, per procedure, the
guard would "lay paper" (charge under the *Correctional Centre Rules
and Regs*) which would cause a Warden's Court trial; and that under
Section 29, inasmuch as the con had apologized and neither guard
nor con was physically damaged, the charge would be dropped.

But it went haywire. For entertainment value, it went haywire for
the good. For the taxpayer, bad. The doctor, having failed to have all
Oakalla hospital security staff fired for brutality, got in his car and
drove down to the RCMP detachment and got them to press charges

against the guard. He tried to have the whole security administration of the hospital charged too, but that didn't wash. Still, his action forced the issue into outside court. Now there couldn't be an internal trial because that would DJ (double-jeopardy) the con and the prison would be in deep shit.

The pranksters now had to play out the hand. The kid in the screw's uniform was an auxiliary. If he admitted that the whole thing was a scam, he would be fired on the spot. The con knew to say nothing except to his lawyer. The lawyer told the Crown to take a hike. The Crown was all hot to trot because any sort of prison animal show would make for good media coverage.

A regular staff guard and the auxiliary involved in the prank paid a visit to the defence lawyer and told him the whole story, which the con corroborated. The criminal lawyer then gave the Crown a call and told him that both guard and con were prepared to get on the stand and say the incident never happened. The disappointed Crown vetted the case and reluctantly dropped it on the grounds that there wasn't enough evidence to warrant even a preliminary hearing.

This whole process took a couple of weeks, during which M. le Docteur was fantasizing courtroom glory. The Crown called him to inform him of his decision and thank him for his efforts.

Ping.

5

Fear and Burnout:
Five Stories

———————— • ————————

A man goes far to find out what he is . . .
   – Roethke

SOME CONS are terrifying simply because they are there; they don't
have to do anything. Others are terrifying because of the people
who want either to help or to hurt them. The most terrifying case of
burnout-inducing stress I endured took place when I was not even on
prison grounds. I was in a hospital, guarding a wounded prisoner
who had a contract out on his life. I had no weapon, no partner, and
no police coverage. The man was moved daily, and no one knew his
room number; each guard had to find him when he came on duty. For
three weeks, we both hit the floor whenever the door opened.

WILKINSON

Wesley Wilkinson was doing two years less a day in Westgate B for
aggravated assault. He was black, skinny, and about as unathletic as
you could get, but short of being effeminate. None of the stereotypes
held by whites applied. He didn't have rhythm, and he didn't have
"soul." Said he was a washout with girls because they found him dull.
He wasn't into any cause or movement. He was an American, but
without a hint of down-home Black English enunciation. He came

from a family of educated people, most of whom were educators. Black was no more beautiful than any other colour of biped. To Wesley, human beings were pretty much human beings. What he did have was an M.A. in math and he was a teacher in the Seattle school system. A career interrupted and quite possibly ruined by his conviction in Canada. I was his case manager.

Wesley had met a single white female teacher at a math conference in the States, and she had indicated an interest in him. So he drove up to Vancouver one Friday night, screwing up the courage to call her once he got to town. After he checked into a good hotel, he found her number. He went to dinner alone, and when he returned to his hotel, he finally phoned her. They arranged that he call her back the next day around noon and perhaps then they would make plans for Saturday night. Wesley read for the rest of the evening, then went to sleep.

However, Friday night, in front of a nightclub dive in North Vancouver, an assault occurred and the black perpetrator drove away in a car of a certain colour.

Wesley awoke much too early to call the lady, so he had breakfast and went for a drive around Stanley Park and the West End.

He was pulled over in Stanley Park by the Vancouver police because he was the right colour and the car was more or less the right colour; he wound up in the city tank. On Monday, he was remanded in custody at Oakalla's West Wing. At that point, the hospital wasn't sure whether the victim of the Friday-night assault was going to pull through. Not wishing to involve his family or the lady he scarcely knew, Wesley looked in the phone book for a criminal lawyer.

The criminal lawyer wanted a huge amount of cash up-front to represent him. Wilkinson called his family. They raised the money. His bail was set so high that he hadn't a prayer of raising it. He would have to remain in jail through preliminary hearing and trial. The high-priced lawyer showed at the bail hearing, but Wesley never saw him again. Wesley kept calling but could never reach the lawyer and the lawyer never called him back. (The trick here is to annoy the client so much that the client will fire the lawyer, who is home-free with the retainer without having had to do anything.) So Wesley went to trial with a lawyer who was ill-tempered because he had been stuck at the last moment with a legal-aid case.

To Wesley, the evidence against him seemed ridiculous. The legal-aid lawyer recommended that he stick with provincial court and a judge without jury. (It is the accused's prerogative to elect the court up to county- or supreme-court level, where it is harder for the Crown to prove its case, but where the penalties are stiffer if the Crown succeeds.) Wilkinson was convicted, not on the basis that he committed the crime and was seen doing it, but that he had no one to provide an alibi for him at the time of the crime. The legal-aid wizard advised against appealing either conviction or sentence; Wesley could keep his nose clean and be paroled in eight months.

I've seen some bad judicial calls in my day, and this was one of the worst. But Wesley wasn't the sort of person to raise hell or scream foul. He didn't like troubling people. He hadn't so much as a single parking ticket on his record. He didn't drink, smoke, or do drugs. Probably the first time he ever saw pot was in Oakalla.

At Westgate, he got along well enough with the cons. He was on a decent tier and he was cordial to everyone and did as bidden. After he had been around long enough for the tier to decide he wasn't a fink, he and I conversed through long evening shifts about every subject imaginable. (At Westgate, guards are locked on the tier with the cons.) We were dismissed as a couple of eggheads talking about academic bullshit. The cons knew Wesley was green as grass and without jail-wisdom, but he was solid enough not to rat out anything to a guard. I always made it a point to sit with him within earshot of the guys playing cards to minimize their suspicion.

I thought I knew Wesley Wilkinson pretty well. Every now and then in mid-conversation about the States or teaching, a kind of distance would come over him, but I dismissed it as homesickness. Homesickness is not unusual. He quickly worked his way up through the gangs. With good behaviour, prisoners move up to levels of less and less supervision. He was sentenced around the first of the year and by the time of early summer, he was allowed out alone to mow grass. He reported back to the unit only at shift-change. Wesley was pulling his time like a champion.

During yard, which on the weekends began before shift-change and ended at dinner time, the cons could play baseball, run the track, or simply sit on the bleachers and enjoy the sun. Wesley usually took a book and sat on the bleachers and read, looking up now and then to check out the ball game.

One day, I came on shift and went out to relieve Tower Five. I took the shotgun and radio and sat down in the tower. When I looked over the yard, I could hardly believe my eyes. There was gangly Wesley humping around the track. Skinny as he was, he couldn't even make a single lap without pausing to rest and puff and blow. But he persisted. He kept it up day after day, and soon everybody got used to Wesley out there on the track alone running lap after lap, faster and faster.

On the tier we talked about his running. He said the usual things: he felt better, it was the first time in his life he had actually been fit, it was interesting to discover what your body can do.

I was on patrol up near the gym looking down on the yard one day while Wesley was running. It was a warm afternoon. I turned for a minute to give a light to a handcuffed con who was being escorted to segregation. I was just about to light a smoke of my own when I heard a brouhaha behind me, then a warning shot.

Wesley had left the track and was running up the asphalt drive toward the fence around the gym. This made no sense whatsoever. No one was chasing him. He was going in exactly the wrong direction for an escape – south, up the hill, toward the fence which surrounds the gym. I started running to cut him off. If he intended to come left, he'd run right into my shotgun, or the one east of me, or the West Wing patrol, or the patrol truck, or all the guns at the gate.

The parts of the scene simply didn't fit together. No one in his right mind would attempt to escape wearing a tank-top and shorts. The fences were heavy hurricane mesh topped by barbed wire slanted inward, topped by concertina wire, which never rusts, retains its razor sharpness seemingly forever, and catches the light like bits of mirror.

There were certain traditions and rules about escapes from West-gate B, the source of most of the many escapes at Oakie. First, you didn't go alone; you escaped in pairs because most of the time the local RCMP detachment only had one mutt on duty. The dog, unable to track both cons at once, would be forced to pause and make a decision. Second, you would get everyone at yard to agree in advance to charge over to the easternmost fence and sit down for forty-five minutes to an hour, so no one could tell which of the 150 to 200 bodies had escaped. That delayed the Mounties, as they couldn't give an article of clothing to the dog to put it on the correct scent. Third, you smuggled out to the yard two chequered mackinaws and two pairs of gloves per escapee, and wore as much clothing as you could under the two coats as armour against the razor wire. And finally, you made sure the guard in Tower Five was not paying attention to anything but the inside of his eyelids; then you ducked around the work-shops to the fence bordering Royal Oak because the fence was lowest there. An athletic type could be over that fence in no time. The Tower Five screw would radio for help and might fire a warning shot, but he wouldn't aim at the escapees because of the likelihood of blowing a few cars off the street just the other side of the fence. It was then a race to make it across the fence and between the houses before the prowl car roared down the hill or the horsemen cut you off on their way up the hill.

When i saw Wesley I yelled, "Stop!" and fired a warning shot into the air. I pulled down my aim on him with the vague thought that a shotgun pointed at him might change his mind. I don't think he saw it or me. He hit the hurricane fence and started climbing. Then I was right under him screaming at him to come down. He reached up with his bare hands and grabbed the barbed wire and kept climbing. He hit the razor wire and gave a final thrust to get himself over. Either the pain hit him or he ran out of gas. For a few seconds he held onto the hurricane wire on the far side of the fence to minimize the pain, then he let go. He was hanging with his full body-weight from the razor wire. Johnston, the other shotgun guard, was beside me by now and the patrol truck was roaring down the lane.

When Wesley let go, the razor wire really did its work on his chest, under his arms, his wrists. It literally flayed him. His black, black skin fluttered in tatters from the deep pink gouges as though someone had gone at his upper limbs with a chisel. It seemed as though every major artery and vessel in his arms had been severed. Blood rained all over the ground and on me as I tried to climb the wire and grab him and lift to lessen the weight. The width of my feet and the damned leather soles of my joint shoes prevented my making any climbing headway. Johnston was also trying to scramble up, but it was useless. We could reach his feet and push up but we couldn't unhook him. I'm not sure Wesley was fully conscious at this point.

I slid down the fence and started to take another run at it, when Johnston got the driver of the patrol truck to pull up under Wesley. We jumped up on the hood. We were joined by a guard who was a fraction of an inch under seven feet tall, and we got Wesley unsnarled, into the prowl, and down the road to the hospital. Wesley was unconscious.

The unit had sent out a couple of guys to cover our positions. As we backed down the road I saw the cons and guards in freeze-frame. No one had made a move for the usual sit-down against the east fence. Wesley hadn't put out the word that he was going to try.

It was a weekend and there was no doctor on at the Oakie hospital. Staff minimized the bleeding and fired Wesley off by ambulance to Vancouver General Hospital, where they transfused and sewed and patched for a week.

I pulled one morning shift at the hospital as his security. He greeted me with a smile, "Mr. Yates, thanks for helping get me down. I don't know anything about what you and everybody want to ask me. I have no idea why I . . ."

His eyes underscored the truth of what he had said.

Shit happens.

Shit happens especially when a man can't pull time and isn't even consciously aware that he can't.

After the stitches were finally out and the bandages gone, the scarring on his arms was beyond description.

PETOWSKI

When guards burned out, they sometimes did so in spectacular fashion, but none so spectacularly as line screw Peter Patrick Petowski. He was proof of the adage that bad things come in threes.

Pat was huge – over six-feet-six. He had kinky hair which was always too long even for the sloppy dress code at Oakie. His front teeth had been knocked out in a prison scuffle a few years before, so he wore a bridge of which he was extremely careful. Whenever heading into action, Pat first removed the bridge, which gave him a menacing Dracula mien. He had an enormous flock of kids at home to which he was devoted, but he confessed it was nice to come to work and get away from the throng. For years he got great evaluations, but then things began to go sour for him.

First, there was a nickel-and-dime escape artist who uncuffed himself on the steps of the Main Gaol and took off toward Deer Lake. The West Wing patrol man nailed him with a .38 wad-cutter slug through the leg without touching bone or artery. Pat got the duty of escorting the young punk to Vancouver General Hospital emergency. He feigned being in such pain that he sucked Pat in. While everyone's back was turned, the kid rolled off the bed and around a corner, found himself a doctor's smock and was out the door.

This was during one of the budget cutback periods. There should have been two guards on duty. The beds in emergency have nothing to cuff the con to. If you turn your back for a moment, goodbye.

Pat pulled a three-day suspension.

Next time up was big-money and big-media time. The Co-ordinated Law Enforcement Unit had spent five years and a great many tax dollars collecting evidence on the Gallo gang. The unit's crowning achievement was catching Gallo himself. Gallo was god-papa of the most powerful Mafia family on the coast.

For reasons I'll explain in a chapter to come, this extravaganza probably cost the taxpayer somewhere between 50 and 150 million dollars. This for perspective.

It is fairly difficult to spring an inmate from a maximum-security institution, but it is much easier from a hospital, or while in transit to or from hospital. At Oakie, the easy way to get to hospital was to inflict yourself with some medical condition which the primitive jail couldn't handle, or to describe symptoms that required expensive toys to run tests. For example, if you were really talented at faking a seizure, chances were you'd be sent downtown for an EEG. Gallo wasn't that talented. So he had to resort to one of the traditional methods of getting medical attention while in prison: a subcutaneous injection of sputum. In a couple of days it looks like early gangrene. Gallo was sent down to Vancouver General.

The higher-profile the inmate, the more comprehensive the medical care and – theoretically – security. However, still in budget cutback gear, Oakie was sending out one measly screw per shift to guard a man it had taken years and millions to put in jail. And guess which lone unarmed screw was assigned to Gallo on the first shift? Petowski the Luckless.

It was a very slick operation. While in hospital our inmates were put in private rooms, because it freaked civilians to share a room with someone handcuffed and leg-ironed to the bed. Gallo was no exception. It was later discovered that he had six *soldati* in the stairwell nearest to his room, and members of his biological family dressed in nurse and orderly uniforms running around on the ward.

A couple of ersatz orderlies wheeled a mobile X-ray unit down the hall until it blocked Gallo's door. They had a white uniform his size ready for him. Doubtless they had a cuff-key. (Smith and Wesson and Peerless cuffs and leg-irons all use the same key for lock and double-lock.) Devices like handcuffs are called "restraints" and that's about the size of it. They slow folks down, but they don't stop them from doing what they truly wish to do. Those who don't have their own cuff-keys can fangle one from a ballpoint-pen filler in a matter of minutes.

Gallo joined his friends in white and pushed the mobile unit down the hall to the stairwell where the heavy fire-power was waiting. Goodbye, Gallo.

And he was gone for a couple of years – until Mafia Multinational informed him that Interpol had cranked up the heat and his absence was fucking up operations. Likely after deals were struck, Gallo took the moral high road and gave himself up. He's probably out of federal by now.

Pat's story was that he baby-sat Gallo until his bladder was about to burst. Private rooms have private johns. He went for a leak and when he came out, gee whiz, Gallo was plumb gone. And that's the way it was. He stuck by the story and he was fired. Then the line screws threatened to lock down the cons and go out on a wildcat. By the time the dust settled and the media circus was over, the union and the politicians agreed on a three-month suspension and Pat was back. He stuck to his story, even to staff. This was a frightened man. He knew nothing. Saw nothing. Solid as an old-time con.

A more likely scenario is that a quiet-spoken gent of Mediterranean extraction waved a sawed-off shotgun under his nose and told Pat that whether he knew it or not he desperately needed to take a leak and that it would take him a specific number of minutes to do so. After that, he could follow *Manual of Operations* escape procedure.

For Petowski, things were going downhill. The three-month suspension hurt him financially and, to make things worse, his wife was pregnant again. By the time he and I were assigned to be present at the hospital as security while serial child-killer Clifford Olson was administered sodium pentathol by a UBC psychiatrist, Pat was getting a little spinny, and his appearance and demeanour spoke volumes about his state of mind. Half the time, he forgot to put in his bridge, and everyone was calling him Dracula. He stank and his pointy little goatee was ratty as hell. It looked as though he hadn't changed his uniform in weeks.

Olson was being given pentathol as a last-ditch effort for grounds to raise the common-law "insanity at the time of the crime" defence. After the injection, Olson was asked to focus on one of the more bizarre of his murders. In astounding, lucid detail he recalled every step of his actions, state of mind, time of day, right down to the length of the spike he drove through the skull of his victim. We and a veritable battalion of guards escorted Olson back to Main Gaol, the defence's experiment having failed. Olson had recalled far, far too much for an insanity defence to stick.

It was dinner time. They had saved a couple of meals for us in South Wing. Pat was a big man and he loved to eat. This night he sat there in the staff room and ate nothing. Stared and smoked and stared. I wasn't really in the mood to take on a heavy Oakie meal myself, but I poked at my tray and tried to get a few words out of the usually very voluble Pat. I tried wing gossip. I tried a couple of raunchy jokes. I even half-heartedly tried a little black humour about what we had just heard at the hospital.

At this, Pat turned to me: "You know, Yates, I'm religious and not religious. I only go to church when the wife blackmails me and reminds me I need to be an example for the kids. I don't take communion or go to confession or any of that bullshit. Tonight, I feel like going to confession. I don't know what to confess, but I feel as though I ought to unload something. All my life I have listened with one ear to all the cock about good and evil. Good is obvious enough. But I could never really get the hang of evil. Satan was never really anything to me. I think that tonight I have really been in the same room with evil. Olson isn't crazy. For the first time in my life, I have experienced evil. Real evil. Church evil. I need to get to confession."

I tossed my tray on the cart and headed back to West Wing. I heard later that Pat had asked to be relieved because he wasn't feeling well. You don't tell your P.O. you need to go to church and talk to a priest.

A few days later during a lazy afternoon shift I heard sirens blasting up from the bottom of the ridge and assumed there was an escape from B-side. But I didn't hear any rushing about to get staff from the wings down for back-up and sounds of rookie warning shots in the air. Something else was amiss.

Pat was in one of South Wing's shotgun towers. Without saying anything on radio to the other towers, much less to Central Control, he stood in the tower aiming the 12-gauge at the bunched-up cons in the yard without saying a word. They froze and pointed toward his tower. Then he raised the barrel and aimed first at one then at the other of the other two towers. The other two shotgun guards instantly tried to radio him.

Pat had clicked off his radio. He was unreachable by the towers and by Control which, by this time, had been alerted that something was going down. The barrel of Pat's shotgun moved back toward the gathered cons as though he was going to gun down the bunch. The moment he moved the gun, the other two guards flattened themselves in their towers and called Control to ask for orders.

Mike Adler, the most respected officer in admin, raced to South Wing and came out at the count position. Pat was still moving the barrel from the yard to the towers. Mike shouted and asked whether Pat had a situation. Pat, lost in his funk, didn't answer. For half an hour, Mike talked and Pat moved his aim from cons to screws. Pat even swung the barrel dead on Mike, who continued to talk as though a man in a tower wasn't giving every indication that he was about to pull the trigger.

As inexplicably as it began, it ended. Pat propped the shotgun in a corner of the tower and climbed down. He later said he had been overcome with an impulse to wipe out the yard and the towers. It didn't make any sense even to him, but he couldn't help himself.

The local wing director is allowed to send any staff-member to occupational health, not to return to work until cleared by psychiatric staff. There was no clearance for Pat. He went off on long-term disability and that was the end of it.

I heard later that he had been placed as a weigh-master on a highway somewhere up-country in B.C. Later, his family situation blew to hell.

KAZIZ

Ben Kaziz was wanted in Egypt for a capital offence. He maintained that he was a political refugee and had committed no crime in Egypt, and if extradited he would be put to death. In order to avoid this and to stay in Canada – even in jail – he attempted to put someone else to death. The incident has become a classroom staple in teaching guards the risks inherent in lowering your defences even for a moment.

Whatever the truth about the extradition for which he was being held, the man could not do his time in population. He looked more East Indian than Semitic, and was so thin and spidery that he annoyed the population cons just to look at him. Every time we tried him in population – including the hospital – he got thumped around. Someone finally suggested the option of signing himself into protective custody. He wound up in the South Wing Observation unit. South Wing was the place where only those who can't handle population were put. South Obs was where you put those who can't even handle time with the other misfits. Obs was also the place where the high-profile media types like Olson resided – those whom everyone wants to kill and those who want to kill everybody. A door locked from the other side separated the unit from the rest of the wing.

The Obs unit had only twelve cells. Six and six back to back, with big department-store mirrors so the desk screw could see every movement in every cell. Observation meant observation – a guard staring at you twenty-four hours a day, seven days a week. Chiefly, his focus would be on the devout wackos who were awaiting forensic psychiatric profile and those committed to suicide. The worst of all was the high-profile inmate who just might in a moment of despair do himself. Oakalla had weathered numberless media hurricanes.

Kaziz was pleasant enough one to one. Before long he had the South Wing Obs cleaner job. In any prison, cleaners are trustees who carry out day-to-day tasks without close supervision and have the run of the landings. They earn the position through good behaviour and popularity. In South Obs, the cleaner was let out to mop the range. If addressed by other cons, he was not to answer.

It was a shitty winter's day and the heat was on too high. A younger guard was sitting at the observation position, his eyes fixed on the mirrors and the cells he could see straight-on. He had taken his tie off and unbuttoned a couple of buttons of his shirt. Most of the cons had their shirts off.

Kaziz was mopping in desultory patterns on the floor. He stuck his head through the door between the range and the office and asked that a couple of windows be opened. The kid at the desk started to get up, but his partner, Jack Denyk, was already pacing around and so went to the corner to get the stick to reach the window lock fastener.

Jack Denyk was an ex-military exercise freak in his mid-forties. He had been a boot-camp instructor and still believed all the "temple of the body" doctrine he fed his recruits. Jack encouraged inmates to do calisthenics and sometimes joined them. He was not crazy about working Obs. The space was too close.

The kid sat down again and stared. Denyk had his arms up above his head when Kaziz jumped on him from behind like a monkey, his left arm around Denyk's throat, a shank (homemade knife) in his right hand. He managed to plunge it into the back of Denyk's neck three times before the kid (violating procedure here) bolted through the door, disarmed the Egyptian, and nearly killed him throwing him into his cell. The kid then ran to the box and hit the button. "Staff up to Obs! Staff up to Obs! Denyk is down . . . Aw, fuck, I think the cocksucker killed Denyk!"

By the time the herd got up the stairs, the hysterical young guard was rocketing around the unit. Kaziz was at the bars of his cell screaming, "Now I not go Egypt! . . . No go! . . . No go! . . . No Egypt!"

Eventually they stretchered Denyk to the Oakie hospital and did what they could while awaiting the ambulance downtown. No one was making book on whether Denyk would make it.

He did and didn't make it. Amazingly, the Egyptian had missed Denyk's carotid, jugular, and spine. It was never clear in the stories that came back whether any of the ganglia at the base of the skull had been damaged. But Denyk never worked another day. At anything. He was a bachelor with only two or three ex-military types close enough to him to qualify as friends. Once out of hospital, his whole body seemed to twitch all the time. Doctors assumed the twitch would go away but it didn't, and life just seemed to leak out of him day by day.

After the incident I saw him at the Safeway a couple of times, but he never spoke or nodded, and then I didn't see him any more. He cut off contact with everyone in the jail and his name was never mentioned again at Oakie, except when the incident was brought up in training as an example of what can happen to those who lower defences just for a moment.

As for Kaziz, he swore that his lawyer had counselled him that there was a surefire way out of extradition. It was to kill someone in Canada. He would be tried in Canada and the lawyer had a whole briefcase full of defences. He could claim that he had gone "stir-crazy" at the time of the crime and could not "appreciate the nature and quality" of his act.

A quick huddle was held involving Corrections, Justice, Immigration, and Egyptian officials. Either the charges were dropped on the

Canadian incident or the proceedings were stayed to expedite extradition to Egypt, where it was assumed Kaziz would meet his maker.
But he beat all charges in Egypt and an Arab acquaintance told me
that Kaziz was back in Vancouver and, having been diverted from the
system, couldn't be prosecuted.

Denyk is alive or not alive. No one I know has heard from him in
years now.

DUMARAIS

There was a Belgian executive named Monel Dumarais who lived in
the West Wing for some time because of a complicated white-collar
case. He claimed to be true-blue Belgian, but I once lived for four
years in Germany – the Belgian spoke German flawlessly. He was a
very cheerful man of about sixty who, because of his age, was not
pushed around. He minded his own business and quickly earned a
job as a cleaner and moved into the "country club" of Two Right. The
tier had an area, much like the common area of the living-unit concept in newer jails, where they could play cards at a real table, get extra
desserts, and other privileges.

The crimes of the accused on the cleaners' tier ran the spectrum
from fraud (the Belgian) to murder. Eligibility for a cleaner's job was
based solely on institutional record. I watched who got the cleaner
appointments fairly closely for reasons of self-preservation. Trouble
came when a Murder One was appointed to the cleaners' tier. He had
been no problem before his arrival, but as soon as he moved in, the
cons in the protective-custody (P.C.) tier were at the gate bitching and
roaring. They contended that he took every occasion to threaten
them and abuse them by throwing things down the tier. I told them I
would keep an eye on him.

I saw him slip up the stairs one morning from Two to Three. I
went up the other stairwell and listened. He wasn't shouting but he
was indeed harassing them. I reamed him out and then threw him
out. The very next day, I caught him baiting the P.C.s again. I couldn't
believe anyone could be that stupid. Being a cleaner is a big deal and,
once fired, you don't get rehired. I gave him the bum's rush down to

Two and told him he was fired and charged, then locked him on the cleaners' tier until I could get someone to take him to another tier.

As it happened, we had some electricians in and I had to do security for them up on Five most of the morning. I'd had a couple of cups of coffee and had to piss like a racehorse. I dashed down to the makeshift john on Two after calling the desk for someone to take over.

As I came down the stairs, I found my Belgian buddy glued to the cleaners' tier endgate with a big smile on his face (which was usual), but what he was saying in German was not amusing. "*Höffentlich, Sie kommen nicht herein.* [I hope you aren't planning to come on this tier.]" In German, I explained that I had to take a leak. The Belgian was cool. He kept a bantering tone as he told me that the cleaner I had fired was waiting in number 14 for me to come on the tier (I saw him stick his head out and peer up the range) to take a piss and he was going to shank me. He added that I might perhaps prefer to piss my pants than die avoiding the embarrassment. I told him to scamper on down the tier. I would wait a while and then handle it. I then went over to Two Left and asked a con if I could use his john. No problem. I needed to kill some time to keep the heat off the Belgian.

I told the P.O. We quietly got some cuffs and clued in two or three staff and waited until one of the cleaners asked to have the gate cracked so he could make a call. When the gate swung open, I flew through the opening with the others on my heels, down to 14 and through the cell door. The ex-cleaner was sitting on his bunk, and I threw a body-check into him that would have made an NHL scout take notice, then tossed him on the floor face down with an arm-lock. The P.O. frisked him and turned up not one but two razor-sharp shanks. The con started screaming at me, "You fucking pig . . . you fucking pig . . . who ratted me out? I'm looking at twenty-five years, and taking you out wouldn't mean shit. I'll get your ass yet." Then he was hauled off to seg.

I made it a point of staying clear of the Belgian for a few days to make sure no one made the connection. Then we went back to German jokes as usual.

Without the Belgian or German or whatever he was . . .

I've had some nasty day and nightmares about that one. The

randomness of it all. The fact that both of us spoke German, that the Belgian was even on the tier at the time I came down the stairs. What if it had been a different guard? The "what-ifs" roll on and on.

I still have the shanks in my little bag of memorabilia.

PAULSEN

I have yet another shank which has special meaning for me. Like most of them, it is the handle of a soup spoon with the dipper broken off, egregiously stamped PROVINCE OF B.C. (there has to be something symbolic in that; one is sure of it around contract time) and honed sharp on a cement floor, which makes an excellent whetstone.

Oakie was dark on graveyard shift, and darker the deeper you ventured on a tier. I was on the third or fourth of my hourly rounds and at Four Right 12. Without the flashlight, I couldn't have seen my shoes.

The range one walked down was between three and four feet wide. Enough room to jump right or left if a con was crazy enough to make a grab for you from the line of cells. Or so I thought.

As I was moving the light from the ceiling of number 11 to number 12, I picked up in my lower peripheral vision an arm flashing quick as a fish out between the bars. The light was in my left hand. With my right I grabbed the wrist and rolled forward with it. I was so startled, terrified, and enraged, I had visions of ripping the arm out of its shoulder socket. The shank clattered on the cement, but I hung on and kept turning the arm. A god-awful cry of pain flew out of the mouth of the owner of the arm and shank – so loud and so piercing that it awakened both sides of the wing.

I pocketed the shank, finished my count of the tier, walked back and called Central Control. They hauled the shanker off to the hospital where I was sure they would find that he had to be sent to a specialized unit for microsurgery to repair the massive damage I had done to the arm.

When they came back with the news (after depositing the would-be slayer in the digger) that his arm wasn't even sprained, I listened in disbelief. I had had his arm across the steel cross-strut.

My rolling with the arm had the effect of causing him to drop the shank, but it also saved his arm, allowing it to bend in its natural directions. Very much at odds with my intentions.

When the con came back into population I went down the tier to talk to him.

"Hey, what the fuck did I do to earn a shank?"

"Nothin', man. You just happened to be the first uniform down the tier."

"Were you at court that day?"

"Yeah."

"What did they lay on you?"

"Fifteen, and they didn't give me any dead-time" (time off the sentence for time already served in remand).

"They usually don't except for Murder Ones. Gonna appeal?"

"Yeah. Conviction and sentence. Looks like I'll be here for a while. Thanks for not charging me in outside court."

"I never do. Nice job on making the shank. I'll display it proudly at home."

"Right on. Are we cool, boss . . . I mean, between us?"

"I thought I was gonna shit myself when your arm shot out . . . but I didn't. You nicked the shirt, but stores replaced it. We'll be cool, as long as you ask whether it's Uncle Mikey before you shank anyone."

"You're on."

6

Celebrities

——————————————— • ———————————————

A cynic is a blackguard whose faulty vision sees
things as they are, and not as they ought to be.
— Ambrose Bierce

Dear Sister:
Yes, you're right. The punkers are going to save us. They will fill the
streets of Vancouver. We will be five people with one message. All the
media will be at the trial. The whole world will hear us. There will be
riots in the streets of Vancouver and the exploitation of women will be
over forever ...
Love and Solidarity,
Bill

THE ABOVE is an approximation of a typical letter that passed
among the Squamish Five, an infamous gang of three male and
two female "revolutionaries" who blew up pornographic video
stores, among other things, across Canada in the early 1980s. The
letter differs from the real thing in that the spelling, grammar, and
punctuation are correct and it is not long enough to contradict itself
several times. But all the elements are there.

What elements, you may well ask? Exactly.

Night after night I read mail like this as it passed between the
men's and women's units. We read mail to determine whether in the

outgoing pieces there was any reference to guards or their vehicles, and in the incoming, any hint of an implicit or explicit drug deal. Inmate mail, every word of which guards are *supposed* to read, is an amazing body of communication.

I hadn't paid much attention to the Squamish Five as they went on their dynamiting spree from Ontario to B.C., so when they came through the door I wasn't prepared for their celebrity status. And what I really was not prepared for was the kind of twist their presence threw into the whole dynamic of the wing.

One day as I passed through the visits cage to go on shift, I saw seven people in a glass conference room. The two Squamish Five women had been brought down from the Women's Unit (three or four hundred yards away) and the three men from West Wing. They had a female lawyer and a male lawyer and, God help me, they were sitting there all holding hands around the table. I couldn't hear what was going on, but the sympathetic look on the faces of the lawyers was a sight to behold. Every now and then I could hear a muffled shout of "Right on!" or "Solidarity!" come through the soundproofing.

The case was very much in the press and very high-profile. The only thing that Squamish had to do with it was that Squamish was the place they were holed up when the Mounties apprehended them. I learned that the Five had come into Oakie that morning, and that their lawyers needed to meet with all of them together. Lawyers' visits are high-priority and considered sacrosanct.

I went on into the wing and got ready for afternoon shift. Eventually the three men filed back into the wing, heads held high, and aloof from cons and guards alike. They were looking at charges of conspiracy, possession of illegal weapons, stolen explosives, all kinds of property crimes. But in their own eyes they were better than the rest of the prison population.

We put the three men on the same tier. I could see them conversing among themselves but they wouldn't even speak to any of the other cons. None of them smoked, so pure were their ideals. One con offered one of them a tailor-made cigarette and the jerk simply turned his back on the con and snubbed him as though he were an insect.

This didn't look good. My heart was not gladdened to observe such behaviour. This was a fairly heavy tier, and I could see cons I had known for a long time looking at them as though they were Martians who had just stepped off a saucer. The three of them were spouting their caca about being political prisoners who had committed no crime.

Later that day an old-time con who was in and out of Oakalla like a yo-yo saw me at the endgate and came up and asked, "Jesus Christ, where did you get these assholes?"

"I dunno. I've been on days off. I have no idea."

"What is this 'political prisoner' shit?"

"I don't know anything about that either. I wasn't aware they were involved with politics. Are they Communists or Progressive Conservatives?"

"Well, it's not going down well on the tier."

I learned later that when they first went on the tier, one of them made a moral high-road comment about the decor of the cell he was put into. All the cells at Oakalla were plastered, walls and ceiling, with the raunchiest photographs of women in every spread-eagle position imaginable, some of them even committing amazing acts of contortion with animals and objects. Each guy who came in tried to add to the graphics. Otherwise all you would have to look at was the yellow lead-base paint. These pictures served the very practical purpose of assisting fantasies when the cons were attending to sexual relief.

The guard who installed the Squamish Three in their cells hadn't a clue what they were objecting to. You get to the point that – after you've seen thousands of these pictures – you can't even see them anymore. What would be surprising would be a cell without them. The three had dutifully gone in and removed every single picture from the walls and destroyed them. This really pissed the cons off because they never knew when they were going to be moved from one cell to another, and it's always nice to have some different wallpaper in the next cell.

For sexual relief, masturbation is always available, requires the least amount of equipment and the fewest number of people (and/or other animals). And you quickly learn in jail that human beings are infinitely resourceful in obtaining sexual gratification under the heading of what I call "guerilla sex." Top of the list of choices was to have a drag queen on the tier. Next, although not treated as grandly as the transsexuals (or sometimes transsexuals-in-progress), homosexuals were teased about being "gearboxes" but were still respected for their valuable service. The gearboxes were known to use long-necked shampoo bottles for insertion in orifices in the privacy of their cells but sometimes gave the whole landing a view in the reflection in the window. Those who worked in the kitchen were revered for certain raw items of food which could be smuggled back to the tier. Like liver. I'm told by the old-time cons that when Oakalla was Oakalla Prison Farms and the fields abounded with ducks, chickens, pigs, cows, and horses that no imaginable form of what the law would call bestiality went untried. If it moved, it was fair game.

The prison rapes which television so loves to showcase do occasionally occur, usually when a rookie is sufficiently clueless to put a young, unmarked, untattooed, smallish person on a tier. An experienced guard wouldn't think of doing such a thing without seeing how many favours he had on the tier which he could call in – preferably from the heaviest con on the tier. If the heavy owes the guard, one of two things will happen. Either the heavy will take the kid under his wing and make him his mascot and go-fer, or he will give the kid one black eye and send him up to request being taken off the tier. The latter is a message that the heavy hasn't sufficient control of the tier at that time to guarantee the kid's safety. In either case: no rape.

The misconception is general that heavy-time cons love trouble, and rape of a "new fish" is their idea of a good time regardless of how much trouble it stirs up. The fact is, the rape is probably not worth the trouble because if the kid comes off the tier traumatized and beaten up (and it takes very little to get them to name all the perpetrators), the trouble is Big Time. The entire tier is likely to go off to segregation for starters. This is a serious disruption of tier routine. Next, all of them could be labelled "skinners" and wind up asking for protective custody. Next would come an exhaustive internal institutional investigation. Then another by the Corrections police force, Inspection and Standards. Finally, the kid's lawyer would demand that the

Crown lay charges in outside court (sexual assault is sexual assault wherever it happens) as well as crank up a case to sue Corrections branch. If you were a con attempting to do your time quietly, the rape of the kid is likely to cause you very, very serious forethought.

This is notable. I think I have seen about as many sexual shenanigans as any guard over the years, but if a man comes to jail a heterosexual, regardless of the number of encounters he has with drag queens or homosexuals, he resumes his heterosexuality on the street. And I don't know of any homosexuals or queens who changed sexual orientation while in the joint.

Perhaps these three Squamish stooges thought someone was going to begin treating them like Solzhenitsyn or Koestler or Faludy just because they had blown up parts of certain institutions they thought were emblematic of society's ills. They came in with such high media profile that everyone assumed that these people were extremely dangerous, extremely organized, and perhaps a cell of who-knew-what seditious and insurrectionist and possibly terrorist group. In their fantasies, they had sacrificed themselves to this visionary idealism.

After seeing their on-tier behaviour and the seance they were having behind the glass, I was quite sure that anyone who would behave as they did was either a cretin or a fanatic. When the cops had nabbed them in Squamish, they were in possession of an arsenal of illegal weapons. One of them looked like a cross between a Mediterranean basketball player and Bjorn Borg. I kept looking at this guy and wondering whether this was the new Che Guevara or a black belt in some esoteric martial art. By the time the whole show was over, I wondered whether any of the Five had mastered use of any of the guns the cops found.

One of them was sent as an emissary down to the shift P.O. to explain they were political prisoners and sorely resented being kept with criminals. The P.O. responded that the place was bursting at the seams. He might be able to split the group up and put them on other tiers if they so desired, but, until he had grounds, other than their claim to be political prisoners, they would stay in the cells assigned to them on the tier assigned to them. Unless, of course, they felt they couldn't handle it in population and wished to sign themselves into protective custody.

What was that?

"Protective custody is the place for rapists, snitches, child molesters, and all others who for one reason or another will not be tolerated by population inmates."

Weighing the options, perhaps that was a possibility as a temporary measure.

"But then, there is a saying that you pull one day of P.C. and you pull P.C. for the rest of your life."

What did that mean?

"That means that once you've done time in protective custody, anywhere else you go in jail someone is going to recognize you and it'll be open season to relieve you of life and/or limb."

Suddenly protective custody didn't sound so good.

The P.O. then offered him the drill on an inmate's options to write his M.L.A., his M.P., the Ombudsman, he could even contact our own internal police force, Inspection and Standards, if he felt that he wasn't receiving treatment consonant with his status.

The Squamish One left assuring the principal officer that he had every intention of doing all the above. I think he actually expected that there would be a special place in a maximum security prison for those mercilessly incarcerated because of their high ideals. Maybe they thought they were going to get the kind of cushy treatment that the Watergaters got. Maybe they had been watching too many Hollywood movies.

There was quite a bright, affable guy on the same tier who was in for a computer crime. His charge was complex and he bragged to me, "You don't have an expert witness in Canada who is intelligent or well-educated enough to testify conclusively against me, so I'll beat it." He was right, and several millions wealthier.

I asked him what was going down on the tier with the Squamish dildos. He had no idea. He had tried to relate to them as an educated, first-time inmate and had failed. When he had first gone on the tier himself, he had been bright enough to adapt very quickly. It had taken him about half an hour to learn how to speak "Him 'n' I" (prison grammar) and to begin picking up prison argot. He said he'd never seen anything like the Squamish Three in the few months he'd been there. Either these guys were stupid beyond belief or they had an ace up their collective sleeve that he couldn't detect. I asked him where they were coming from in their *raison d'organisation*. Damned if he knew. No information there.

They wrote and received copious letters, most to and from the Women's Unit. I kept expecting to see long passages of Marx, Engels, Che Guevara, the Russian anarchists. No one was ever quoted. There was no philosophy. Then I thought they must be writing in some sort of code. But, if there was any plan to their blasting things off the planet, I certainly never discerned it in the letters. Whatever they blew up deserved it and that was about as far as their collective intelligence and insight carried them. In short, what they had done made about as much sense as a bunch of kids walking down the street and scraping a key along the paint of a brand-new car just for the hell of it. Except that these people's ages ranged from nineteen to twenty-nine. That was the only difference. The Squamish Five was a group of fuck-fumbles. What really amazed me was that they actually got it together enough to set off the explosives without blowing themselves to bits.

At first, the cons on the tier were much more patient with the three of them than they normally would have been, probably because they were baffled by them. Tiers have their ways of taking care of people who fit into certain categories. Eventually, the new cons will be made to fit in on the tier one way or another. It is quite literally a do-or-die situation. But with the Squamish Three I think that initially the cons were looking for something that really wasn't there, just as I was. None of us had ever seen anything like this.

However, the cons do not suffer idiots gladly, and it was time to bring this disruption to a cease.

A *blanket-party* is called this because a blanket is affixed over the head of the victim so he can't identify his assailants.

A *sock-hop* derives its name from the ready and practical weapon of a bar of soap in a provincial-issue sock. It has several advantages. Staff cannot keep soap and socks off the tier. The weapon rarely leaves marks. Like nunchuks, the bar of soap strikes with several thousand pounds per square inch, and the victim will feel the beating for a couple of weeks. Unlike fists against a face, there is virtually no sound when the soap in the sock strikes the person under the blanket. Finally, using the soap obviates using a fist with resultant tell-tale skinned knuckles.

When coming in as a new fish, the inmate is advised by staff and by cons in the change room to drift down the tier and ask questions. If told to fuck off, ask someone more voluble. Someone will come and tell you the drill sooner or later. But do not go on the tier with a chip on your shoulder and test the whole tier. Unless – and I've seen it happen – you really are the baddest cat on the tier, in which case, you are the instant new boss. But this is the exception.

If you go on the tier with a "when in Rome" attitude, you will not draw heat from guards or violence from the tier. Keep quiet and the tier will come to you. No one is so heavy that he can whale on some-one's head whenever he feels he needs a workout.

Prisons simply don't work that way. On the other hand, there are those like the Squamoleans who just don't get the drift – neither from guards, nor from the inmates.

But then the cons' patience wore out. It took only one blanket-party and sock-hop one night to get the Three into cadence, as it were, with the rest of the tier. The following morning, a little worse for the wear, the three of them came off the tier for breakfast aping con body language, speaking when spoken to by tiermates, using prisonese, and talking about ordering chonies (chocolate bars) in canteen. They were about as convincing as Gene Wilder and Richard Pryor. They whistled around the tier collecting beaver pictures and gluing them to the wall. Turns out these dudes had resources for survival unknown even to themselves. My computer buddy and the others roared for days over the metamorphosis.

At the time, I was dating a guard at the women's jail. After each shift, we exchanged reports. There were two romances going on amongst the Five, and one odd man out. And he was odd. So odd that he later severed his trial and liquidated their solidarity. The two Squamish women continued to pledge undying love to their lovers in Oakie. Meanwhile, their political-prisoner stance had also taken a turn for the worse. Women's prisons are predominantly lesbian, and a new con joins one "family" or another or suffers the consequences. They were persuaded to acclimatize. No problem.

The men put their new pictures to good use and went along with whatever was happening on the tier. And, of course, continued the rant against the exploitation of women in their letters to their girlfriends.

Jack Dunham died at length. But not before this – the closest that serial child-killer Clifford Olson came to death while at Oakalla.

The old-timers who remember Olson from his brief stay in the seventies at New Haven (an institution run on the Borstal honour-system program; Olson walked away) say he was never the sort of inmate you could become friends with, but he certainly wasn't disruptive or tough. By the time he hit Oakalla, facing eleven murder counts, he was a garrulous, institutionalized prima donna (thanks to his media celebrity), and a horse's ass.

Few inmates at Oakalla had ever been more disruptive than Olson. Almost all day-to-day operations were snafued. He had visitors almost daily – publishers, movie producers, his wife – at which times the entire Centre Hall had to be cleared and the guard trebled. When alone in his cell, he was happy enough to have a guard to talk to. He had several mattresses piled on top of one another instead of a bunk. A bunk could be taken apart and used to hurt others or himself. But he never did impress me as being self-destructive. He had survived too many institutions and brushes with death.

He was a slight man of about forty then. Black hair, no grey. Without conscience, yes. Enthralled with the limelight, yes. He told me he had twenty-two more bodies buried and that would give him the biggest record by one body. But after he was convicted and sent off to protective custody in Kingston, Ontario, he was flown back to B.C. to show the cops the burial place of his other victims, and he couldn't produce one. Monomaniac, yes. Megalomaniac, yes. Psychotic, no. Suicidal, no.

He indulged in bursts of gratuitous petty savagery whenever he had an audience. I was guarding him one day while he was having a visit (secure visit, glass and telephones) with a Hollywood type. It had taken us half an hour to clear Centre Hall. He was locked in the visits cage. But no one spotted the East Wing kid who was the Centre Hall cleaner, a good-natured youngster who had gotten messed up on angel dust and broken into an entire business block on a Sunday in broad daylight, piling up his booty on the curb. He couldn't remember any of it. It was his first offence.

The kid had been in the far corner between the gates to East and South sweeping when Olson was brought through. The other staff had gone back to their wings until time came to move Olson back to South Wing Obs. I was smoking and talking to the Centre Hall man when the cleaner passed by with the broom on his shoulder. I heard a voice from the gate to the tank. Olson had left his guest and was standing at the gate. "Hey, kid, got a light?" The cleaner nodded and started over. I don't think he even knew that it was Olson in the tank. It looked innocent enough. When the kid got close enough Olson hocked and spat in his face. Instantly, I had a punch-up through the bars on my hands and got whacked a couple of times separating them.

Olson had done it simply to grandstand for the producer. I was really angry. I had taken a couple of punches and banged my hand against the bar and it hurt like hell. Centre Hall took the kid off to East with instructions from me that he was not to be charged. I told Olson his visit was over and Centre Hall brought a platoon from the other wings to escort him back. I told Olson I was going to charge him. His response was, "Damn, Yates, what're you gonna do? Put me in jail?"

He was right, of course. He was already segregated. I wrote up the charge and he was convicted in Warden's Court. It was included on his institutional record, but there was no penalty.

Almost daily for much of the time that Olson was at Oakie, it seemed that there was a new script for hitting him, snitched out by whoever to whomever. Olson has seen a lot of prison. He knows exactly the chapter and verse and odds of guard behaviour and that of population cons. He knows how to play one against the other. He has experienced a great deal, including being shanked nine times while in Prince Albert prison. The shanker – who had no regrets, except that the bastard didn't die – was so highly celebrated by population cons when he later came to Oakie that the West Coast media speculated (doubtless some joker inmate phoned them) that he had intentionally got himself arrested to have another shot at Olson.

It was near the time that Olson was to go to trial on the first of the eleven counts of Murder One that Jack Dunham started to feel ill. At first, he tried to write it off to twenty-plus years in service, heavy smoking and hard drinking. He even thought he might be a candidate for a by-pass. Finally, he went to his doctor, who launched a battery of tests. One afternoon he learned he had no fewer than seventeen malignancies sitting like land-mines in his body. As he walked down the hill from the main gate for graveyard shift that evening, he was not exactly part of this world.

Clifford Olson was being held in the South Wing Observation unit, which is virtually protective custody inside protective custody.

Jack was on the desk. Sprott was in the P.O.'s office. Both were senior screws. They sent an auxiliary screw up to Obs to stare at Olson all night and locked the door to the stairway to Obs behind the kid.

It's difficult to stay awake in South Wing Obs. The night lurched on. Ollie Brent, the night-jailer, did his rounds fairly early.

Jack couldn't concentrate enough to read. He couldn't doze. So, with purpose, he rose and walked to the P.O.'s office where Sprott was sitting with feet up, eyes closed.

"Sprott. Can't find my fucking locker key," he said.

"Wake up a con to pick it for you."

"It's a cheap lock; I'll cut it off with the bull-cutters. Be back in a few minutes."

Dunham walked to the South Wing gate and called Centre Hall. The Centre Hall man walked slowly over and keyed the gate. They walked together across the common area to the visits cage. The Centre Hall man keyed this gate and opened it. Dunham walked through and called Front Hall. The Front Hall man came and popped his side of the visits cage. Dunham walked down the hallway and turned left into administration, which included Central Control and the armoury. Stan Barnaby was the P.O. on duty.

"Hi, Barnaby. Lost my locker key and I need my chewing tobacco out of it," Dunham said.

"Filthy habit, Jack . . ."

"Piss off and give me the key to get the bull-cutters." Stan passed him the flat to the armoury through the opening between the bars and the high counter.

Dunham keyed the door to the armoury, which is like a safe door. He opened it just enough to slip in. Barnaby was busy muttering to himself and sorting the mail.

Inside, Dunham breathed. To the left was the line of 12-gauge shotguns and below these were the Smith and Wesson .38s. He took one. Below the hand-guns was the drawer containing ammunition. He palmed five rounds, slid the drawer quietly back in, and put the .38 in his inside jacket pocket. Then he grabbed the bull-cutters by one handle and stepped out the door, which he closed, and keyed the lock.

"Here you go, Stan. I'll bring the cutters back after next count." He slid the flat across the counter to Barnaby.

"Yeah, fine." Barnaby had piles of mail all over the cage.

Jack went into a toilet close to the stairs and once inside he loaded the gun, leaving the hammer on the one empty chamber, as per standard operating procedure. He replaced the gun in his inside left pocket, flushed the toilet, and stepped into the hall. The Front Hall man was sitting on the steps waiting; he stood, turned the flat in the lock, lifted the locking bar and Dunham went through. The Centre Hall man was waiting on the other side and popped him through. They retraced their steps across the hardwood floor and Dunham was soon back in the wing, bull-cutters in hand.

Sprott was still sitting with his feet up, eyes closed.

"I'm going up to spring the rookie for a coffee."

Sprott grunted. Dunham at the desk dialed Obs and the sleepy kid answered, "South Wing Obs."

"Coming up to spring you for coffee," Dunham said.

"Great."

Dunham started slowly up the flights of concrete steps to Five Landing, listening to the gritty noise of his joint-issue shoes.

At Five, he took the large brass lock in his left hand and his right slid down the long chain to the key which could unlock every padlock in the wing (except his locker's). He eased the chain through its loop, swung open the door, and climbed the two short flights to the Obs landing.

"How're you hackin' it, kid?"

"Fine, Jack, fine."

"Go and get some brew. While you're down there get Sprott off his ass and do the three o'clock count. You need the exercise. Don't forget the lock."

"Right." The kid dove down the stairs.

On this night, only one cell was inhabited: Olson's. Dunham eased into the chair behind the desk and looked into Olson's cell. Olson twitched a little in his sleep but didn't waken. Dunham sat and gazed. Then he reached inside his jacket pocket and eased back the hammer on the double-action .38. A muffled click. He withdrew it from his jacket and rose. As he moved around the glass barrier between the office and the short line of cells, Dunham trained the weapon on Olson's head, which was mere inches from the bars of the cell. He moved toward Olson until the crown of the barrel was no more than two inches from Olson's temple.

He could hear every part of Olson's breathing. He could hear his own. He had squeezed the trigger on a weapon exactly like this one on more than one occasion. He felt calm. Calm. Perfect. It was absofuckinglutely perfect.

A con fucks up. You reprimand him. He observes, "What're you gonna do, put me in jail?"

What would they do with Dunham? Sentence him to death? He received that very sentence from the quacks the previous afternoon.

Fuck 'em.

A couple of weeks later, I heard rumours of Jack's disease. Then I had occasion to work one graveyard shift with him before they hospitalized him for good. He was exactly my age, forty-six. As we spoke, I was somehow looking into the eyes of my own death, and there was nothing to do but put death on the table between us and open it like a bivalve. He was, by turns, agitated and obviously in pain, then dazed.

Whenever the pain became too great, he would disappear to the staff-room and return with dilated pupils. He was on heavy dope by this time but had told the brass nothing. He had cancer. So what? It is an adage that there are only two real requirements of a maximum prison screw: Be breathing and be on time. Jack was handling both of these. The eight hours of conversation was more relaxed toward the end than the beginning, and we put in words that he was dying and I was not. Rather, his dying was kicked into turbo and my dying was bumbling along at the usual rate of 4500 heart-thumps an hour. He also told me about Olson.

"Looking back, it was maybe the most brilliant idea I ever had." He had just downed his pills. The linkage between thought and speech was a little stiff. "I didn't plan anything. Never gave it a thought until that night. I simply listened to all the wild-assed notions the cons had about hitting him. I didn't know anything you didn't know. Except that afternoon when the doctors dropped the guillotine on my life, it just happened of its own accord. Can you imagine what a fuck it would have thrown into the whole system?"

I was amazed. "It was probably the only hit that would have worked. The one good shot the cons had at it, they muffed. You had it all together. You had Olson cold. He was history."

"Yeah . . . he was history . . . Why didn't I squeeze it off?"

"I got no questions," I said.

"Sometimes, in my funk, I'm sure I did blow him away. I'm not religious, never been religious. But who knows what's on the other side and what sort of mood whatever is running the universe is in? Maybe there is something to the Ten Commandments. Maybe God, if there is one, is friendlier toward skinner-killers than knuckle-draggin' Oakie screws. The way things have been going for me since I went to the doctors, it seems that way. How do you figure it?"

Six months later he died in hospital. Maybe he got his answers.

One day in 1982 as I came in to work and headed down to One Landing, I noted that the guards on Two didn't look entirely comfortable. Mafia Gallo Gang Lieutenant Dimatteo was standing near the door to the desk cage on Two with something strange and round in his hands. It was about the size of a human head and slightly pumpkinish, with brown lumps bulging from it. I stopped to watch.

Dimatteo was taller than the tallest guard – who was at least six-feet-seven and had to duck under everything we had in the West Wing then – and, at around three hundred pounds, heavier, too. Dimatteo liked comfort. He wore his joint-issue runners with the heels tromped down like slippers, which made him sound like everybody's mama slapping around in the runners. We had a hard time finding clothing big enough for him and his T-shirt was always hanging out. He looked like the Mount Rushmore version of Cheech. His curly hair was all over the place, and his moustache was haywire and full of food half the time.

I watched Dimatteo advance on one guard after another with the large brown warty sphere held out at arms' length with both hands. "You wan some Italian bread? Is very good."

Guards usually like free food, and the round loaf Dimatteo was holding looked as though it was full of nuts and fruit and all sorts of good stuff, yet the prospect of taking a bite was freaking out the legendary heroic crack troops of the West Wing of Oakalla. They were spooked.

I have no idea what they thought, collectively or individually. Did they suppose that anyone would be dumb enough to jap food and then offer it to a guard with whom he would live in the same wing for an indeterminate length of time (in the case of the Gallo family, a very long time)?

Georgie MacDiarmuid, a large man who looked tiny beside Dimatteo, writhed and lied that he had eaten just before coming on shift. (To eat before coming on shift would be unguardlike. Meals were part of the wages. And the cons at Oakie were great cooks in the olden days before the caterers got in.) Then Dimatteo went after Eggie Dillingham – ex-British military, nearly sixty, a strange and bitchy old crank. "Get away from me, you crazy big bastard with your evil-lookin' fookin' food."

Dimatteo kept a straight face but his Sicilian eyes glinted with delight as he blew away one guard after another with the mere offer of a hunk of bread. God, I loved it. I knew Dimatteo pretty well from the Scared Straight program (in which juvenile offenders are obliged to visit an adult jail with the aim of terrifying them into giving up their lives of crime) and liked him; he had just the right touch with the kids. He was a great actor. He would take the little apes down the tier, make them strip and do push-ups while he sat on his bunk and lectured them with his best *mano negro* accent and expression. Then he would make them continue the push-ups with his foot on their asses explaining all the while what would happen to that ass should they pull time.

Then it was my turn. "Looks great to me," I said truthfully.

Now, until this time Dimatteo himself hadn't taken a bite. The bread was a culinary artifact. But when I accepted a piece, he held the head-shaped loaf up and, in a ritual gesture, ripped it apart. You could tell that the act puckered the guards' sphincters. He handed me my hunk, tore off a wedge for himself, and we began chewing at the same time. It was delectable. Sweet and full of all sorts of chewy surprises.

They had been had, oh, supremely had, by a loaf of bread.

I headed up to my landing, with Dimatteo shuffling behind me, and we sat down and polished off almost the whole loaf before Georgie MacDiarmuid peeped up the stairwell and asked, trying to save face, "Have you got any of that wop shit left?" Dimatteo was gracious in victory: "You no want before? You eat before work? Well? Here . . . sure." He gave him a hunk, and Georgie brandished it in triumph as he descended to Two Landing.

Dimatteo was a member of the notorious Gallo Mafia family that ran a large drug and rackets operation in B.C. They were by no means in control of the West Coast, but they had been around for a long time. Gallo himself hadn't a trace of an accent, so I assume he was born in Canada. The same could not be said of his ranks, most of whom retained their Sicilian citizenship for occupational reasons. (Once convicted in Canada of an indictable offence, chances are good the Canadian system will deport them; this puts them on the fast track to get back to North America by buying the people who push the papers in both countries – with no jail-time to serve in either country.)

Over a period of five years, the costly but effective Co-ordinated Law Enforcement Unit, made up of the cream of the local cops and Mounties – the A-team of B.C. law enforcement – concentrated exclusively on the Gallo gang, collecting some eight thousand hours of videotape before they busted twelve of the boys and hauled them to us at Oakie. Try to imagine how many people that operation involved, how many specially tricked-out vehicles, and how much the cost of the toys inside those vehicles – because most of the tape was shot with starlight-lens technology – as well as the cost of police overtime, technicians, lab assistants, paper-pushers, and so forth. Not to mention the cost of phony drug-buys.

Such an undertaking makes the taxpayer not only one of the drug-lord's best customers when he is out of jail, but also his benefactor when he is inside. The Gallo gang pulled the better part of two years of "dead time" (remand time: awaiting trial, awaiting sentence); that's about $85,000 a year per man – in early-1980s' dollars – times twelve, not counting court costs for a trial that went on for 165 days. Try to get your mind around how much money the whole extravaganza cost, and then imagine how much gang money is still stashed safely in bank accounts in Switzerland, the Cayman Islands, or the Bahamas.

When the Gallo gang arrived at Oakalla in late 1981 and early 1982 charged with conspiracy and a long list of other related crimes, they were all housed on the same tier. There were about a dozen of them – including, originally, Don Gallo himself, who escaped.

As long as they behave themselves, there is no reason why you cannot house two or more co-accused on the same tier. The only time that this policy becomes a problem is when one or more of the co-accused have a falling out and their trials are severed. But the Gallo gang were more than solid – the *cosa nostra* commitment is a condition of solid beyond solid.

On the street and at their trials, members of the family wore very expensive, tasteless clothing, custom-tailored, of course. And even in jail they all took – especially *Consigliere* (second-in-command)

Senatore – meticulous care of their hygiene and appearance at all times. Senatore had chiseled features and looked like he had just stepped off the set of *The Godfather*. He was always complaining – with a big pearly smile – about what an embarrassment Dimatteo was because of his appearance.

When you have a dozen of a group like the Gallo family in a remand wing, as we did, very few of the traditions of prison apply. For instance, while the average con who had no desire to participate in a riot did so anyway when it was expected of him by his tiermates, to avoid being killed or having to sign into protective custody, the Gallos could sit out a riot with perfect impunity. They reeked of power, and it gave staff and cons the booglies. You had the feeling that they could have the entire province erased with a telephone call.

They entered jail with their rank long-established. There was no jockeying for position on the tier; no horseplay; no loud arguments. They thought and acted as one well-engineered, well-conditioned, well-oiled machine. It was beneath their dignity to get out of line and cause the staff problems. They were jail-wise beyond belief. When they socialized outside their group it was only with the super-cons (white-collar criminals with big connections, and mega-heavies like Mike Garcia, who was looking at his third life sentence and was the real warden of Oakalla). These guys were professional criminals who accepted time in stir as an occupational hazard and made the best of their time. They were never any trouble on the job.

Contrary to media depiction, a prison "heavy" is not a person who lifts weights, is covered with scars and tattoos, and lumbers around like an ape. These goons are the lackeys and go-fers of the real heavies. A heavy is a pipe artist: someone who could walk up behind anyone of any size with a pipe or similar instrument, crush his skull, ditch the weapon, then have a big lunch and a long, dreamless afternoon nap. A heavy is not a troublemaker. He does control the tier and sometimes an entire prison. He knows when he owes a guard and he remembers that certain guards owe him for his assistance in times of crisis.

As a group, the Gallo gang were heavy. They didn't have to do much to establish their dominance. Their reputations preceded them.

They took jobs as cleaners and they really shone in their participation in such programs as Scared Straight.

If the Galloeans liked you, they joked with you and played harmless practical jokes on you in the wing. After you had been had, they would give you the open hand under the chin and "*complimenti!*"

I don't know for a certainty that the following occurrence took place compliments of the Gallo family. It is only in hindsight that I suspect them. There were other high-profile criminals in the wing at the time.

One day early in my first year on the job I had been home perhaps an hour after morning shift when the telephone rang.

"Yates? This is Winston Caldwell, you know, up on Five Right?" I almost filled my boots. I had two Murder Ones in the wing – one a murder-dismemberment. One had the last name of Winston. The other was Caldwell.

Bear in mind that I was green as grass. No one had bothered to suggest that I de-list my telephone number. Most peace officers do not list their numbers.

"You must have the wrong number." I hung up. It immediately rang again. I clicked on the answering machine and sat down in stark panic. My estranged wife's telephone was still listed under J. Michael Yates. I called her. She said a man had called for me a little earlier but declined to leave his name. She had told him I didn't live there. I called the wing and talked to the afternoon brass. They had no idea what a line screw does in such circumstances, other than deep-six the listed number, and suggested I talk to the director in the morning. I called the phone company and explained the circumstances. They gave me a unlisted number within twenty-four hours.

I sat on the couch, stunned, all evening. A couple of times I picked up the phone when it rang. Same voice. I simply hung up. They knew they had me on the run and the fun was just beginning.

I went to work the next morning feeling completely paranoid. I watched every con come through the line – including the Gallo people – for some inkling of who was responsible. All shift I watched. I was so busy watching the cons, I fucked up a couple of minor procedures and caught hell for it. At the beginning of the shift, I reported the calls to the director, who suggested I get an unlisted number, and contacted the Burnaby Mounties, who suggested that the wing monitor the outgoing calls.

I thought about quitting, but soon it became a challenge to outsmart them. It was clear that the brass and the cops were going to do nothing. Two days after I had the new unlisted number (which, as required, I had given the brass in the wing, my wife, and no more than ten trusted others), the phone rang and "Winston Caldwell" was at my service again. I slammed down the phone.

I methodically called everyone who had the number and accused them of breaching the security I requested. I called a few more than once and really pissed them off. When I got my unlisted number I had to tell my wife why, and she accused me of putting the lives of everyone we knew at risk. It only fortified her point that I was an asshole for stooping to such an unsuitable job. War-time. I was scared and mad – at her just as much as the caller – but rational enough to worry about my kids.

I decided to distance myself from my family in order to protect them. I thought of one woman I knew who met the two criteria I had just invented: she lived about as far away from Burnaby as you can without having an Alberta visa, and she had a roomy house left behind by an escaped husband. I drove out and suggested I move in with her, explaining up-front about the telephone. She didn't think it a problem; her number was still listed under her husband's name. There was no way the Voice would puzzle that one out. I wasn't so sure and decided to put a second line into the house.

She came over and we packed up my apartment, the movers came, and I vanished, smug that I had 'em licked. Even if "Winston Caldwell" and company found out where I was, it would be evidence that I no longer had any connection with my ex-wife and the children.

These are the thoughts of a madman. Who, particularly one's ex-wife, is going to go for such bullshit? You don't dissociate yourself from your children just because you part ways with a wife. My new living arrangements only got me into a situation of "extreme prejudice" with her.

I called the phone company to arrange for the second line and on the first morning shift I had off, the telephone dude installed the new line. I made not a single call on that line or on the line belonging to my new landlady. I was alone in the house. I read and wrote all morning, then I ran into a snag writing something and so walked into the bedroom (as was my habit at such moments) for a creative nap. I zonked until the brand-new telephone on the brand-new line rang. It was between noon and one.

"Hi, Mike . . . Winston Caldwell here." Wham.

Now, you'd think I might have deduced that, inasmuch as I had not told a living soul that number, the caller or whoever was behind it must have someone at the phone company on his payroll. Wrong. I spent the afternoon apartment hunting. You can just imagine how delighted my landlady of a few hours was when I informed her that I was moving because I feared for her safety. I was playing an insane and expensive geographical shell-game that I couldn't possibly win.

I was so spooked that I hit the road there and then and spent the next few nights in a sleeping bag in an empty apartment in north Burnaby until the movers brought my belongings. I ordered a new phone line (having a phone was a condition of employment; I was on call twenty-four hours a day, seven days a week). More calls.

I was wacko. Every decision I made contradicted the previous one. I had to move again.

My friend and co-screw Teddy Daignault lived in an apartment block right across from the gate to Oakie. I made yet another needless move into his building. New line. More calls. Teddy was about as laid-back as they come and even he was peering out from behind curtains and opening the door of his apartment to check out the hall. One day the phone rang and it was my man.

"Look, asshole, if you jerks really want me, I can be had in the joint or on the street, you know it and I know it." The fact was, it had taken me three months to think of it. The Voice gave me a belly-laugh and the phone clicked. That was the last phone call.

If the Gallos own that one, it was the grand-daddy of their jokes. I think the hair on my chest turned white in those three months.

7

The Queen of Drag

•

Some things are better than sex, and some are worse,
but there's nothing exactly like it.
– W. C. Fields

Because of my teaching background I was often pressed into service as a training officer for auxiliary staff. I enjoyed this. The only thing I enjoyed even more than this was working a tier where we had a drag queen or two in residence. The most fun of all was to have a rookie *and* a drag queen or two on the same landing.

For afternoon shift, I was assigned Randy, a young turkey whose uncle was in federal corrections and had recommended it as a career. Randy was big, he could handle himself, and, so far, he demonstrated ample possession of the most important faculty in a line screw: common sense.

Day after day on afternoon shift I had been going over with him Section 28 of the *Correctional Centre Rules and Regulations*. When an inmate commits an infraction of the *C.C.R.R.* he can be charged by a Corrections peace officer and go to trial in Director's Court, known in earlier times as Warden's Court, and since time immemorial by the inmates as Kangaroo Court. Indeed, to get proceedings under way one infamous unit director used to bellow, "Bring the guilty cocksucker in here!" (In fact, he was a fairly lenient judge.)

Each day I reviewed with the rookie one of Section 28's twelve sub-sections and gave him a verbal synopsis of case law: trials I had

113

participated in and heard of, how each section had been interpreted. Some of the language could be misleading as hell. And there were other considerations.

"You have to consider the circumstances every time you're about to lay paper on [charge] a dude. For instance, time. On morning shift, no problem. There's lots of staff and if the guy decides to jackrabbit [escape] on you, there is all kinds of light for chasing him down over the flats, and the Burnaby horsemen can head uphill with their mutt squads."

"Right."

"Afternoon and night shifts present entirely different problems. Tonight you may well catch several cons having a blanket-party with some poor sonofabitch. You catch them cold. It's a good bust. The perpetrators are going to do serious digger-time [segregation]."

"Okay."

"Any difference between the seriousness of the breach of the *Rules and Regs* on afternoon and night shift?" This is my trick question.

"No. If a guy fucks up, he goes to court."

"How about the way we handle it?"

"Same."

"Not necessarily."

"You trying to tell me that sections of the *C.C.R.R.* mean one thing at one time of the day and another at another?" The kid was baffled.

"Nope." It was about 2100. Good shift, good jail. The Stanley Cup semi-finals were on and the inmates were laid-back and watching the black-and-white TVs covered in sparrow-shit on the catwalk. (We had real jailbirds in the Old West, our name for the West Wing; they had nested above the catwalks for years and didn't fly south for the winter.)

"Look at it this way. If you lay paper on the guy after dark, you have one less bad-ass for the night. But there are eight guards on an afternoon shift and an inmate count of damn near two hundred. S.O.P. [standard operating procedure] is that two max guards have to escort the guy to the hospital so that we can certify that he isn't thumped up [injured], then we have to walk him down to A-side [segregation] and skin-frisk him with seg staff, then hoof it back.

This all takes about forty-five minutes, longer if the hospital is busy or if the nurse is on call in one of the wings."

"I see where you're comin' from. We got staff tied up."

"Security diminished by twenty-five per cent. Now, if you were an inmate and had some serious tier business, wouldn't it be a good ploy to get a couple of stooges to fake a rumble and get them charged, knowing that you were getting a couple of screws out of the way?"

"I get it."

I had developed a few bromides as a training officer. First, I explained to the recruit that there were twenty-one rookies hired at the same time I was. Within a year, I was the only one left. Almost no one can be a maximum prison guard for any length of time, and of those, very few ever develop any talent for it.

Next, very few are capable of determining when an inmate is a fellow human being and when a jail is a jail. That means that if you are not a shrewd assessor of human character, then you had better learn to be one fast. Some people are inside because they never had a break in their lives and some are in because they were "born to lose" (the text of one of the more popular jailhouse tattoos). You give the former the benefit of the doubt and you bend the rules for the latter only when it suits your purpose. In certain circumstances, you think of the inmate as an individual, a fellow human being. In others, you must think first of the good of the institution in general. It's a matter of making judgement calls, and it can't be taught except through experience.

Then: Read the book, but don't throw the book. Do not go prescriptively into any situation. Read the circumstances and take the entirety of the whole wonderful living organism of the prison into account.

"We're gonna swap tiers. I'll do a walking count of yours and you do mine while I cover."

"How come?"

"Same cons, different eyes. You might see something I been missing all night and vice versa."

I crossed over the landing to Four Left.

Randy keyed the lock and levered the bar. I swung the bar and the hurricane-wire endgate open and walked slowly down the range before the cells, giving every six-man (look-out) plenty of time to warn whomever. Stopping to ask this guy about his family and that one when his preliminary appearance is coming up, it took me about ten minutes to get down to cell 20 and count them again on the way back. I tried not to get in the way of the guys glued to the TVs.

I walked out the endgate and Randy secured it. Then we walked over to Four Right and I opened the endgate and Randy started down the range. I could see him imitating my easy saunter. He would have loved to pussyfoot and catch someone doing something. He didn't yet understand that he wore one uniform and the inmates wore another uniform. Inside each uniform is a different life. The courts have seen fit to do certain things with the lives of the inmates and it is not up to guards to second-guess the courts or to meddle in lives inside the institution unless it disrupts MODS (management, operation, discipline, or security) of said institution.

He reached the end of the tier. I saw him move closer to the bars of one of the end cells. Then he looked toward me at the endgate for a reality check. Christ, I could see the whites of his eyes. From the look on his face, I thought he had found someone strung up.

He headed toward me, picking up the pace as he came. By the time he reached the endgate, he was almost sprinting. Some of the cons peered out of their cell doors as he rocketed past, wondering what was up.

I locked the gate. Randy was dancing and moving toward the middle of the landing and motioning for me to come over.

"Jesus Christ! Holy fuck! Mr. Yates, I caught 'em."

"Caught who doing what?"

"It was down there on top of a guy."

"Slow down, Marshall. Who is it?"

"That transvestite thing with the tits."

"The it you're talking about isn't precisely a transvestite," I said. He was talking about Sherrin, a transsexual-in-progress. The entire psychiatric and surgical process takes several years and involves some fairly radical physical transmogrification. To a rookie, it must look very strange to have something with facial hair but with breasts, as well as other features normally attributed to the human female, walking around on a tier with yard-apes who spend much of their day doing push-ups and curls with their hinged bunks, and walking around as though they had a rash under each arm, so overdeveloped are their lat muscles.

Even the old-time guards splutter and don't know which pronoun fits a drag queen. But regardless of how early they are in the process, queens prefer to be referred to in the feminine. That's no problem as far as I'm concerned, adult male institution or not.

The state dispenses hormones to them – their "itty-bitty titty pills," as guards affectionately call them – and, in some cases, the state pays for castration (the nip) and the creation of a vagina from the penis (the tuck) if they happen to be incarcerated at the time that the psychiatrist in charge decides that they are ready. This practice gets mixed reviews at all levels of Corrections. But then all levels of the bureaucracy are paranoid and deem it safest to err on the side of the rights of the inmate.

They remain legally men until both the tuck and the shrink pronounce them otherwise, at which time the authorities attempt to instal them in women's institutions. But this presents other problems – the women's jail tradition is as long and irrational as the male open-contract on anyone accused of a sex offence. By tradition, even after transsexuals become women legally, they are not tolerated in population and must go into protective custody.

The inmates, of course, joyfully play all sides off one another. Sherrin, one my favourites, who poor Randy was so excited about, had a doctor so well trained that whenever Sherrin's dark roots began to show, she had only to hand in a medical chit (request) and she was taken to the hospital, where she could peroxide her hair. This event always caused great grumbling from staff over the contention that these "freaks" were given "special privileges."

I liked working the drag-queen tiers. A drag-queen tier is a clean tier (I generalize, of course). And a drag-queen tier is a mellow tier. I can't remember violence ever occurring on a tier with a dragger on it.

Back to poor Randy, who was certain we had an institutional emergency on our hands.

"They were doin' it and she was on top. In cell nineteen."

This projected a very strange image on the screen of my mind. I had been over Sherrin's file many times. She had been in jail on my tier dozens of times for prostitution, assault, theft-under – any number of nickel-and-dime beefs. I knew she had not had the tuck, but she had had the nip. No gonads. Was she functioning in the male role? Couldn't be.

Just about this time, an apparition appeared at the endgate. Sherrin wasn't even five feet tall, and she was wearing a T-shirt long enough to be a nightgown. Like most drag queens she was grotesque in the abstract sense of the word. She did not evince womanliness but an outrageous and stupendous caricature of womanliness – close enough to woman that a drag queen usually works the street with a "real girl" rather than another dragger, but wide enough of the woman-mark that women are not threatened by them.

"Doing *it* with Sherrin on top?"

"You got it."

Sherrin over at the gate couldn't make out what we were saying but she was getting impatient.

"Mr. Yates, are we taking names and numbers?"

"Hang on, Madame, we'll be with you shortly. Just as soon as I can wring out of this young officer just exactly what he thinks he saw." Back to Randy. "Do I understand that you're accusing her of handling the boy part of the operation and he was doing the girl part."

"Oh, no. He was . . . uh . . . just lying on the bed face up and it was bouncing up and down on top of him just like a woman on top of a man."

"*Mutatis mutandis.*"

"Yeah . . . huh?"

"With minor changes from, say, what you might expect as a man with a woman on top."

"Yeah. Yuck. How can they do that?"

"That's really not at issue."

"Well, do I charge them?"

"Not even the director can tell you when to charge an inmate and when not to. You are the reporting officer. You make up your own mind. Give me your copy of the *C.C.R.R.*"

He handed me the small cream-coloured book. I turned to Section 28 and read sub-section 10, "No inmate shall use indecent language or gesture or participate in an indecent act."

He listened carefully, took the book back, and seemed to be checking the shape of every letter.

"You've got to make up your mind before end of shift."

"Christ, I just don't know what to do."

He agonized for several minutes while I strolled over and talked to Sherrin. I refused to discuss whether she and her partner were to be charged.

Randy called me back, saying I had to help him or he'd have a nervous breakdown before end of shift. This got my attention. He could have a nervous breakdown after end of shift but not before. I demanded his book of rules and regs again. I read the charge out to Sherrin, who sang along with me because she had memorized the section.

"Were you, Madame, caught by Mr. Marshall in full fornicatory motion as reported?"

"Boss, you know damned well I was. I don't bullshit you. I just want to know whether I'm going to seg, bag and baggage, for the night."

"Then I have only one final question."

Sherrin had caught on to my tone of voice. Randy was still standing as though petrified.

"Were you doing a decent job of it?"

"Count on it."

I closed the book, replaced it in Randy's jacket pocket, and walked over to my chair and sat. "Problem solved. See you both on shift tomorrow night."

I should explain that while certain guards seem (or pretend) not to be able to handle drag queens, on the tier (and on the street) they are treated with the greatest of deference. He who manages to capture the attention and services of the tier drag queen is one who is held in high esteem. If he shares his transsexual paramour with the rest of the tier he is held in the highest of all possible esteems. Pimping, in or out of jail, is virtually irresistible. Two walls in each cell are available for the stacking of decks of tailor-made cigarettes, and I have seen them quite literally stacked from floor to ceiling with packages and cartons of cigarettes in the cell of an enterprising drag queen with an attentive pimp. I was privileged to see one marriage on the tier (without benefit of chaplain, but nonetheless solemn and sincere). She got out before he did (having gone on to federal); the last I heard, she was living in the Fraser Valley outside Vancouver so as to be near the husband, who was in Kent penitentiary.

This may seem like sexual custom from another planet. Perhaps this is a comment on me rather than society in general or prison population, but I found the ceremony just as moving as any I ever saw in the usual places in society.

We all have certain needs for bonding, contact, and sex; why should someone sentenced to time not have similar needs? At what point do we delimit our parameters of "punishment"? If we cannot starve prisoners because of U.N. guidelines, how can we deny them other appetites? Is one more important than the other?

Oakalla turned a blind eye to "guerilla sex"; Vancouver Pretrial, where I worked later, went out of its way to pretend that the sex drive did not exist: it was a chargeable offence for more than one con to be in a room at once; therefore there were many dry hands and requests for hand-lotion from the nurse after a racy movie. Blue magazines were forbidden. When will we learn that certain things cannot be legislated whether by statute or standing institutional order? The inconsistency between Oakalla and Pretrial (both supposedly maximum institutions) was outrageous. The reason cons view the system as arbitrary is that it is indeed arbitrary. His needs, nay, human nature, are rarely considered in the Brave New World of Corrections.

When I entered corrections, certain things altered my perspective. First of all, there was my perception of the significance of human size, and its use and abuse. All around me were people in the same

uniform who were a head taller and a hundred pounds heavier than I
– and I am six-feet-one with a big frame. Big guards. Big cons.

In jail, the small ones who survive are wily, very wily. When I
was green as grass I had a very small training officer, name of John
Chapman, from India. (East Indian inmates never suspected that he
spoke Punjabi, Hindi, and Bengali, as well as pidgin-Canadian. They
often learned this to their chagrin.) One day early in my training
Chappie looked at me and said: "You're a pretty big guy. That's helpful
in this business." Not knowing him, or enough to be suspicious of a
remark like that, I took it to be a compliment and nodded. He went
on for some minutes about size and strength, then ordered me to follow him. I did. He unlocked a door. Inside was a schemozzle of badly
maintained gas-masks, truncheons, and helmets. He picked up a
couple of plexiglass shields and stood them side by side. "See? Same
size. All of them the same size." I nodded. He put one of them in front
of him. "Ya see, a little fella like me can get behind one of these and
virtually my whole body is protected." I nodded. "As for you, you
overgrown, pea-brained, rookie stiff, one day they'll call down here
saying that there's a riot at the women's jail. They'll give you one of
these and you'll go through the door with it in front of you. Women
don't fight fair. They never heard of Queensbury rules. The first
three-hundred-pound female you see with a leg of a chair in her hand
will fake you high by waving it at your head. You'll lift the shield to
block it. Then she'll kick your nuts up to your fucking earlobes." I
nodded. Intuition told me that he was right. I needed lessons in
becoming smaller.

In the Scared Straight program, the big guys, especially the heavy
dudes, really shine. Prisoners and staff work together to dispel any
illusions these young men might have about what would happen to
them should they end up in our institution. We never know when
young offenders will show up for the treatment – nor could we imagine that one day drag-queen Sherrin would outshine us all in our
efforts.

Half-way through one eventless Oakie morning on Four Landing
in the West Wing, my partner and I heard steps coming up the stairs.
We looked over to the left. We saw a head, then shoulders, then the

rest of the body. It finally arrived on our level and its head damn near touched the ceiling. Every muscle in its body was taut, flexed. And it couldn't have been any more than sixteen years old, in jeans and a T-shirt. It had a look on its face that said it was absolutely fearless.

More steps. The special-services officer who was escorting the kid was looking downcast. He explained that this was a Scared Straight number.

"Your sense of success doesn't seem overwhelming," I observed.

One of the cons at the endgate called the kid over and gave him a homily that had worked on other kids. Phillips, the special-services officer, complained, "I've had this punk in tow all morning. Nothing works."

"What about One Landing," I suggested. This was where the Gallo gang lived. "Senatore? Dimatteo?"

"Dimatteo [who was as tall as, and far heavier and stronger than, this child] took him back into his cell and made him take off his clothes and do two hundred push-ups with Dimatteo's foot on his ass."

"And?"

"The kid told him to get fucked. Dimatteo told him that if he ever wound up in a jail like this he would be raped every fifteen minutes and the kid said bullshit. He'd kill the first nerd who unzipped his fly. Never saw anything like it."

"He's juvie?"

"Sure."

"Tried and found delinquent?"

"Bingo."

"What for?"

"What else? Assault. He beats the shit out of tall trees just for practice."

"Sounds like he's got the makings of a real dog. We'll have him here in a year or two – or sooner if he winds up with a manslaughter charge and is raised to adult court."

The cons on Four Left were clearly striking out at getting through to this young gorilla. Phillips pushed the kid over to Four Right to give them a kick at the cat. They tried everything. They pointed to the scars on their bodies, their jailhouse tattoos. They told him horror stories about being beaten and raped, they showed him bullet wounds, and showed him legs terribly scarred from the teeth of "alligator" dogs (attack police mutts). He told them about a police dog he killed with a two-by-four. Needle tracks didn't impress him. Slash scars from attempted suicides didn't impress him. He was impervious. Phillips asked whether we had any ideas.

"Sounds like you've done all the standard stuff," I said. "Phillips, my son, you can't win 'em all. If the judge sentences them to the treatment, all you can do is submit them to the treatment. The cons are giving it their best shot. Listen to them. They're as frustrated as you are."

On Four Right, while all this palaver had been going on, the little drag queen, Sherrin, had been standing in the background, too short to be seen, listening. I heard her voice calling "Boss, oh, boss!" I walked over to the gate. She had elbowed all the machos out of the way and was standing there in her nightgown-length T-shirt, staring up at the kid.

I looked at the kid, whose granite expression was twitching a little, but this didn't seem significant to me. Sherrin probably wanted a phone call. Normal landing operations had been suspended while staff and inmates directed attention to the task at hand: scaring the kid straight.

"Mr. Yates, open this gate right now," she squawked in her amazing falsetto.

My right hand slid down the chain toward the key reflexively. "What d'ya need?"

She pointed at his crotch. "I'm going to suck his dick!" She was so short she could have blown him standing at full height.

The kid went nuts. He crossed and uncrossed his arms, he reached over and hung onto the hurricane wire. He shifted his weight from foot to foot. He began to change colour. And – I couldn't believe it – his damned knees began to go on him. We thought he was going to faint.

Sherrin could smell blood. "C'mon, boss. Mr. Yates, open the gate. Right here, right now, I'm gonna suck his dick right off."

This was the variable the kid hadn't figured; the proverbial ball of fire in the night. Right on. I was into it.

"Makes sense to me, Sherrin; a girl needs a little young stuff now and then." I inserted the key in the lock, kicked the lock off, and grabbed the bar to open the gate. You can make a hell of a clunk and clang with the gate, as though you were opening it, without actually activating the opening system. I clunked and clattered.

The kid was now holding himself up on the screen. When he thought the gate was about to go, he wailed "Noo-ooo!" and burst into tears. Then he covered his face with his hands. My partner had to help Phillips pack the kid down the stairs because his knees had turned to cooked spaghetti. He wailed all the way down and was still sniffling when they arrived back at Willingdon Detention Centre for Juveniles.

This is how it is, Will Rogers. I never met a drag queen I didn't like. Sooner or later.

8

Bugs, Dog Meat, and Stringers: An Oakie Lexicon

———————— • ————————

When we remember we are all mad, the mysteries
disappear and life stands explained.
— Mark Twain

SAMMY Schmidt, a very bright, easy-going screw, was behind the desk with a harried look on his face. Coming in from Centre Hall, I could hear *whap!* then swearing, several times, long before I went through the gate into the West Wing. A thin, flat sort of whap. Nothing one would normally associate with the known collective larynx of Oakalla.

Sammy noticed me and smiled. "Morning, Mikey."

I was about to answer when, without breaking eye contact with me, Sammy smacked the counter with an eighteen-inch ruler. Perhaps we had an infestation, perhaps this was a new form of Tai Chi.

"Good morning," said I.

Sammy's eyes flicked to his left and he whapped the counter again, to his left this time, without changing his business-as-usual expression.

"Bug," he announced.

I stepped through the door of the cage and peered at the counter where he swatted, expecting to see the corpse of some sort of beetle. Nothing. He whacked the counter again.

I figured I'd been had at approximately 0645 hours by a kid. "Stand there and watch both stairwells at once," Schmidt said.

I did. The stairs left and right went down about ten steps then switchbacked for another ten. I could see the nearly-shaved top of a head and eyebrows appear in the stairwell on my side. The ruler whizzed by me and whacked the counter near my elbow, and the head disappeared. Then it reappeared in the stairwell on the opposite side. Whack. It was like the midway game where gophers stick their heads up and one smacks them with a mallet except, in this case, just the noise was sufficient.

"He's nuts," Schmidt explained. "And if I stop hitting the desk, he'll be on the landing and all over me in a second."

"Lock him on his tier."

"Can't."

"Why?"

"He's on One Right and the maintenance crew is working there, so the gate's open."

"Put him in his house and throw a chain around the door."

"Can't leave the desk."

"I'll put my stuff in my locker and come back for the lock and chain."

Bugs (crazies) worried us more than any other kind of inmate. This one understood that the whack of the ruler meant "Don't come up here." After I locked him in his cell, I stood by the endgate for a long time watching and listening. If he had begun ritual noise-making, we would have had a serious problem. But he was quiet. Population cons will tolerate a bug only as long as we seem to be doing something about him. They know we'll get him off the wing and to forensic medicine for a psych profile just as soon as we can. On a weekend, this is impossible.

This was Saturday. We couldn't get him out until Monday. Sammy was keeping him off the tier so that the other cons weren't disturbed, and keeping him off the landing so operations could proceed, by turning his ritual behaviour into a game with the noise of the ruler. This guy had not said a syllable since being booked in. He had a face-sheet with only a face on it.

Heavy-time cons have no qualm about exterminating a bug, especially a noise-maker. A continuous noise in a jail can drive you

around the bend, and for most cons this is not a long drive. I knew
that if we didn't keep an eye on this small, wild-eyed wraith, we could
find him piped behind a garbage can.

The twilight-zone creatures truly vex the law. Having allegedly
breached the Criminal Code of Canada, they must be remanded in
custody by the judge. They are jailed because it has not yet been established that they cannot appreciate "the nature and quality of their
acts." It has not yet been established that they were insane at the time
of the crime. It has not yet been established that they, for reasons of
insanity, are unfit to stand trial. This can only be established by
Forensic. They are our problem until then. We must keep them
alive. Some have made a true disjunction from the generally accepted
reality and are therefore psychotic and suffering from mania, schizo-
phrenia, paranoia. For some a trauma has shut them down mentally.
Others, after several thousand hits of LSD, angel dust, free-based
cocaine, alcohol, are little more than vegetables. It is not ours to
diagnose.

Some, like this one, seem harmless. Others hallucinate at no
apparent provocation and come at you with whatever as a weapon.
Not because you have angered them, but because they think you are
Satan, Jesus, or a gremlin. The good news is that when they are hallucinating rather than seeing you, their reflexes are lousy.

When you are locked alone on a tier full of murderers and bank-
robbers, you go about business. And you can't go about business
without turning your back on them. Sane criminals are generally not
a problem. They are self-serving. Cutting the throat of a guard would
not serve them well, normally. Bugs, on the other hand, have no such
focus on their best interests. On bugs, you do not turn your back.

We got through the Saturday with the bug. Schmidt and I looked
in on him from time to time. He was a little strange at the food line –
didn't want to eat at all. We managed to persuade him to take a tray.
He trotted with it to his cell, scraped off its contents into his shitter,
and flushed it.

Sunday morning on the tier began with the announcement that I
was on church duty.

Any way you look at it, church is a major pain in the ass because it is the least complicated way to make a major drug pass between one wing and another. When there is some big action going down, as many as fifty cons per wing will turn out for church.

It was widely known that I would do almost anything to get out of church duty. I usually wound up losing the argument.

We had a brand new rookie in the wing. This was his first shift in max. His eyes were so wide open, I don't think he had dared to blink since the top of the shift. I was told to take him with me to church.

Landing by landing, we collected the herd and headed for the church on Five. I looked around and noted that we didn't have a huge herd of West Wingers. This gave me joy. Obviously, we would not have to deal with a big drug transaction. As they filed past me and up the stairs I noticed that the silent bug himself was going to church.

I oriented the rookie. The West Wing cons sit in these chairs near the West Wing door, the South Wing are in the middle, and the East are on the other side. Notice the nice broad aisle between the wings. They don't cross the aisle for any reason. They don't toss things across the aisle. Feel free at any time to get up and stroll the aisle. Fuck the sermon. Security is first. Check anything you want to check. You want to frisk anybody down, let me know. We'll get the East P.O. to let us through the door and one of us will check it out. No problem.

I continued, "Now, as soon as you hear the Bible-thumper begin to wind down, although we've told them all a thousand times not to, he's going to say, 'I have some pamphlets here for those of you who wish, blah, blah, blah,' and they're all going to jump out of their seats and mix East with South and West. All the big action is going to happen right there in the confusion in front of the pulpit. The minute you hear him begin to say 'For those of you,' you jump up and sprint toward the sky pilot. Stand in that fucking aisle. Order our West Wingers to stay seated until we tell them otherwise. Pick up a chair and threaten to thump somebody with it. Whatever. You let a West Winger move a hair toward the other wings and I'll hand your *cojones* to the P.O. after church. South and East can have an orgy up there in front of the preacher. That's their problem. They have their staff here.

But we aren't taking more problems back into the wing than we came in with. No contact. Am I coming across?"

"Loud and clear."

"That's just marvy. Now, plant your ass in that chair back there and get ready for action. I'll be taking notes on how you handle yourself." Sure I will.

Well, the preacher was a little bit late. Then, what finally appeared from a back room was fairly unbelievable. He was a kid, twenty, maybe twenty-two years old. He was so terrified he couldn't even make eye contact with the cons. Even my rookie wasn't that afraid of me. Damn. The regular protestant minister liked to fish; he was probably off somewhere dangling a line.

When the preacher finally quit talking to the podium, he began to explain at a factor of about ten times longer than necessary that he was going to preach his Christmas sermon. At Christmas he hadn't had a chance to use this sermon, and he'd worked really hard on it, so they were going to get the benefit of hearing it for the first time. This was March. Late March. Any other group of people on earth would have turned into unlawful assembly steaming toward riot at such news. Our cons sat still.

The preacher started his sermon and I started to doze. If I nodded off, one of our nerds would go for it, sure as hell. I had to come up with a plan.

The rookie was sitting to my left and about five rows back. I turned around and glared at him, making sure I caught his eye. Then I looked very slowly and suspiciously around the room as though I was looking for something in particular. The rookie had no idea what I was looking for. I had no idea what I was looking for. But it was good for about ten minutes of the rookie imitating me: he stared around the room as though he could see right through people – into their pockets, into their very skulls.

When I finished, my chin sank toward my chest and I passed out. I'd prayed that the clerics would complain about my antics in church to the brass, who would disallow my ever taking cons to church again. My prayers were not answered.

I snored and it woke me up. I turned around and made eye contact with the rookie and showed him with my eyes what correct professional church security is. He surveyed the room, looking hard.

I looked out over our West Wing cons. Everything looked good. Our guys were being really polite to the Christian, who probably should have been shot for insulting their lack of intelligence.

The bug was sitting alone only about five feet from me, not bothering anybody. None of the other cons would sit in the same row with him, but that was okay. The bug didn't mind. And the bug wasn't causing any trouble. This gave me a warm feeling inside and I went back to sleep.

I woke up again and went through my little ritual of winding the rookie up again. He must have been getting eyestrain. The veins were standing out on his neck. He was white-knuckling his chair so that he could launch himself if need be into the middle of what he supposed would be a hellish fray. I looked back over the backs of the heads of the West Wing cons again. All was well. The bug was sitting in the same position, except that he'd brought his left foot up from the floor and now had it on the seat of his chair. That was okay, the bug wasn't bothering anybody. I went back to sleep.

The next time I woke up and checked out the cons, he had both feet on the chair. I slept again after first getting the rookie to turn his head around like an owl.

The next time I snored and scared myself to consciousness and looked over my flock, the bug had eased his ass up to the back of the chair. I could see he had good balance and he wasn't making any noise. The preacher was mumbling so hard into the lectern that he hadn't even noticed that the bug was sitting on the chair back, presumably so that he could hear better.

Once more I dozed but, for some reason, not to the previous depth. When I focussed again on the bug, he was standing on the seat of his chair. I still didn't see any problem. The man had been in the West Wing for two days and hadn't said a word. I was not going to get up and disturb everyone and scare the hell out of the preacher simply to tell the bug to sit down. I sat there with my legs and my arms crossed, blearily blinking my eyes, watching him.

His penultimate move was to stand up on tiptoe and open his mouth. For a while, nothing came out. And then he bellowed in a voice that could shatter a rock: "FAAHHWUCKK YOOU!"

To the preacher, this had to be the voice of God on high, the signal that he was under siege, that an entire prison riot was about to erupt. He was about to be crucified in his own church, murdered in his own cathedral – which might not have been a bad idea, given his cruel and *usual* Sunday punishment. In mid-exhortation, he dropped behind the lectern and bobbed up only enough to show his eyes.

I did the professional thing. I bent double and vanished into gale after gale of laughter. I laughed until all the staff and cons in the room were roaring. The bug was still standing with his mouth open. Nothing further issued from it.

I gave the East Wing P.O. the eye and nodded toward the West Wing door, and he moved over my way. I went over to the rookie and told him, "This is probably just a scam; there's something big going down. I'll get back if I can. Don't worry about a thing. You'll handle it." He looked terrified, but on full alert.

I walked over to the bug, reached up, and tapped him on the shoulder, and beckoned for him to come down. He did so. The East Wing P.O. popped the door, and we spiralled down from Five to One. Without another word, the bug jumped into his drum. I snaked a chain around his drum and locked it and there he stayed until Monday morning when he was transported to Riverview for his psych profile. For the duration of his stay in the West Wing, he made not another sound.

Attempted escapees are often called dog meat because of the Mountie dogs that are usually sent to fetch them back. This story illustrates the point.

The year was drawing to a close and the days were shortening conspicuously. West Wing yard was over. The P.A. system had called the cons in. The Tower Two man was down and had sprinted for the main building with a full bladder. With the yard clear, the Tower One man had vanished inside, too. The count man was on the inside of the corrugated wall doing a sweep of the yard, nosing around for drug-drops and hidden weapons. I was doing a last sweep of the outside of the yard wall in case any of the visitors had stuffed anything in any of its seams or tried to toss something over and hadn't been successful.

I was giving the padlock on Tower One a last yank to make sure it was secure when the radio erupted. "Red Alert. Hospital."

I wheeled around and looked down the hill. I could see hatless bodies near the door in staff uniform. I could hear a vehicle burning it down the drive toward me but couldn't see it until it whizzed past me. It was the prowl truck.

I squeezed the radio. "Mainland base, this is portable 2401."

"Go 2401."

"2401 responding to Red Alert at hospital. Inform West Wing."

"Roger."

I sprinted down the drive to the stairs and started down them. The guards at the hospital door were unarmed and required by policy to remain at their posts to maintain hospital security. They were yelling and pointing in the direction that the escapee had gone. The prowl truck screamed around the switchback from the Main Gaol level to the hospital level and locked up its binders. The door popped open and remained open.

Young Jacques Duhamel, the driver, jumped out on the run. He disappeared around the east corner of the hospital leaping into the tall grass. Jacques hadn't been in the service very long and was nervous about working the wings. So they had planted him in administration from where you are dispatched to be the Front Hall man, Centre Hall man, work the gatehouse, or drive the prowl truck. As I rounded the east side of the hospital I heard him shout, "Stop!" Then I saw Jacques unholster his .38. I could see a figure in prison greens going like hell down the grass toward Deer Lake. I bellowed, "Stop!"

Jacques fired a warning shot in the air. I couldn't quite see what he could see because evening was falling so fast.

The con had escaped from the hospital, a fairly heavy-duty Native kid, and I could now see him bouncing down the hill toward the flats like a kangaroo.

There were guards at Oakie who shouted for the escapee to stop.

Then they fired warning shots in the air. Then they fired a round or two into the ground. Shucks. Missed. Less paperwork. Not long before, there had been a case up north where an escapee had made it to the perimeter fence. The guard aimed at his leg, but just as he squeezed the round off, the runner dove over the fence and suddenly there was a dead con hanging by one foot from the concertina wire.

In the distance, I could hear the sirens of the horsemen. Jacques was holding his gun with two hands just as Henry Abbot, the training officer, had taught him. He fired in the air after yelling "Stop," and then he pulled down and aimed carefully at the bouncing, moving target and let off another shot. The con dropped out of sight. I figured that the shot had scared the runner and he had flattened in the grass. I had my .38 out but never fired a shot. Jacques was always too close to the line of my fire.

Then the con was up and bouncing down the brown grass again as though the slug hadn't touched him. He didn't seem to be limping. But this would not be abnormal even if he had been hit. We shoot wad-cutters. Jacques fired again. The con went down again. He could have been crawling around anywhere in the tall grass – or have been down for the count.

At the time it was noticed that we had a Red Alert (escape) some-one contacted the Burnaby Mounties, who had deployed two mutt squads. One car came in the main gate and followed us. The other mutt squad came up from the Gilpin Street RCMP station. Off through the dusk I could see a dog leaping up through the grass and a Mountie leaping along behind. The kid didn't have a hope in hell of escaping. Before we reached the place where he'd gone down, we were walking through bloody grass.

We found him. Jacques had got him with both rounds. The first was by the book: an amazing shot from at least thirty yards at a target moving all over the place. It had gone neatly through the flesh of the kid's right leg about mid-way between hip and knee. He was bleeding considerably, but the bullet hadn't hit an artery.

The second shot was amazing, too, especially as it had been loosed at a running target. It was amazing that the escapee was still alive. The second shot had got the kid in the back of the neck – straight through the back of the neck. The wound was bleeding, but the slug had missed carotid and jugular, spine, and everything else vital that it might have hit.

Except for his exhaustion, the escapee could probably have gotten up and gone for it one more time. But he was out of gas. He was whimpering and snivelling a little and holding out his arms to receive the cuffs.

I arrived with the pistol still in my hand. Jacques was standing over the guy, radio in one hand and pistol in the other, both hanging at his sides. The con was breathing hard, but he was not out. I holstered my gun and cuffed him as he lay on the ground. Then the RCMP mutt arrived and stood there like a pointer. His master, while still running down the hill behind us, gave a command and the dog began to rip at the con's leg. The con tried to pull away but the more he did, the more the dog sank his teeth in and growled and ripped and chewed flesh and clothing.

I yelled at the Mountie, "What the hell is going on? What the fuck are you doing?" The cop was puffing and blowing and running and egging the dog on as he approached. I took a couple of kicks at the damned dog, and the dog took a couple of snaps at my foot. I yelled again, "The con is down and cuffed and wounded. Call the fucking dog off!"

Jacques hadn't moved. At this point, the con was bleeding from the shot to his neck and from the shot through his leg, and now his other leg was all bloody because the dog has chewed it all to shreds. The cop did nothing to call the dog off. "Call off the fucking dog!" I snarled.

I unholstered my pistol again – in case the dog wanted another go at my leg. The three of us had pistols drawn. Jacques continued to stare.

The cop said, "The dog needs practice."

The mutt kept on growling and pulling and biting. The con was screaming. I took my .38 and drew the hammer back and hunkered down, keeping the bead on the head of the German shepherd.

"You call the dog off right now or I'll blow this flea factory all over this hillside. Maybe they didn't teach you about a little statute that says you use excessive force and you go to jail. You come to jail, you asshole, and you belong to me." The dimwit thought a bit. I continued, "I'll personally call your N.C.O. and lay the information."

He called the dog off, bitching and moaning that guards were assholes. I radioed to Mainland base and told them it was all over. We had the escapee and we needed an ambulance.

I looked at the cop, who had the dog chained up, and said, "You get the fuck out of here."

Jacques moved for the first time. He unbuckled the Sam Brown belt which held his gun and radio and started up the hill to the driveway. He dropped the belt. He walked up the drive. He took the gun, opened the cylinder and emptied it on the ground. He dropped the gun on the ground. He pulled the keys to the patrol vehicle out of his pocket and dropped them on the ground. He turned and walked toward the gate. That's the last we ever saw of him.

The kid who didn't escape healed quickly. He was back in Oakie hospital in a week or ten days, scarred terribly from the dog. Beside these scars the little bullet-hole wounds hardly seemed significant.

In jail, stringers are not free-lance journalists, they are cons who hang themselves at the end of home-made rope. How a guard deals with stringers has a great deal to do with his longevity in his chosen career.

Once when I reported for morning shift, I went upstairs as usual and looked at the sheet and the board and saw the names of all kinds of new inmates. I also saw that I would be working Five Landing with a kid named Klocker, whom I'd never seen or heard of. Since I didn't see any unfamiliar faces around, I presumed he was already up on Five drinking coffee.

Normal procedure in the morning was to open the tier-box, lift the night-bar, and then lift the day-bar. You could go up a landing and do that yourself, but you could not open the endgate even with the cells still closed and walk down the tier without back-up.

Your landing partner is your back-up. In this case, I was Klocker's back-up. In order to get from One to Five Landing, I had to climb ten flights of stairs, because of the elbow and half-landing as the stairs reversed. You had to be in good shape to run up to Five from One or Two. The more junior you are, the higher the landing the desk man assigns you to.

Each half-landing was fully glazed, and in the West Wing gave a magnificent view of Deer Lake and the North Shore mountains. I ambled up toward Five, pausing on each landing and each half-landing to gaze out, have a swig of coffee and a drag of cigarette. A few voices on the tiers could be heard as the cons were waking up asking one another the time and the day. When I got to Three Landing, I could hear very loud talking. At first it sounded like an altercation between a couple of inmates, growing more angry in tone. I picked up my pace. When I arrived on Five Landing, I could hardly believe my eyes. The endgate had been left wide open.

As I ran across the landing, I heard a man shouting, "I'm giving you a direct order."

On every landing there is an intercom or squawk-box. I ran for it. The rest of the staff of the shift were on Two Landing when I left it, so I knew that my rookie partner was up on Five alone, and I hit the box.

"Go Five."

"Get me staff up to Five Landing."

Not only was the endgate to Five left wide open, so was the tier-box. The night-bar and the day-bar were up for the entire tier. The shouting was coming from about five cells in. Klocker was half in and half out of the cell with his back to me. "This is a direct order! Come down from there!" he screamed.

Some of the cons were starting to drift out of their cells, curious at the noise. I shouted down the tier: "Back into your drums! Right fucking now! And shut the door. Now!" They jumped back in, and I could hear their doors rolling closed and clicking. I dropped the bar, leaving open only cell 5 where Klocker was standing. With the rest of the tier sealed off, other potential problems were averted. I could see hands holding shards of mirror trying to get a view. Just then the staff arrived up both stairways, puffing and blowing.

I ran down the tier to cell 5. Then I stood there wondering whether I was asleep and this vision before me was a dream. The rookie was screaming orders at a corpse that was hanging from a beautifully braided rope made from government-issue sheets. Not only was he ordering it again and again to come down and reminding the corpse that he was giving it a direct order, he was also poking it in the chest with his middle and index fingers, causing it to sway and turn in balletic arabesques and arcs.

I looked around at the regular staff of the wing, who were peeking in the bars and looking over my shoulder. They were as amazed as I was. You always think you have seen everything in a jail, but this is never true. The rookie was unaware of our presence. He continued to scream and push the corpse. I put my hand on his shoulder. He didn't turn around. I said, "Mr. Klocker. He's dead."

Klocker continued to scream. The kid had separated himself from reality. I looked at a couple of our bigger staff and stepped aside. They walked in. Each one took the young guard under an arm and, lifting him off the ground, escorted him off the tier and down the steps. He screamed all the way, yelling about direct orders and the responsibility of the inmate to accept such an order. Nowhere in his stream of hysteria was there any acknowledgment that he had looked upon the face of death – much less that he shouldn't have been down the tier without back-up at the endgate in the first place.

The rest of us followed standard operating procedure. One man grabbed the corpse around the knees to lessen the tension on the neck. We tried to untie it, but the knot wouldn't untie. So we cut it. (Strictly speaking, maximum guards are not to carry pen-knives. One always appears when needed. We needed one.) We carried the corpse out to the landing. By the look of eyes, tongue, skin, and vital signs there was nothing we could do. He was quite dead. But standard operating procedure required that we administer artificial respiration until the paramedics arrived, and this we did.

That was the one and only time I ever saw Mr. Klocker. I'm not sure whether he ever sent his uniform back.

9

The Oakalla Riot
of 1983

•

. . . whenever it is a damp, drizzly November in my soul . . .
– Herman Melville

NOVEMBER 22, 1983. Vancouver Pretrial Services Centre.
"Lock down! Lock down!"

It was Ted Colley's voice. It came over at the emergency volume of ninety decibels, rather than the normal seventy. And there was an adrenal stridency to it. Most curious was that the "Attention, all units . . ." which preceded every announcement affecting the prison entire was missing.

Colley didn't rattle easily, but this order was the soul of urgency.

It was about 1900 hours and wet out. It had been raining for days as only it can in Vancouver. A few months earlier, I'd transferred from Oakalla to Vancouver Pretrial.

The evening news was just winding down on TV, and I was only half paying attention to it anyway. Old Burton, a favourite con friend of mine, who was sixty-six years old and had spent forty-four of those years in prison, was telling me about the old days in Alcatraz and Leavenworth and Kingston, and as usual I was fascinated by his quiet narrative. It had taken me the Oakie years and the time I had spent at Pretrial to receive the compliment of hearing such an oral history from this tall, quiet, gentle, and wise, wise man who was completely institutionalized and loved the adventure of his life of living in institutions.

He read Colley's voice exactly as I did and we came out of our chairs like pilots ejecting. He strode swiftly to his room and slammed the steel door.

I leapt up on the big wooden hassock.

"Lock down. Right fucking now!"

I jumped down and ran from door to door checking that there was a con inside.

Greg Mooney, my partner, had the door waiting wide. He slammed it and rolled the bolt with the flat.

"Look." He pointed at the window in the door to the other unit, Three South. The rookie guard in there, Whitley, hadn't even begun his lock-down.

Greg and I, both ex-Oakalla, sprinted for the unit door of Three South. I nodded at the lock; he cracked the door.

I went in like a rhinoceros.

"Lock down. Now!"

One con was fucking around the sink fixing a cup of coffee to take into his room. "Goin' Boss, wait'll . . ."

I whacked the cup out of his hand, threw his arm up behind his back and shoved him into his drum, coffee all over the place.

Whitley began, "Yates, this is my unit . . ."

As I was still wrestling the con through his door I cut Whitley off: "You, asshole, get in the hall . . ."

As I was closing the con's door, he whimpered mockingly at the top of his voice, "Just because they got a riot at Oakalla . . ."

"How the hell do you know?" I ask.

"The fuckin' radio."

"Right."

I checked the rest of the rooms on the South and pulled the doors. Secured. I headed for the gate. Greg was already chewing Whitley out so I had to boot the gate a couple of times before he came over and let me out. When I emerged from the unit, Whitley started for me. "Hold that thought, Whitley," I said, walking past him to the staff-station and the telephone.

Ted Colley answered, "Control."

"Oakie is up," I said.

"Good guess."

"No guess. Radio."

"But I killed the radios at the same time I called lock-down."

"Not soon enough. The media probably knew before the cons did."

"Some shit has been cooking out there since afternoon. Couple of staff got trashed, but now it's really gone up."

"Which wing?"

"Where else?"

"The Old West."

"Bingo. The team is going out. Two SWATs from the Mounties and city SWAT are already there or rolling. We're going in too. The fuckheads never practised the tac team going anywhere but across the street to the police station. There's a vehicle problem. You might have to take your own."

"Might, hell. I will. I'll get there alive. Be sure they get all the gear in. Like mine."

"Wish I was going."

"Stick it. And bring me an elevator."

I put down the phone. As I came out the staff-station door, the rookie began on me. I grabbed the front of his shirt and his tie and lifted and slammed him against the wall.

"An emergency order came over the P.A. You fucking ignored it. Just shut up and read my lips, asshole. There is a full-scale riot at Oakalla. When one prison goes up, you lock up all nearby prisons and go into media blackout as far as the cons are concerned. There is a reason for this. Sympathy riots. If all the major prisons in this province go up, there aren't enough people to do anything about it. If you can't take orders, get the fuck out."

The elevator door finally opened. Colley's voice came over the speaker. "You wanted a limo, sir?"

"Yeh, take me home to Oakie. I've had enough of this high-tech hell-hole."

The elevator opened on One Landing and Colley popped me

through to the staff area where I picked up my patrol jacket, put the rain-condom on my hat, and headed out the several doors to the alley-entrance. I made the three block walk/sprint to my Suzuki cheap jeep and fired it up. I was away. It would be twenty minutes from downtown to Burnaby and Oakalla.

As I bounced up Cordova through the sheeting drizzle, I tried to construct the scenario I would encounter.

Oakalla had been unstable for some time. Its instability from a staffing point of view was the reason I had transferred to Vancouver Pretrial in September 1983. It was a natural enough move, given my credentials, from remand to remand. Vancouver Pretrial was supposed to replace the West Wing, Oakie's remand wing. All remands for Vancouver jurisdiction would now be housed at Pretrial in Vancouver. Only remands from outside Vancouver would go to Oakalla. This meant big cuts from Victoria. If you could eliminate the staffing of one wing and close down tiers on some of the others, "cost-centre directors" would begin looking good in the eyes of the ministry hierarchy. So the West Wing was closed.

I had seen poor old Oakie take several beatings. The riot damage was costly to repair, but the money never went into upgrading the place. After this or that riot, they could have put bars of high-tech alloy like the thirty-hour bar at Pretrial. Instead, they repaired the old pot-metal bars that anyone with a wire-saw can get through in about thirty minutes. They could have replaced the porcelain toilets with stainless steel. Many things could have been done, but weren't.

I could see the lights of numerous police wagons whirling as I approached Hastings. Huge snarl-up. They were turning back traffic. A city bull with his red-cone flashlight came to my window. "You'll have to detour . . ." He saw the flashes on my shoulder.

I reached in my pocket and grabbed my ID. "Can you fire me though? I'm Vancouver Pretrial SWAT on my way to Oakalla. Your SWAT is already there."

"Yeah, yeah, right, right . . . uh . . . Swing left and your jeep should be small enough to make it between the firetruck and the curb. Where are your unit vehicles?"

"Remember the Keystone Cops?"

He grinned and got me through. Sheriffs' vehicles, fire-department vehicles, and ambulances seemed to be heading in the same direction as I was.

Unlike in the movies and television, riots do not happen spontaneously. There is always a pumping-up period during which snitches let you know what's happening, chapter and verse. The information is handed up the chain of command. Everybody knows it's coming, but in ten years I have never seen the brass take any measures to prevent a riot.

Food was the immediate catalyst of the '83 riot. Vancouver Pretrial had opened in August 1983 with catered meals and no inmate involvement in the kitchen. The cons at Oakalla could see the dollar signs on the wall. Oakalla food was not fancy but it was solid, fresh, and provided a number of inmate jobs. There had been rumblings and skirmishes for a month prior to this November night as soon as rumour turned into announcement that Oakalla was soon to be catered.

But the mixing of inmates (remand and sentenced) who by law should not have resided together had served to turn Oakalla into a powder keg before this announcement was made.

With the closing of the West Wing, the lay-off of auxiliary staff, and the scattering of regular staff like me to other units and institutions, suddenly there was a problem of what to do with the non-Vancouver-jurisdiction remands. The brass in its wisdom decided to stick them in the East Wing (a sentenced unit). It was against the law and against the manuals, but who'd notice? The remands didn't like it and their lawyers screamed. The sentenced inmates didn't like it, either; who wants to play cards with a stooge who knows nothing about jail culture, doesn't even know the lingo, and is scared to death? And then there was the problem of what to do with the P.C.s – the rapists, the molesters, the flashers, the streakers, and the rats.

If the West Wing was empty, rendered redundant by Pretrial, how could a riot involving more than one hundred and fifty cons occur? You may well ask.

When they closed West Wing, they stirred all the above immiscible elements into the East Wing. Inmates made their demands clear: they wanted the protective-custody people out. But the brass took no

action. It would have cost money. There were a few sit-ins and skirmishes. Then a mini-riot that did enough damage to require repairs
to be made without inmates peering over the shoulders of tradesmen.
Someone got the bright idea to move the East to the West. Good
thinking. They were in the West Wing but answered the phone
"East Wing." Except for a few jokers who answered "Weest Wing" and
"Est Wing."

Inmates had very little to do other than observe the cuts, the political pandering, and the bad morale of staff. When enough is enough,
a jail goes up. The average riot requires three to five perpetrators. The
rest go along to the extent that they must to avoid being labelled and
having to sign into protective custody. Once in motion, a riot has a
life of its own. The perpetrators keep it cooking. The followers just
want to get it over with without hurting anyone or being killed or
having extra time added to their sentences.

During the next few hours (and in the following weeks) I learned
the details of the exordium:

About a year after I began work at Oakalla they hired a fresh herd
of auxiliaries. In this group was a good-natured mountain, name of
Colin Tucker, a retired bobby from London's tougher districts. What
a breath of fresh air compared to the ex-military types and ex-
Mounties in corrections. Colin had been trained with emphasis on
crime prevention, rather than law enforcement. His presence inclined
one toward reasonable behaviour. He was there to be helpful, to
defuse potentially explosive situations.

Colin was a jewel. About fifty years old. He liked his family and
food and the job at Oakalla. He was six-feet-seven or -eight and
weighed something more than three hundred pounds. His forearms
looked as big as my thighs. He spoke quietly. If two cons were rolling
around on the concrete, intent on killing one another, Colin needed
only to stroll up and inquire whether there was a problem in order to
end the fight.

On the afternoon of November 22, 1983, the East was in the West
and all was not right with the world. Nor had it been right for some
time with the cuts, the moves, the mixing, the overcrowding. That day
yard was held despite the rain. The inmates of the East didn't very

much like living in the West and the yard was one of the reasons. The East yard had a view. You could see who was coming and going and say hello to your visitors as they came in. The West yard was a maximum yard, with solid metal walls topped with deadly concertina wire. The only view from the West yard was of the building, the guard on count position, the sky, and the two occupied shotgun towers.

During yard that day there were various scuffles – staged – to lure staff out into the yard crowd. It didn't work. The cons then tried a sit-in, but many were hungry and it didn't take a lot of coaxing to get them back into the unit. The cons agreed that, after dinner, when the cells were opened on One Left, they would grab the first line screw who ventured down and take him hostage.

Colin Tucker and his back-up went down after dinner and began opening the tiers. They were about to go on to the next tier. There was a call from One Left. "Hey, boss, you better have a look at this guy in twenty." Nothing especially suspicious about this, and it could have been Colin's back-up who took a stroll down the tier, but it wasn't.

As Colin walked down the tier, the cons began coming out of their cells and packing in behind him. When he neared cell 20, the last cell on the unit and farthest from the endgate, they threw a blanket over his head and pulled weapons from their pantlegs, pockets, and inside their shirts. Colin thrashed with his huge arms and fists and sent numbers of them flying. But he was hit and he was hurt and then he was down.

His partner locked the gate, per maximum procedure, and yelled, "Staff to One! Staff to One!" at the top of his voice. Colin was being piped (whipped with a pipe), but he kept his arms over his head and so his arms were broken instead of his skull. He was badly cut up with shanks of various types. And when he went down, his legs were piped and some ribs were kicked in. But massive Colin kept getting up. He simply wouldn't let himself be dragged into a cell.

Finally, staff entered the tier and began slamming cons into the cells. An ambulance was called. Colin had dragged himself half-way up the tier. He had two broken forearms, one broken leg. The shanks hadn't hit any vital organs, but he was badly shredded. Any more kicks to the ribs and his liver would have been punctured, and it would have been the end.

After the medics packed Colin off to the hospital, the wing began to turn frenzied. The inmates on all tiers began pumping up, looking for the final catalyst for a solid confrontation.

Now the line staff were plotting what to do. It is possible to bring out one man and explain verbally and physically that breaking the bones of guards is inappropriate behaviour in a maximum institution. It is quite another problem to address this message to an entire tier.

On every tier, except the one where Colin was injured, inmates were going from cell to cell ensuring support. The phone was ringing constantly as staff from other wings tried to find out what was going on.

The local director, who had already gone home, was called. He was on his way back, as was the wing senior correctional officer. The principal officer discussed with administration whether to try for a lock-down using present staff, or have the other two wings lock down first and then have their spare staff back up the West Wing lock-down. Administration finally decided that they would quietly lock down the other wings, then lock down the West.

A riot will occur whether or not the inmates are locked in their cells. With his adrenalin sufficiently up, an inmate can use the very cell itself to destroy a cell. On the tiers, there are always weapons squirreled away: weapons hidden deep in mattresses or high on cross-struts of bars. Weapons whose two or three parts are scattered around the cell so that the average screw would never put together in his head the sum of those parts.

Toothbrush knives, made from one or more disposable razor blades heated and sunk into the non-bristle side of the toothbrush, and string wrapped around the handle to guarantee a good grip; shanks, made from metal spoons, but also made of pieces of glass with strips of sheet wrapped around for a handle; heavy objects of any kind in a woollen issue sock; braided strips of sheet which are tied to metal handles of water spigots or anything else heavy; zip-guns, made out of a pipe with a wooden handle strapped onto it, using a rubber band and something hard enough to strike the cap of the smuggled-in bullet – unfortunately a zip-gun is useful only at close range, and there is no guarantee the bullet will exit the front of the weapon – even the cell furniture, such as the bunk, may be reduced to several weapons.

Things were heating up on both sides of the bars when staff from South and East wings arrived to back up the West Wing staff in the lock-down. They locked down One Left last – where the assault had occurred. The other nine tiers were noisy, but there was no violence during the lock-down. There were more staff than inmates when they went in to lock down One Left. Not a peep. Staff from other units returned to their posts. The local director and the S.C.O. arrived to read the incident report on the injuries of Colin Tucker.

At about 1830 the noise, trashing of cells, and burning began. Precautions were taken among the inmates, and instructions passed to novices. These included: Keep materials that can be burned against the north wall where they would be harder to hit with the fire-hoses; stash matches and lighters under the mattresses, which were covered in plastic; when guards and firemen come out on the catwalks to extinguish fires, hit them with pieces of heavy, sharp porcelain from the toilets which the inmate was to smash later on signal.

When a full riot hits, staff begin to operate by the book. They call local police for back-up. With a full wing up, Oakalla would bring in off-duty officers. A command post made of Oakalla brass must be established, and liaison officers for the fire department and police appointed. The media must be called and hook-ups established for their equipment, if they don't bring their own.

Lines must be kept open to the ministry in Victoria. The regional and district directors had to be summoned to the jail, as had the district director from Vancouver Pretrial and a team of his men, including me.

When I finally reached the intersection of Royal Oak and the Oakalla gate, there were guards, Mounties, and miscellaneous others trying to hurry traffic along. I could see that there were still a few places I could tuck the jeep among the fire and rescue equipment and zillions of cop and press vehicles in the parking lot.

I stopped and turned on my left signal. The cops directing traffic swarmed across to dismember me. I rolled the foggy window down a little. "We have a situation here, sir, you'll have to keep moving," barked the Mountie.

"That situation is precisely why I'm here."

A couple of Oakalla guards with flashlights were looking on with big grins on their faces.

I said to one, "Marshall, why don't you take this defective rent-a-cop back and get one that works."

The horseman became upset at that and began dancing around. "I'm ordering you to keep moving."

I popped the clutch and the Suzuki lurched left. The cop jumped out of the way, the hand reflexively reaching for the snap on his holster. Two Oakie guards, Marshall and MacDiarmuid, were standing there with 12-gauges. The Mountie made eye contact with them. They shook their heads. I flew down the drive.

A semi bearing a CBC logo was in the lot, as well as a vehicle from every rat's-ass radio and TV outlet in town. One nitwit was doing re-asks to test the equipment in the rain. His made-for-air grey flannel suit was soaked. "And what, in your opinion, did the guards do which was the last straw, the thing that really precipitated the riot?" he intoned.

The cameraman was cursing. The guy with the shotgun mike was trying to see if the rain was soaking through the black plastic sock. I walked by them in mid mock-interview, and couldn't resist. "Well, you see, the guards gave a TV idiot a real cock in the ear." They heard. "You, guard, what's your name?" The cameraman pointed the camera, but the light wasn't on. "Bessasson, Charlie Bessasson." Gave them Oakalla's director's name and kept on walking.

At the gatehouse, guards, cops, and fire-department brass were milling around. Anyone could have walked in. No one would have known the difference. Off-duty guards were trying to find out what was going down and make up their minds whether to leave or stay for the overtime. The same with the cops.

Around the parking lot and upper ball-field, vehicles had been pulled nose to the fence with engines running and lights on to flood the back area around the South and West wings with light.

On cherry-picker arms, portable lighting units were being hoisted up over the tin wall of the West Wing yard, trained on the stairs at the west end of the wing, which led down to the yard.

I could see that the fire-doors, installed since I quit working there, had been ripped out. How the hell do inmates, supposedly beginning with no tools in a maximum-security institution (until 1983 the highest-security joint in the province) rip doors, frames and all, out of their brick and cement collars with their bare hands? Those installations were fabricated of 12-gauge steel.

Rioting cons had the complete run of all the tiers, the fire-escape and the yard. One would dash out on the fire-escape at Three or Four Landing and do a dance and scream, "Come on in, Campbell. I'll do you personally."

Deployed over the hillside above and on both sides of the Main Gaol were North Vancouver Early Response Team (the proper term, these days, for SWAT) and the Vancouver City SWAT, both with their sharpshooters strategically placed should anyone try to get over the concertina wire. In all likelihood they were peering at the whole circus through their starlight-lens scopes. As I walked down the drive, I passed the Burnaby horsemen's SWAT vehicle, a black milk-truck full of toys. The team were all standing around with canisters of gas in their hands arguing about which gas to fire. As far as they were concerned, using gas was a foregone conclusion.

I had seen this movie before. The cops fire in the gas and then hang around outside and watch while corrections teams go in and have their skin and eyes and lungs destroyed. Just listening to them gave me the screaming itchies. (The gas makes everything unbearably itchy.)

The cops were dressed in their umpire uniforms – foot and shin guards, crotch cups, chest pads over flak jackets, and helmets not on yet. They didn't need any of this gear because they had no intention of going in and exposing their bodies to bullets from zip-guns and flying objects of all description.

There was a horseman there I liked by the name of John Lardas. I walked over and we had a wet handshake, both genuinely glad to see one another. It was a little tough to carry on a friendly conversation over the din coming from the prison looming above us.

"I didn't know you were SWAT," I said.

"I'm stuck with running the show, it looks like." He rolled his eyes as we could hear a couple of his men discussing the properties of the various gases. They were almost coming to blows over which gas to shoot. John looked at them and they lowered their voices.

"John, my friend, tell me you aren't going to piss that nastiness into the wing and then invite me to stagger around trying to find bodies."

"Well, they managed to get sixty-odd of them out, but there are eighty and change left in the wing according to the last report I got. As you can hear, the frolic goes on with no sign of let-up. My guys are not eager to go in."

"John, drag your feet on the gas, if you can," I asked. "I want to talk to the command post and get a better picture of what's going on. Things may not be as bad as they seem."

I started up the front stairs of the Main Gaol two at a time. The front doors were thrown wide open. As I hit the top of the stairs, I found the Pretrial SWAT men sweating like bulls in all their gear. They were taking cuffed prisoners coming out from Centre Hall and chucking them into a truck for transport to the segregation unit at Westgate A. The real villains went to the "Oakalla cow-barn" – an ancient, dungeon-like segregation unit from the Dark Ages, located beneath what used to be a cow-barn.

Pretrial line screws, Corelli and Wade, did not look like happy campers. At the order of our brass they had suited up, ready for action. It was November and wet, but very hot inside. They shone with sweat.

"Why are you wearing all that shit?" I asked.

"Because Humpty and Dumpty told us to put it on and prepare to hit formation." Wade hocked and spat in a long arc past the truck door and into the darkness beside it.

"How you gonna *formate* if you haven't got them all together in the yard?" I asked. "Near as I can see, they've turned the whole wing into a Swiss cheese, ducking out of one landing and up or down the fire-escape to another." The footing inside – the marble foyer, the wooden hall, the painted cement – was slick from the rain water.

Windfors was part of the ferrying-command bringing cons from Centre Hall and East Wing for transport to Westgate A to the segregation unit. He had on the bottom of a tux and pieces of the top. He had been on his way to a date when he saw all the toys turning in at Oakie gate. He'd made the mistake of turning in to find out what was going on and had been nabbed by an S.C.O. at the gate. I asked Corelli about my equipment.

"I dunno. I think we had a full twelve bags [all the equipment for each individual was packed neatly in a duffel bag] at the outset. But, by the time we did musical seat and musical vehicle so that the guys with the bird-shit on their hats could be sitting in the proper places, some of the gear got rearranged."

"Is my gear here or still out in the truck?"

"Damned if I know. It could even be still in the closet downtown."

It was five hundred or more yards of gauntlet of fire-hoses and vehicles and people back out to the parking lot and Christ knew who had the keys to the vehicles.

"What am I doing here?" I asked.

"What are we doing here? Captain Queeg insisted that we suit up in the parking lot, get in formation with sticks and helmets and double-time all the way here to the Main Gaol. Then we stood around like assholes being laughed at by horsemen SWAT and everyone else until the brass caught up. I think they thought they were going to run the show. Queeg and company went inside to the command post and got told they were off jurisdiction. We asked if we could take these fucking suits off. No. We were to stand ready. The Oakie guys backed up the truck here and obviously needed a hand, so we've been helping load bodies ever since. It's something to do. The brass haven't said anything."

The Oakalla guards, many of whom we worked with when we were at Oakalla, appreciated the help. They had their coats off, sleeves rolled up, and shirts unbuttoned. The truck was pulled up to the

main steps and the Pretrial tactical squad was gathered around sweating and cursing. Just inside to the right was the door leading down to
records. The next door on the right led to Central Control and the
armoury, and that hall was perpendicular to another hall which led to
middle-management administrative offices, staff-lounge, and Protestant and Catholic chaplain offices. Most of the latter had been taken
over by command post, with direct lines of communication out to
Central Control and press.

"Hey, Yates." On the left, across the marble foyer, was a waiting-
room with no door. It was dark. The voice came from there.

Instead of heading down to the command post for assignment, I
walked across to the unlighted room. I looked in.

"Yeah?"

"Yatesie, c'mon in."

"Who is it?" My eyes began to adjust to the bad light.

"George Mastryk." His cigarette brightened and dimmed in the
dark as he smoked.

"Havin' a break?"

"Sit down."

I sat.

"Listen, I'm not just taking a break. It's scary as shit in there. You
can't . . . I can't . . . You're supposed to stay till it's over. They think it's
going to be a long one. After we had locked the West down they
started rioting in their cells . . . banging and chanting at the same
time. You should have seen Tucker, he was hamburger. The fucking
noise was everywhere. I ran to the bars over One Landing and puked
my toenails up."

"Come on, Georgie, you're an old trigger-puke. You puked your
way through every venue at the academy when we were doing the
physical."

"I puked because I was terrified. I never knew noise could make
you puke."

"How bad is it in the West?" I asked.

"All the staff is just milling around," he said. "We got about fifty
cons out after the lock-down, and every fucking one of them will have
to sign into protective custody. I think there are still about a hundred

of them running around in the West, setting fires. They destroyed all the shitters, of course, and we could see sharp pieces of porcelain flying around all over hell. I think they still have a lot of porcelain left."

"Didn't you tell me they were locked in their drums?"

"Yeah." Mastryk lit a new cigarette from the one he was smoking after blowing on the tip. He offered me one. I shook my head.

"When I came down the hill I could see them running around on the fire-escape, and in and out of the fire-doors, like mice in and out of a Swiss cheese. How the fuck did they get out?" I asked.

"Bunks." Mastryk said. "You know how the bunks are bolted with a collar or a toggle into the plaster. You lift the bunk enough times and the bolts pull out of the wall. No big deal. Every now and then they pull out of the wall just as a matter of wear and tear. The bunk breaks into pieces of angle-iron, very strong and just about perfect as wrecking-bars to smash the old pot-metal bars and pop the spot-welds. It's easy to bend a hole big enough to squeeze through. You give guys pieces of bunk for a crowbar and get them under the collar of a fire-door and the whole thing will pop out like a rivet out of a hole."

I was getting the picture.

"I'm too curious to hang around here with you all night. You deal with your own demons. You'll think of something and do it. You always have, man. Bear in mind you've been here for fourteen hours and fatigue may have something to do with your view of the world."

I walked back toward Centre Hall. I saw Godfrey Jutra, a principal officer in East Wing, there and wanted to talk to him. The roar coming from the West Wing was deafening.

"Jutra, I've got an idea." I announced. "How many guys from the Old West are there around?"

"Counting you and me, maybe six who are close by. I just saw Sprott and O'Dell near the gate in the South with coffee cups in their hands."

"Good, that's four. Six would be a good number, half a tac-team wedge. Any more than that and we'd be too big a target and if the shit came down we'd be falling all over ourselves.

"Derek [Van Hendrik] and Windfors are in here, too."

"Get one of your lackeys to round 'em up," I said. "Can you handle going in?"

"If I don't get in there and do something, I'm gonna pass out in the water and drown," Jutra answered.

My mind was racing. "Who's in the command post?"

"Mike Adler and Ollie Brent."

"We gotta get their okay and have them tie some piano wire around the nuts of the Mounties before they fire that gas."

Jutra yelled at a rookie hanging around the gate in the East and told him where to find the guys we wanted and to have them wait for us in Centre Hall.

"When we go in, I figure we got to have a good plan," I said.

"What's the plan?"

"Get up high enough in the wing that we can yell at them, tell them who we are and call in some old favours."

Jutra thought for a moment. "The smoke is deadly up high. We'll need the fire guys to bring it down with fine spray. And they can hard-stream the assholes back into the cells who come out to chuck porcelain or pot-shot with zip-guns."

"Now you're cookin'. Let's go for it. Centre Hall!"

The Centre Hall kid cracked the gate and we went through the visitors' cage. The Front Hall man was waiting at the other gate and had it open.

Uniforms of every description were milling around: ambulance staff, trauma team, SWAT, line screws, firemen, horsemen, and the press, who had been given a room down the hall and a rookie screw to run back and forth. We threaded our way through and made it to the command table. Ollie Brent and Mike Adler were running the show with Bessasson upstairs in his office on a hotline. Mike looked up.

"Mr. Adler."

"Jutra and Yates. What can we do for you?"

Jutra began: "Yates tells me that the Mounties are thinking of firing in gas."

"We haven't okayed it. It has, however, been mentioned a couple of times."

"We'd like thirty minutes of slack to try something," I said. "Mike, we've got, counting ourselves, six West Wingers who know the wing by feel. We want to go in. The firemen have an emergency lighting system they can string in behind us after we're in position."

"Who are the four others?"

"Sprott, O'Dell, Windfors, and Derek Van Hendrik. We think we can get the rest out without the gas and without weapons. We have a good idea who the perpetrators are."

Mike sat back in his chair. "There are eighty-seven monkeys swinging around in the wing."

"Yessir, but I have all the triple-uglies down at Pretrial. We think that most of these guys are just doing the usual go-along-or-be-labelled number. And even if they are heavier than we think, what's it going to cost to try?"

Mike was listening hard. But I just didn't have the magic word to tip the scales. Jutra did.

"Mike, if they fire the fucking gas, and you send every guard on grounds in there, you're going to have over a hundred staff off on compensation tomorrow and maybe a couple of stiffs, too. You'll be running on pure auxiliary power manning the rest of the jail. All we're asking for is half an hour to see whether we can make something happen. They've been jacking around in there at full speed for quite a few hours. A lot of them are bagged. If one of us gets beaned, you got one off on compensation. If we get nowhere, we'll back out and you can send everybody in boots and saddles."

Mike liked the numbers. "You guys understand that you're volunteering for this?"

"Yup."

"Ollie, you witness that I'm not ordering these six men?"

"Witnessed. And remember I said it's probably a waste of time." Ollie winked at me. He liked the idea. He and Mike had eaten enough tear-gas over the years to know exactly why we didn't want any part of the Mountie games.

I turned and saw John Lardas at the door and wondered whether he had heard much of the conversation. He was smiling his most inscrutable Mountie smile.

Brent turned to Mike Adler: "I think we should discuss this." The two of them rose and went over to the window overlooking the West Wing yard.

Jutra and I lit up and waited. Little did I suspect that this would be the last night of my life that I would smoke with enjoyment. My old friend, the cigarette, and I were about to part company.

Mike and Ollie returned to their chairs and sat down gravely. Mike looked up toward the door: "Officer Lardas, would you join us for a moment?"

John came in and nodded. Mike continued, "Would you please inform your people that we're going to delay the firing of gas for thirty minutes?"

"Yessir," John replied. He was itching to ask questions, but he was a savvy professional. He knew he'd find out more by keeping his mouth shut and allowing corrections to bring the info to him. He turned and headed for the door.

When he was out the door, one of the rookies was told to close it and Mike and Ollie asked us what we needed.

We wanted the firefighters right behind us with charged hoses and the portable lighting system, but no lights until we gave the word. Then we talked about gear. Apart from a few army-surplus gas-masks, there was none. Oakalla hadn't had an organized tactical team for years. The government had decided it was too expensive to buy the equipment and find a secure place for it, let alone spend the money on man-hours to train staff to use the equipment.

"Get us the masks, a couple of sticks just in case, and maybe three sets of cuffs per guy, and we'll go for it," Godfrey said.

We headed for Centre Hall to pick up the rest of the team. The firemen, being the kamikaze pilots they are, all wanted to come up with us when they heard our plan, but we persuaded them to cool it, and they pared their initial follow team down to three. Godfrey had a radio and O'Dell had a spare, turned off. It was agreed that we would use the radio as little as possible and at the lowest possible volume until we were in position. Mike and Ollie had our portable numbers. We headed for the West Wing gate with the Centre Hall man. From here on we could only talk in whispers.

As soon as the wing gate closed and locked behind us the noise was on us – pounding, screaming, the sound of metal against metal, wood against cement. If we stood at the centre of the landing, no one in either of the two tiers could see us. Godfrey pointed to Sprott and Derek to check out Two Right and Two Left and make sure the gates were secure. They flattened themselves against the tier-boxes. We had flimsy joint-supplied plastic flashlights stuffed in our ass pockets and one of the firefighters had a mega-light, but the plan was to use the light from the windows to check out the tiers. The cons would chuck pieces of toilet or shoot their zip-guns at anything that looked like a light on the landing. Derek and Sprott nodded that the endgates were secure and inched back to us.

Derek said, "Good news, good news. They've got the tier barricaded about five feet back from the gate. They fucked themselves for keeping six on the landing."

"Same on the right," Sprott said. "They can't see shit unless they're between cell six and the end of the tier. But the fire-door is wide open. I can see the lights outside."

Derek told us that the fire-door was open on the left as well. I said we'd better check out One Landing. It was below ground. Godfrey agreed. I went for One Right and Windfors headed for One Left. I hit the floor, belly-crawled across, and started down the stairs, feet first. It was too quiet. I could see shadows falling across what I took to be the wet floor as romping cons passed between the windows upstairs and the lights outside. It was way too quiet. I reached the half-landing beneath the window. From here I could see the tiers on the other landings above. There were fires in a few of the cells and bodies were moving back and forth between the barricades and the fire-doors. This made me all the more suspicious about the silence on One Landing. I stared as hard as I could into the darkness in the direction of the endgate and continued slithering down the stairs, keeping as flat as I could. I knew I was too low down to be seen. I looked across the landing to see if I could see Windfors moving. Then I bumped down another couple of stairs and . . . yaaaah.

Suddenly I understood why One Landing had no action. At the bottom of the stairs, the water was groin-deep and christly cold. Then from the other side of the landing I heard Windfors yell, "Shit!" as he took the plunge, too. He flicked on his flashlight. Suddenly there were shouts from Four or Five Landing.

"Douse it and get over here," I stage-whispered. Windfors turned off the light and virtually walked on water to the cover of the tier-box. Behind him there was a hell of a crash and shatter as someone chucked a hunk of porcelain down. We stood there in the water, dead-silent.

We could hear the cons above speculating whether so-and-so saw a light down on One. Fortunately the commotion outside in the yard was in our favour. A bunch of cons were racing around the yard and lobbing whatever they could get their hands on over the metal wall, hoping to bean a guard or a cop. Another couple of chunks of debris fell in the general area where Windfors's light had been, but the chuckers lost interest when the light did not reappear. After a few minutes of standing stock still in that swill full of ash and defecation we figured it was safe to exit, stairs-right.

Back on Two Landing I reported to Godfrey that One Landing was clear because of the water, and thanked the firemen very much for not pointing out that they had been shooting water into the wing for hours. They thought it funny as hell. Godfrey kicked on the radio, relayed our report to the command post, and told them we were heading up to Three Landing.

One of the firemen suggested that his people could douse the hell out of Three, Four, and Five and it would chase most of them out into the yard and give us some cover going up.

Godfrey got back on the radio. "Command, this is 2743. Can you have the firemen on both sides of the wing shoot all the water-power they have on both sides at our signal?"

"Just a minute," Mike Adler said.

We waited. Then Mike came back. "Say when."

Godfrey lined us up. Sprott and Windfors dropped back behind the firefighters to help pull hose. We would go up as low as possible, up the right stairs, flattened against the wall, under cover of the water from outside, then fire our own hose down Three Right to keep the ones in their cells inside and keep the ones in the yard outside until we checked the endgate. Then we would move to Three Left and repeat the procedure.

Godfrey squeezed the radio, "Hit it now!"

We were flattened against the wall when the barrage of water hit. What glass was left in the window frames blew all over the place. We were face down, covering the backs of our necks, and were soaked to the skin in seconds.

"Let's do it . . . now, now, now," Godfrey shouted. We started to drag hose, but it snagged somewhere on Two. Our leather-soled shoes were slipping on the painted concrete. I had one fireman by the collar of his slicker helping him pull the hose. It freed up and we were suddenly on Three firing a strong stream of water down the tier, inmates yelling every insult they could think of.

"Try to get an angle on the cells." Godfrey yelled. "Fill 'em with water. The colder and wetter we can make the cells and the cons, the better our chances."

Instantly the air was full of flying pieces of metal bunk, porcelain, and large hunks of wood from the trashed desks. Fortunately, the rioters didn't know whether we were coming up Three Left or Three Right or both. A cross-strut of a bunk cleared the bars, whanged against the painted brick of the wall end-first, then batoned over and conked Derek on the head. Most of the energy was out of the projectile by the time it rapped him on the napper, and Derek was wearing a hat that took the brunt of the blow, but it gave us a sudden and profound sense of vulnerability. We pulled hose with all the adrenalin that uncut terror could produce.

Godfrey yelled, "Now!" The hose bucked and the stream leapt into one cell after another through all twenty on Three Right, except for 3, 4, and 5, which were blocked off by the barricade. But we could even get some water into them over the top of the barricade. There were only two or three cons on the tier and they ran for the fire-door, wet as drowned rats, and well-propelled by a stream of water in the backside.

Sprott dashed across the landing and peered around the tier-box on Three Left. There was a sharp, loud crack, then the sound of ricochet. A zip-gun. The shot wasn't loud enough to have been made by anything larger than a .22, probably fired from deep down the tier, almost at the fire-door. Zip-guns are notoriously inaccurate and often do more damage to the shooter than the target. The inmates were just hoping scare hell out of us.

We humped the hose across the landing and fired the stream down the tier full-bore until there was no more movement or sound on the landing. We shut off the hose and went back to the centre of the landing and listened. The only sound came from above, below, or outside. Mostly outside because the streams of water were still coming in the windows.

Derek asked the firefighters, "Where is the best place for us to be so that you guys can douse fires and cons as necessary? Five Landing?"

The head firefighter said, "Probably Four. We could reach anything above or below."

"Yeah," Derek agreed. "I think that if we get as high as Five, we'll be too exposed. The endgates are secure so far, but we don't know how much they hammered them before we got here."

By the time we got to Four to douse Left and Right, the cons had set everything inflammable alight. It was awful, breathing in that smoke. I ripped off my glasses and put on the old World War Two gasmask. I couldn't see a damned thing because the plastic eyes were scratched, I didn't have my glasses on, and the smoke was too thick. The firemen were shooting a heavy stream into the cells to flood them and then switching to a fine spray to bring down the smoke. The good news about the smoke was that the cons couldn't see where to aim the pieces of shitter, although hunks kept hitting the endgate and all of us felt that we were covered in ground glass.

Suddenly the cons were there lighting fires (and, we found out, covering up inflammable materials to be lighted later), but while we were yanking masks on and off and firing water at an angle down into the cells burning most brightly, the smoke would make the tier seem to be empty.

Godfrey yelled that he thought they'd torn down all the fire-doors. So I got on the radio. "Mainland control. Tactical squad in

West Wing. We're on Four trying to determine whether any of the fire-doors are still secure. Would you have one of the searchlights you have out there train on all the doors, one after another?"

"Roger."

"We're on Left. Have them start with Left. Then swing to Right. And ask them to hold on each door for maybe thirty seconds. The smoke is pretty thick."

"Roger. Do you have any bodies in custody?"

"When we get 'em, you'll have 'em."

"The RCMP SWAT are getting pretty antsy."

"One canister of gas and they'll swim back to their detachment. We can't do anything until we get the smoke down and get the lay of the place. So far, it's looking good."

"Roger. Y'all stay in touch, y'hear?"

"Get the lights cookin'. "

The smoke was thinning. One by one, the big light revealed that there wasn't a single fire-door left. The rioters had taken out even the frames. Each opening was surrounded by irregular brick.

Derek whistled, "Jesus, they've got complete run of all the tiers behind the barricades, the fire-escape, and the entire yard."

Whang! A brick was lobbed up from about Two Landing and broke in two as it hit the landing bars. Made a hell of a noise. We retreated to the centre of Four Landing. The firemen kept pouring water in.

O'Dell asked, "What's the fuckin' plan?"

"No plan," Godfrey replied.

"No plan?"

"An objective is close enough. Dummy up!" Derek said.

Windfors protested. "If you're going over the top of those barricades with nothing but a fucking stick and a gas-mask, count me out."

I joined in, "These assholes have been wearing their asses off for hours trashing the place and running up and down. I figure they're tired, for starters."

"And wet," said Derek.

"And cold," added O'Dell.

Godfrey had about fifteen years in at Oakie. "Listen, I've seen things make or break just on how you talk to them. We got to be careful what we yell down the tier. Never use the words 'surrender' or 'give up.'"

"How about just asking whether anybody else wants to come out."

"Yates, why don't you do the talking. I hear they teach you to talk at Pretrial."

"Suppose someone decides to come out," I asked.

Godfrey said, "I've got that part figured. Standard procedure. Yates yells, Derek backs him up. Yell around the tier-box until they get tired of chucking things. O'Dell and Sprott will frisk and cuff. No shirts. No shoes and socks. No belts. No personals. Anybody brings out any personals, take your stick and whack any Walkmans, watches, anything – books, whatever. They could have shanks in any of that shit, and most of the watches are used for brass knuckles, not for telling time."

The firemen had done a great job of clearing the smoke. We could now see almost all the way down the tier. We checked that all the tier gates were secure, and unlocked the tier-box to Four Left so that we could pop the gate when necessary.

I cupped my hand and shouted around the tier-box and waited for the noise to subside. "Hey, you guys in there!" There were still some men in the unit – we couldn't see them because of the barricades – and others were racing up and down the fire-escapes outside; still others were in the yard.

The expected response came. "Fuck you, screw . . . fucking pigs . . . come on in here, we need a hostage . . . Hey, Clem, you ever fuck a rookie screw? . . . Step out to where I can see you; I have a present for you."

I tried again, "Listen, it's Yates from Pretrial."

"Oh, shit. Holy cow. V.P.S.C., the fancy-dancy made-in-Tokyo jail. Heavy number. You used to work here in the West, didn't you?"

"Yeah. Listen. For one goddamn minute, listen, then, if you want to carry on, do as you like." There was a bit more hooting and trashing, but I could tell from the volume and cadence that they would hear me out. Then there was silence.

"There are two Mountie SWATs and one city SWAT and a Pretrial

SWAT outside. That fact is not a problem, until and unless someone authorized reads you the Act. [The Riot Act gives them thirty minutes to disperse and desist or they can be shot with impunity by peace officers.] We're up here to try to get the last of you out before the horsemen shoot in the gas. They're going to gas the unit and the yard. Then we have to do the mop-up. You guys are wet and cold and we're wet and cold. Perfect conditions for the gas to make you feel like your eyes are on fire and make you wish your skin would fall off. And the same goes for us. You know and I know that they're gonna have a hell of a good time dicking around with the gas and concussion grenades and never step foot in here and risk broken eardrums and fucked-up eyes. If there are any more of you who want to come out before the SWATs go nuts on the place, we'll take you down one at a time. Come out the Four Left gate. We'll escort you down personally to Centre Hall and guarantee your safety. Most of you will be taken to the East [the renovations had just been completed]. Anybody who wants to jack around once he gets out here on the landing goes to A-side [segregation]."

"No cow-barn," a voice yells.

"I was told it was filled to capacity when I arrived. No cow-barn." Long silence.

I went on, "If we don't bring anybody down in ten minutes, they're gonna start shooting the gas and we're outa here." More silence.

"How many of you out there?" one of them asked.

"Six. Just enough to frisk, cuff, and escort. No more."

More silence.

"Who?"

"Me, Yates, from Pretrial. Godfrey from East. Sprott and O'Dell from South. Derek Van Hendrik and Windfors from records."

"Bullshit!"

"Send someone over the barricade to check it out at the gate. I won't unlock the gate."

Silence except for heated debate in stage-whisper. In the distance we could hear people rattling up and down the metal fire-escape and yelling in the yard. I gave them ten minutes and radioed command, "I have 2115. We move out at 2125. No gas until we get to Centre Hall. Flying pieces of shitter are bad enough without taking a tear-gas canister in the head. No gas till we radio from Centre Hall!"

"Roger."

It was a gamble. I knew that if they believed what I said, the rioters knew where we were, and how many of us there were. On the other hand, if they didn't believe me and one guy came out and saw I told them the truth, it would boost our credibility.

If they'd been quietly taking down a barricade on another tier, they could have used a fire-door as a battering ram to get through an endgate on a lower tier and trap all six of us above them. We knew this. The fire dudes knew this. They fired a few streams at the spot-fires they could see on lower tiers. Every now and then a shadow streaked down a tier and out a fire-door or rushed in the door and ducked into a cell.

Derek hissed, "Listen."

We could hear movement but couldn't see anything happening on the tier. The barricade was fifteen or twenty feet down the tier. Then we saw a head appear above the junk of the barricade. By the time the first guy made it over the top, we could see another one following him over. The first guy looked over his shoulder. He looked like he was about to run toward the gate.

Godfrey shouted at the first con, "Okay, guy, put your hands on your head, lock your fingers, and walk toward us." The other one was down off the barricade and standing there. "Hang on, fella, we'll be with you in a minute."

I opened the gate and O'Dell and Sprott had the inmate assume the position against the wall, pat-frisked him, and had him take off his shirt and shoes and socks. He had a pen and some other stuff in one of his pockets. Sprott pointed to the table. The con dumped it on the table and Windfors whacked the stuff with his riot-stick and swept it across the landing.

Godfrey shouted out, "Next guy, same routine. Right here. Lock those fingers tight."

Sprott and O'Dell had cuffed the first con, and I walked over and took him by the cuff-chain and his left arm. He yelled, "You guys!

They were telling the truth. No firing squad!" From the tiers on the left came shouts of, "Right on!" "Fuck 'em. Burn, baby, burn!" "Dummy it, asshole!" It sounded good to me. They were tired. They were no longer one collective bag of hysterical adrenalin.

Derek got on the radio to command post, "Officer Yates is coming down escorting one. Please have someone escort the inmate to Centre Hall. We have several more up here and we need Yates back immediately . . . and, uh, get the gas brigade to back off. Remember our deal."

"Roger."

Going downstairs reminded me of movies I had seen of Hawaii where you can walk under waterfalls. There was a wall of water pouring off every landing, down our necks. I was beyond cold, but it was good to be moving. The painted stairs were slick and the con was slipping and sliding. I had to hold him up. "Glad to get out of the shit?"

"Right on, man. It's almost prelim time for me. I needed this bullshit like an extra asshole."

Then we were in the light of Two Landing and heading for the dry floor of Centre Hall. Bailey was waiting by the gate. He took the con and I dashed back up the stairs as fast as I could without falling on my ass. I tried to hit the walls of water where the downpour was the thinnest.

Upstairs, the cons had begun to come out. I ferried down about four more. Then they started to come over the barricade so fast, Godfrey looked a little worried. We locked the Four Left gate after each guy, and Godfrey kept the next one about ten feet back until we were ready for him. Then we ran out of cuffs and Godfrey had to radio down for more. By this time we had ten or twelve out.

When I surrendered the next con on Two Landing, they handed me at least fifty pounds of cuffs and stuffed my pockets with "spare cuffs." These are nylon straps which only pull one way. They work well and bite less than metal cuffs but you have to cut them off. I packed this load back up to Four, only to find the landing full of smoke. I dropped the cuffs and looked around for my gas-mask. Windfors already had his on and pointed under the table. My respiratory system felt like a prairie fire. My eyes were tearing and streaming down my face behind the mask and the plastic was steaming up from the tears and sweat. I couldn't see a damned thing. The firemen were shooting fine spray all over the landing and down the tiers to knock down the smoke, then shooting hard streams as soon as they could locate a bright fire. We supposed the perpetrators had taken back control of the situation and it was the end of Operation Stop the Gas.

The cons were putting inflammable materials against the wall closest to the landing and against the back of the cell. The firemen called for back-up and more hoses. It took almost an hour to douse all the burning shit and get visibility back; to be able to take my mask off and put my glasses back on.

Little did we know that, except for the firemen with their Scott air-packs, we were breathing all manner of toxic fumes, from the burning paint and plastic mattress covers. I've since learned that the most damaging gases are invisible and odourless.

Then a voice from the gate on Four Right shouted, "Hey, you guys, I want to come out."

All of us gave one another glances that said, "No way." We had the Left Landing well covered and well watched. But they could have had fifty cons on the right stacked up like cord-wood in the cells and behind the barricades.

Godfrey yelled, "You wanna come out, you go back down the tier and outside and come out on Four Left like we said."

"Come on, man, I'm right here. Just pop the gate," the con pleaded. Sprott caught the eye of one of the hosers and gave him the signal to hit it. The fireman not only blasted the guy away from the gate, he got him square in the ass as he was going back over the barricade. That was the end of that.

Then, when we were nearly ready to throw in the towel and pull out, the stream of cons began trickling over the barricade again. The next guy over was not a happy rioter. He didn't really want to come out, but he had cut his hand badly on the sharp steel of the fire-door frame while prying it away from the brick. He was one of the housedogs of this mess. (Housedogs attach themselves to whichever power group they think will prevail.)

Once out on the landing, he didn't want to go along with the search. His hand was bound up in a huge ball of torn sheet. Godfrey told him his shirt had to come off. The con replied that he couldn't take it off because the bandage wouldn't go through the sleeve. The con liked that bandage entirely too much. Derek locked the tier door. We jumped him and unwrapped the bandage and out dropped a shank. "Great," I said. "Another one for my collection."

We plastered him up against the wall and cuffed him. Windfors took off his shoes and socks and checked to see whether he had anything taped to the bottoms of his feet. He had a hexagonal wristwatch in his pocket which felt like it weighed a pound. It didn't even work. A big wristwatch with sharp edges is more effective than brass knuckles as a weapon. You adjust the strap so that it fits snugly over your fist when you clench it. We tossed it on Windfors's table and Windfors almost ruined his truncheon trying to smash it. All he managed to do was put a little crack in the crystal. The con was screaming that it was given to him by someone near and dear. Windfors dropped it on the floor and jumped up and down on it with both feet. It was indestructible. I reached down and put it in my pocket. The main thing was that there be nothing within reaching distance which could be converted into a weapon.

The con was cuffed, but he was turning into an orangutan. Godfrey ordered Sprott to help me escort him down. Sprott was an ex-SAS commando. As Sprott approached, the con stood on one leg and attempted to kick him in the nuts. Sprott side-stepped and kicked the standing leg out from under him, and the con fell on his ass. We each took him by an arm and started down. The stairs were very slippery and the con was yanking us this way and that. We crashed into a lot of walls on the way down – con-first. We had to steady him at every waterfall on the way down, with him under it. By the time we got to Two, he was mellow.

There was no pattern to the flow of cons. There would be a herd of up to five, then none for half an hour. I'd go back to my shouting routine: "Anyone else coming out?"

We had no idea how many we had taken out, nor any sense of

space and time up there in the darkness and smoke. Despite the waterfalls, we took turns taking them downstairs just to keep circulation up. At one point Windfors was doing jogging in place to keep warm. He was so wet he didn't want to do escorts and take a splash in the waterfalls. But he was jogging where the light outlined him. An incoming chunk of toilet smacking the bars and shattering took care of that effort.

We'd reached that point of fatigue where you keep on keeping on without feeling anything. Daylight was now on us and we cut the lights, but I had no idea what time it was. I had put my watch in my pocket to keep from drowning it under the waterfalls. When a new fire started, none of us bothered putting on our masks.

No one had come out for what seemed an eternity. Then a poor old con laboured his way over the barricade, his arms full of legal papers. He must have been in his sixties. Christ knows where he had holed himself up during the night. They dumped his papers on Windfors's table. Windfors was going to sweep them into the watery trash-heap on the floor when Derek said, "No, just look through them. I know him. He's harmless. He's defending himself in court and the trial's in progress."

When I took him down, I tucked the papers inside my jacket to keep the water out. They cut his spare cuffs downstairs and gave the papers back to him. Then I went back up to Four for perhaps another half an hour. By this time, other guards were drifting up for a look and I could see staff down below going over the top of barricades and partially dismantling them to sweep the tiers. I had a serious crick in my neck from peering down Four Left around the tier-box.

Someone tapped me on the shoulder. Bob Trevelyan. "Count's clear," he said.

"Bad joke, Bob, I'm not in the mood." I said. On the other hand, Bob was not a joker.

"Really. The board downstairs doesn't lie. The count is clear."

"Fuck you. The ringleader is still in there."

"No, he's not. He's in hospital."

"What?"

"No shit. He's been on the waiting list for some kind of nothing surgery and they kept him in overnight."

"He dreams up this fucking circus, then misses his own riot?"

"You got 'er."

"What time is it?"

"O-six-hundred and change."

"It's all yours, brother. I'm outa here." I started down the stairs, and I was so stiff I had to hang on to the banisters and take it one step at a time and rest on each one. At the time, I still lived right across the street from Oakie. All I could think of was going home to a hot shower and bed.

But when I got to Centre Hall, Percy Deverell, an S.C.O. from Pretrial, was standing there. "All Pretrial tac-team personnel back to the unit for debriefing," he said.

"Sir, I live right across Royal Oak."

"Standard procedure, Mr. Yates."

It must have taken me half an hour to get from Main Gaol to the parking lot and get in the car. I was tempted to go home and get into dry clothes first, but I knew I'd never get back out of the apartment without passing out. Pretrial was a long way from Oakie. It meant driving downtown through the morning rush-hour traffic.

During the debriefing at Pretrial, half of us dozed while the rest of us sat there shivering. Nothing of value was said in the debriefing, and they could have kept their compliments on how well the team comported itself. I had some spare civvies in my locker so I changed into them and tossed my uniform in the trash. Then I drove back to my apartment near Oakie. It was 0800 when I crawled into bed without a shower. Then I got up again at 1300 and was back at Pretrial on shift at 1500. The only one of us stupid enough not to book off on compensation.

Two days later, my voice completely gone, I was ordered to go home and put in for compensation (disallowed by Workers' Compensation). My respiratory system was full of infections. I spent the next three weeks in bed on antibiotics with a humidifier humming. I could never tolerate smoke or smoking again.

I received a commendation (much harder to get than a Ph.D.) for bringing the last eighty-seven cons out without injuries – with a lot of help from my friends, namely the other team-members and the cons who appreciated the way we handled the situation.

The government reported the damage at $200,000. But the work-men who repaired the wing compared notes with other contractors. That's how I learned that repairs cost between five and six million dollars.

PART TWO

Vancouver Pretrial

10

Doing Time with Picard and Data

•

The trouble with our times is that the future is not what it used to be.
– Paul Valery

GOING from Oakalla to Pretrial was like going from the prehistoric caves of Spain to the Starship Enterprise. Pretrial is the highest-security institution in North America, and the most high-tech prison in the world. It is definitely the wave of the future for criminal justice, in philosophy, structure, and methodology. And location. The downtown districts of large cities are unusual places for prisons.

When it opened in August of 1983, Vancouver Pretrial Services Centre was the *nouvelle vague* in corrections design: not a skyscraper, but very CN Tower in spirit. It occupies one city block – across the street from the Vancouver police headquarters and across the lane from the provincial court building – and is connected by tunnel to both.

In theory, Pretrial was to replace the West Wing of Oakie, which had been the British Columbia super-max remand wing. But after the construction of Pretrial, it became evident that, given the demographics and crime rate, Pretrial was not going to replace the West. After I transferred to Pretrial, the ministry had to reopen the West Wing. For a time, Pretrial was the remand centre for Vancouver District (with some flexibility – for extremely heavy-duty, high-profile criminals) and Oakalla max remand was for prisoners who had been taken into custody outside Vancouver jurisdiction.

Even getting to work at Pretrial was tough. There is no place to park at the jail, so line screws went in forty-five minutes early to drive around one of the roughest parts of Vancouver to find a space. Pay parking was prohibitive for line staff; only brass and administrative staff could afford it.

At Pretrial, you were taking your life in your hands if you went to work in uniform. Burnaby, where Oakalla was located, was full of guards. Those who lived near enough walked to work in full uniform without the slightest worry of being stared at or hassled. Everybody went to work in uniform at Oakalla. A place which has no staff toilets is not likely to have a staff change-room.

I tried going to work at Pretrial once on the bus in uniform. I almost got gang-bashed by a herd of drunks who I'm sure didn't even know one another. One guard got pelted by beer bottles just walking the few blocks from his car to the joint in uniform. You had to come in wearing civvies, and carry in your uniform, then change in the locker-room. Needless to say there was no overtime paid for the parking and changing time.

At low-rise Oakalla, only a maximum of five tiers high and spread out over spacious grounds, you could see great distances and spectacular views, which had a soothing effect on both staff and inmates. At Pretrial, there is only north and south. All views from the tiny windows facing south revealed only the street below. It was forbidden – and irresistible – to shout out the windows. It would buy a prisoner fifteen days in the hole. And on the north, only certain rooms, mostly on the northwest side, gave you a view of the harbour and the north-shore massif. At Oakalla, except for the noise the cons made and the televisions, when on, it was quiet; at Pretrial, it was like trying to sleep in a flophouse with the window open – sirens, drunks, traffic, and endless white noise. And deafening unit doors which fired like weapons.

Vancouver Pretrial discipline and training for guards was a grotesque caricature of military law. Those who came there from military service could not believe the measures being instituted, jackboots style. The attitude of Pretrial management was that everyone should behave the same way, have his hair cut the same way (only Mountie moustaches, no beards), every uniform should be identical to every other uniform except for insignia of rank and the custom designs of the Most High.

The net effect at Pretrial was to grind the individuality out of everyone. And the harder the brass ground, the more we tried to find ways to rebel against it. But in that high-tech atmosphere, Big Brother was watching from every direction, inside and outside the building.

At Pretrial, management went crazy about the nonsense of "conduct unbecoming an officer," which had never been a part of corrections practice. One guy was suspended because he was on tranquillizers prescribed by one doctor, fired the doctor, then got another prescription from the new doctor; he was accused by the institution of playing the multiple-prescription game and suspended. He appealed and came out on the good side of the inquiry and came back to work just long enough to tell them to shove it. Another had his family fall apart, attempted suicide, and was suspended. Another (whose brother was a cop) blew close to the limit on the breathalyzer, was relieved of his licence for twenty-four hours, and was suspended. If you drank and frequented the Police Athletic Club, you had to watch your ass. If you had one too many – even if you took a cab home – it got back to the brass and you were looking at a suspension. Even your life off duty was made the business of the prison.

There was no room for the safety valve of humour at Pretrial – no pranks or put-ons or the armour of gallows wit for self-defence. Management attempted to clean up the language at Pretrial, too. It was unbecoming for an officer to swear, for example – except, of course, for the brass.

All the things that humanized that funky place called Oakalla and made it tolerable were summarily banned at the holy vertical jail known as Pretrial.

Everyone had to be capable of functioning on a tactical team. Everyone trained. An hour on afternoon shifts was devoted to physical training. Most of that time was spent with a partner wearing pads; you beat the shit out of him or her with a truncheon while an "animal trainer" supervised. Or you practised karate moves: the horse stance, the T-stance, this stance, that stance.

When the trainer commanded "Assume the horse stance" to those of us circled around him, I began free-form dancing around like an idiot with serious palsy.

"What are you doing, Mr. Yates?"

"The horse dance, sir."

"Stance! I said 'stance'!"

"Oh, certainly, sir. I misunderstood you." The horse stance requires you face your non-existent assailant frontally, tighten your buttocks, and "stick your balls forward." Needless to say, I never used this manoeuvre under any circumstance. Nor, I think, did the female guards.

I did this to the poor gung-ho bastard time after time. The rest of the team would collapse on the floor laughing. But he couldn't nail me with a disciplinary write-up simply because I hadn't heard him clearly. I was never written up or reprimanded at Pretrial; I planned my moves carefully.

This jail tried to substitute physical structure, formidability, and show of force for the traditional Oakie-style human contract between line staff and inmates. The idea was to make all staff as robotic and interchangeable at as many jobs as possible. But some areas, like classification and records, are very intricate. Sentence management in general – which is the business of dealing with warrants, habeas corpus, Crown counsels, and lawyers – requires years to learn. Yet, at Pretrial, they threw green people into these jobs and chewed their asses off when they screwed up.

Backfires were frequent. For example, a rookie guard screwed up the papers of a low-level hit-man in for murder and on his way to court. They fell into the hands of a rookie sheriff at the courthouse. The sheriff told the hit-man he was released. The con walked straight out the door without even seeing the inside of the courtroom and was gone for several months before they apprehended him and dragged him back to Pretrial. God knows how many hits he carried out in the interim.

And it was idiocy to throw just anyone into a position like Central Control, where you have people coming on shift, people going off shift, people going to court, people returning from court, bays to be opened for vehicles, doors all over the building being accessed, elevators rising and descending with doors which must be opened only at secure moments, whole units going off to library, gym, rec room, cons going off to visits, and two radio frequencies (internal and radio contact with vehicles outside) to monitor. All this was the responsibility of two control officers who tried to run the whole show with parallel equipment and a huge bank of closed-circuit monitors. Rookies and long-time staff have been known to emerge from a shift in Central Control as gibbering idiots. Some people are more predisposed for "multi-tasking" than others. Some who are lousy in Control and lousy at the pressures of segregation are, at the same time, extremely good living-unit officers.

At Oakalla each line officer learned the ways of the jail by spending about a year and a half under the watchful eye of a seasoned old-time guard who knew every brick in the building by its first name; you were chewed out every time you made a bad move in handling the cons. Pretrial hired young people straight off the street – often students from the Simon Fraser University criminology department, since the emphasis at Pretrial was on hiring people with degrees – and put them in classroom training, then shoved them on a unit with the idea that they were in charge, that they were gods. And some of them tried to play god – with unfortunate results.

Those of us who transferred from Oakalla to Pretrial for all formal purposes went along with what we were told to do. But once on the living unit with the door closed, we carried on with the staff-inmate contract that was pure Oakalla. Ironically, those screws who were ex-Oakie generally ran Pretrial. It never seemed to dawn on management that if the ex-Oakie staff were getting into the least amount of trouble and assuming the greatest responsibility, the Oakie experience must not have been all bad.

Some of us approached the brass with the proposal that rookie staff rotate into Oakie for six months. It would give Oakie staff a look at their destiny, aside from the obvious benefits for rookies. It went nowhere. Many of the experienced staff transferred back to Oakalla after a few months.

There are times when one's duty is very clear. That is perhaps the chief attraction of maximum security, especially maximum-security remand institutions like Pretrial. Very little of the rational, sentient human being is required. There is little to no nuance in the code of behaviour for either prisoner or guard. A prisoner gets up when told. He cleans his room when told. He showers when told. He goes to bed when told. He grinds out a cigarette on the wall-to-wall carpeting and he can expect fifteen days in the digger.

It's not much different for the guards. You train and train until decision-making is ground out of you. You shine your shoes until they look like deep-brown obsidian or you get written up. Your insignia will appear exactly a certain number of inches up your sleeve or you will be written up.

At Vancouver Pretrial, Fridays were clean-up days. The operations director came around with a senior correctional officer, or with the program director accompanied by an S.C.O., and each cell on the unit was checked.

I called these men, along with the district director, the Most High. You never knew the exact time that they would show on the living unit. Should one of the cons have to use the shitter in his room shortly before they arrived, and should he shed a single pubic hair while doing so, and should this hair be discovered, the unit officer would be written up.

This is a typical Friday inspection: Each con is standing by his door. The Most High enter at the firing of the unit door (goddamn, I hated those ear-splitting electronic locks). They first goose-step over to the shower area and side-step to examine each stall. There is mumbling and whispering. The S.C.O. is writing on the clipboard. They then proceed to each cell and finally the kitchen area.

While the Most High converse about finding the odd waste in the bowl of a shitter, the lowly unit officer can stroll ahead to the next room (in which case the Most High will likely change their pattern of room-checking), or head out the door to the staff-station and have a smoke.

If they find the curly hair they're looking for, the officer's ass is grass. But he won't find out until much later, and not from the Most High. Via the chain of command he will learn of his disfavour and the likelihood of his being written up from the tower principal officer, who will do the chew. If he is in sufficient disfavour, the tower P.O. will tell him what time he is to report to the office of the S.C.O., accompanied by a shop steward should he wish one; a formal verbal or written reprimand is in the offing.

He is, of course, expected to penalize his unit, in the event of a less-than-perfect inspection, with restriction of TV or recreational privileges. But there isn't a hell of a lot you can do to penalize a whole unit. You can't charge them all and send them to segregation. The standard response to too much heat from the line staff is, "Whadaya gonna do, put us in jail?"

Unless they absolutely despise the unit officer, the cons are very co-operative about the Friday inspections. It isn't hard to convince them of the value of cleaning the place thoroughly at least once a week to prevent scabies, lice, and other conditions more dire even than the heartbreak of psoriasis.

It is the job of the unit officer to "keep a lid" on his unit. This is sometimes very difficult when the cons know that heavy heat is coming down on the unit officer and he is not likely to be in a decent mood.

This was often the case on Fridays. One never knew at what time the Most High would be around. There were twelve units to be checked for the inevitable pubic hair. One never knew in what order they would be checked. If an ex-Oakalla buddy happened to be in Central Control, one could call down and ask him to "give you six" (prison lingo for "watch your ass, here comes trouble"). But one could also presume that the Most High would come up with some tactic which would thwart the warning.

Inasmuch as the dreaded door might pop any time between 0800 and 1500, regardless how hard the prisoners had worked cleaning up the unit, it is reasonable to assume that of between thirteen and twenty men on the unit, someone is going to have to use his shitter during the wait. Here comes the *pindejo* (the curly). Unless the officer is prepared to stand in the centre of the living unit and dash into the cells and check each time a prisoner enters one – and some people have blond or white pubic hair, which in the wrong light is impossible to see – the Most High will find that hair.

Word went around that the Most High on Friday reached into their gaunchies and ripped out ten or twelve pubic hairs and planted them.

Personally, I don't believe this. I think rather that the S.C.O. on duty was required to subtract the proper number of curlies from his pelt of less rank. This would be much more in keeping with military law gone berserk at Pretrial.

One became accustomed to fearful Fridays. In this atmosphere of childish rigidity, line-staff morale plummeted.

Then came the invention of the Magical Mystery Tour. On any day, at any time of morning or afternoon shift, the door could go and *surprise!* The Pubic Patrol.

The prison guards I have known and worked with for what has become a considerable chunk of my life are a fairly resourceful, intelligent, and imaginative lot. If they screwed up excessively, they were promoted at the earliest opportunity (a principle which holds true in all bureaucracies and large private-sector structures) to keep them from starting trouble that might result in media black-eyes for the institution. But never, never have I met one so resourceful that he could keep a group of men busy for eight hours scrubbing floors and shitter bowls, wiping ashtrays, floors of showers, and counter tops.

Morale went through the basement floor and the volume of line-staff turnover became astronomical. We often went off shift emotionally exhausted because of rage. But I never went off shift fatigued because of more intelligent activity than the human brain was designed to handle.

11

Condition Yellow

————————————————— • —————————————————

You can check out any time you like,
But you can never leave.
– The Eagles

I HAD BEEN at Pretrial no more than two weeks when I experienced my first Condition Yellow (C.Y.), "a life-threatening situation to which all unit officers must respond." There had been many Condition Yellow drills – each treated as though genuine. Not even Central Control knew a dry-run C.Y. from an "officer-down" C.Y.

There was no such thing as a Condition Yellow at Oakalla, because there was no need for such a directive. If there was a scuffle, a howl for "staff up!" over the ancient intercom was enough to produce back-up.

The Condition Yellow phenomenon, like so many other procedures, is just another paramilitary affectation in an institution that has deluded itself into believing it is the ultimate in corrections professionalism and had, in fact, taken the Keystone Screws to altitudes undreamt of even in Hollywood.

But at Pretrial, when the voice booms over the P.A. system at ninety decibels "Condition Yellow, Six North," procedure demands that you run to your unit door and wait for it to fire. Then you dash like a dog on a kitchen floor around the corner to the elevator lobby. These are centrally controlled elevator doors, so the two unit officers spin like tops waiting for the doors to open. Central Control then takes the troops to the appropriate landing and they proceed north or south. Unless Control has become a two-screw hysterical shark-frenzy (which happens disconcertingly often), the door leading to the problem is open.

At the time of one Condition Yellow I was working in records, which is located on the lowest floor. I was in my mid-forties, my partner, Bentall, in his mid-fifties; he was lean and long of leg but a very heavy smoker. We flew back from our computer terminals and almost damaged one another trying to get through the narrows of the doorway. I let Bentall lead, and lead he did, until we got to the records doorway, where the rookie with the flat – this was a manual door, one of the few, for reasons unknown – was so nervous that he couldn't get the flat into the huge slit of the lock. There were six or eight of us pushing to get through and screaming at the rookie, which only made things worse. Bentall finally wrenched the flat away from him, unlocked the door, and the herd of turtles went bouncing off the walls up the narrow hallway, which was carpeted. Control had us on camera and cracked the door to the elevator lobby at just the right moment. The first man banged the door back and plunged through, only to hit the waxed tile floor of the lobby and fall on his ass. Several guards right behind fell over him. Bentall and I managed to keep our footing.

The Condition Yellow was in visits. This meant we had to get through the door to the administrative area. The S.C.O. was cowering inside the doorframe of his office (wise man) wincing; he could well imagine the number of staff who would half-kill themselves by the time we got to visits and end up breaking the Workers' Compensation bank.

We hurtled through a right turn past the offices of all three of the Most High: the district director, the operations director, and the program director. These were empty. With less adrenalin up, this might have tipped us that something was up. I can remember rounding that turn with my body-weight ahead of my legs' ability or inclination to stay under it, into a lean to keep from hitting the steel doorjamb, and seeing S.C.O. Murdoch's face as he closed his eyes to save himself from witnessing a disaster.

I made it.

Ahead was the maze of the open business area, now an obstacle course. The secretaries in the steno pool and the accounting flunkies didn't know where to hide. One was spun aside into a divider, which came down with a crash on an expensive electric typewriter. One officer made it no farther than this and was off for several weeks with a nasty ankle and various contusions.

Having cleared this forest of booby traps, we slammed against one another again as we went through the door to the telephone operator's lair (she had backed her chair into a protective corner between wall and switchboard console) and headed up the four stairs to the door to visits.

When we entered, there stood the Trinity who comprised the Most High. And one very small Japanese man with very thick glasses. All were staring at their watches, timing us. The operations director had a body alarm (the one assigned to visits) in his hand. He had activated it to show the foreign journalist what a Condition Yellow at the highest-security institution in North America looked like. There were no visitors other than the Japanese journalist.

The room was filling with brown uniforms. My brain noted that my forearm hurt like hell from smashing against something. I looked at my partner. He was ashen and his knees were wagging. Even the youngsters looked bagged.

The Great One looked up from his watch and almost smiled. The Japanese journalist was beaming.

"Forty-three seconds. Not bad. Return to your units," was all the Great One said.

The first Condition Yellow occurred before they had even opened the place formally, while we still had some empty units. Management decided to have a dry run of a riot/hostage-taking on one of the empty units.

The prison, modelled on those in San Diego and Chicago, is designed to prohibit any more than twenty inmates getting together for purposes of mischief at any one time. But if they do, it is not easy to hear them. At Oakalla, anything shouted loudly and clearly on Five

Left could be heard clearly on One Right. But at Pretrial, a unit on the south could be trashing itself and not be heard across the landing on the northern unit.

In this mock riot were a melange of veterans from Oakalla, rookies, and cops (V.P.D.) from the cop-shop across the street.

Essentially, it was an exercise for the Vancouver city bulls' SWAT team. They came along to supply concussion grenades, tear-gas, and other toys (the tear-gas wasn't used because it was determined it might be detrimental to the decor), and to gather a supply of laughter to last for many years to come. The wise Oakies were not at all interested in putting on greens and playing inmate, although weighed against losing points with the big bosses, some of them finally did.

We knew that this was an industrial-strength re-enactment of the infamous Zimbardo experiment, in which a university professor had divided his class in half between prisoners and guards, to tremendously violent effect; nevertheless, Professor Zimbardo published a paper based on the experiment that has become famous among rat-runner scientists. We had been forced to study the project when we trained at the University of British Columbia's Justice Institute.

Volunteers took the roles of inmates. Many rookies (read here: those hired straight in from the street with no peace-officer experience, although one had an M.A. in something) volunteered for the inmate dress-up. Rookies will volunteer for anything. They made a wonderful meat squad. If any were lost, the experienced line staff would still be intact to run the new jail. The greenhorns had no idea what was coming at them.

Normally, in a hostage-taking situation (whether cop lock-up, courthouse, or prison), the officers who run the place do not participate in the negotiation.

A team is brought in from city police, RCMP, or Co-ordinated Law Enforcement Unit. If a hostage-taking occurred across the street at the police lock-up, then the Pretrial negotiating team would be employed.

Each team has designated negotiators who have been to school to learn the techniques.

First, a command post is set up (in this case, downstairs) and then, if the negotiations go on for long, they bring in the high-tech stuff. For example, you can string fibre-optics up through the plumbing, emerging at a toilet, to determine positions of perpetrators and hostages and watch everything go on. And, if need be, sound equipment can be put in place to hear everything.

On this exercise, they made perfunctory contact with the hostage unit. Then took their ERT (Early Response Team, SWAT; there are now many names for these teams which include the negotiators, the rigging experts, the sharpshooters, and others) and split them into those who rappelled from the roof, those who came up the fire-stairs, and those who went in the main door at the order of the leader at the command post located downstairs. They had pistols, M-16s, concussion grenades, the works.

First they lobbed in the concussion grenades, then the team entered with M-16s blazing. They sprayed every cell, even the showers. Had there been real hostages and real bullets, nothing would have been left alive.

But lose some they did. One went off to the hospital with both eardrums shattered; he had tried to chuck a concussion grenade back whence it came. Chuck Foote, who drove him to the hospital, told me the injured guard went into shock on the way to Emergency and he had thought he was going to lose him. Not a lucky guy. It's likely several others lost some hearing with that many grenades and pop-guns going off in close quarters.

The Most High read the event as a great triumph; this is the light in which they read all their scripts. They had proved unequivocally that, first, only small riots could occur in Vancouver Pretrial Services Centre, and, second, once they had their own SWAT teams trained, such riots could be suppressed with acceptable loss-margins of personnel.

Management's nightmares were later realized when they had a real riot on one of units. The rioters were not many, but they found to their ecstasy that the fire-hose boxes were located inside the units (another great Pretrial design enigma). After the guards shattered the glass of the door to the unit (we don't know why they did this, inasmuch as they could see that the cons had the hose and it was charged with water), the inmates blew guards all over the elevator lobby and kept them from entering the unit with the strong stream of the hose.

No one on shift knew how to turn off the water. By the time the proper authority (who guarded such knowledge with his life and his job) was contacted, the water had seeped down through several units on the south part of the building, even into the administrative area where it ruined equipment, carpet, wallboard – the usual stuff that water damage does. Having seen the damage of several riots, I would guess that this little one cost about as much to patch up as a minor riot in one of the wings at Oakie – calculating the difference in capitalization costs between an aging dungeon and hi-techy Pretrial.

"Condition Yellow, Six South!"

South, South? What the hell is Six South? I well knew what Six North was: the seg unit. But Six South? The duty roster didn't even list anyone for security on Six South. It was the general assumption that the hospital unit was still under construction there, not yet staffed. The all-units alert didn't figure.

The south part of the building had some architectural peculiarities which later caused consternation. For example, although the doors of the hospital were accessed like all the other doors in the prison (they could also be keyed with a flat in case of emergency), they opened inward instead of outward. Doors that open inward are not a great idea in a prison, especially when there is anything movable inside which can be wedged against the door to block it. No one could explain this.

I was on Five North at the time, and so it was fairly easy for me to dash out to the elevator lobby, jump in, and be one of the first to respond. Bill Corelli, a friend of mine, was right there with me. Control had already opened Six South East, the main door to the hospital. In we went, leaving the door open for others to follow. We could hear conversation coming from room 6S07.

When we looked in the door of 6S07 we could see Sally Hengest, a nurse, cowering in the southeast corner, and a halfbreed kid I was fond of and had had in the West Wing of Oakie several times, name of George Charbonneau, in the middle of the north wall holding a chair above his head. He screamed when he saw us: "If you come in here, I'll kill her and I'll kill you!" and so forth – all the things you might expect of someone hysterical and terrified and resolute.

I knew this kid. He wasn't very big. He didn't work out with the yard apes. He had an acne-ravaged complexion and thick glasses. He was quiet and liked to read. He frequently engaged me in talks about Melville, Hemingway, and Faulkner. He had been in federal and had a couple of years toward an English major. He most certainly was not violent.

I looked at Bill and switched places with him so that I'd be closest to Charbonneau. No shields had arrived, no sticks, but Sally didn't look like she could hold out much longer. Bill and I made eye contact and nodded. He knew I wanted to be closest to Charbonneau because I knew him. We walked straight into the room and over to Sally Hengest.

There was blood all over Charbonneau's part of the room. Hackles of blood flew out above his collar like feathers on a fighting cock. Charbonneau kept moving side to side and waving the chair – not to threaten us but to cause himself to bleed faster.

As we passed him I said, "George, hang on, just stay where you are, I'll come back and whatever the problem is I'll help you deal with it. You got nothin' against the nurse and you sure as hell got nothin' against me."

He tried to muster a threatening expression as we crossed the room, as though he were going to swing on us. He didn't. Corelli and I each took Sally Hengest under an arm, and with me still between Charbonneau and the nurse, we got her out. At the door, her knees went out from under her and we carried her the rest of the way. But she gathered herself up very quickly and got busy getting equipment ready to deal with Charbonneau.

Charbonneau was still waving the chair about.

"Yates, I got nothin' against nobody, but you got to let me die. Shut the fuckin' door and let me die. I won't hurt anybody."

"Hey, hey, what's the problem? I got a selfish interest in having you around to argue about literature." Where was the back-up? Bill and I wondered whether we should go in Oakie-style and try to get the chair away from him. I thought he would have parted the hair of one of us.

Finally more troops arrived, and cuffs and sticks and shields (these were the pre-Mace days) and all the rest of the paraphernalia. Charbonneau stood there, chair still brandished above his head, and bled and bled.

"Yates, keep them away . . . Ah, shit . . . Man, I talked to my common-law . . . Ah, shit . . . She's . . . Ah, shit . . . Just keep them away. You owe me, man. From Oakalla and from here. I never caused no trouble on the unit, man."

One never knows just how fragile incarcerated people can be. Apparently he had talked to his girlfriend and she had Dear-Johned him by phone.

The first problem was that the moment we got Sally Hengest out, Charbonneau was smart enough to realize that the more he flailed around the quicker he'd bleed to death. This man had cut his carotid artery on one side and the jugular on the other side, and there was so much blood that we never noticed, almost until he was ready to be transported to the hospital, that he had cut his wrists as well. Whatever the woman had said to Charbonneau, it was sufficient to bring him to this.

A guard owes any inmate who doesn't disrupt his unit. Both inmate and guard know this. And from bit (remand or sentenced time) to bit, each calls in his markers as needed. The inmate needs something from personals or a special phone call. The guard needs a particularly vulnerable young inmate looked after. It is an invisible ledger, but it is real. The more institutionalized the inmate, the more often he comes to jail. The ledger fattens.

At Oakalla, inmates shaved with the old Gillette double-edged razors which had to be opened with a wrench (kept at the desk on Two Landing) to change the blade. It was a one-for-one exchange. One razor per tier. At Pretrial, to establish the new high-tech era in prisons, in the inmates' doggie-bags (government issue toiletries) they handed out Trac-Twos and Bics. With the aid of a cigarette lighter or matches, it was very easy to get the blade out and make a weapon out of it for purposes of homicide or to cut your own throat. Or to set up booby traps for guards when they came around to frisk the unit for drugs, weapons, or other contraband. There is nothing quite like running your fingers along a ledge and having three fingers laid open to the bone by a well-planted razor-blade that has been Christ knows where. Once you get a little jail-wisdom, you do not go in and frisk without gloves on and something like a toothbrush that you can run along that ledge in order to knock things off that you're not tall enough to see before you ever, ever, ever put your hand up there.

The hospital was the last unit finished at Pretrial and nobody had spent much time figuring out how it would be manned and what the security procedures would be. It was not even being used yet. As far as anyone knew. It was reasonable to have a nurse over there working on the set-up. It was not reasonable to have a prisoner over there with no security cover. This was a suicidal con's dream come true.

The beds were all very fancy. They could crank up at the foot or at the head and they could be nicely dismantled to make a miscellany of weapons. The commons area, like the main unit, had wall-to-wall carpeting. But there was a walkway of gleaming unscuffed linoleum around it that was white beyond white and highly polished, as well as new.

By this time, everyone had arrived: the district director, the operations director, the director of program, S.C.O., tower P.O., and every guard in the tower. We had the doctor, we had the psychologist (who would have been interrupted from his usual description to the cons of his tennis game, his Italian shoes, and how much money would come into his hands should certain of his wife's relatives benevolently die), we had the psychiatrist (who also had a law degree and therefore doubled his money and doubled his fun). Everybody was stumbling over each other outside the room, but nobody was going in.

Before the helmets and shields could get through the door, Charbonneau chucked the chair and dove onto the bed, where he

correctly calculated that he could wedge himself very well. He hung
onto the bars of the headboard and wound his feet through the bars
of the footboard.

Although I had hunted and fished, and once even assisted with the
slaughtering of a pig, and had to do with all manner of events involving death and blood, certain things came to me in this instance as
though revelation. Blood just escaped from its human container is a
very greasy liquid. When there is much blood, it has the consistency
of hand-lotion.

Some of our largest and strongest guards were present. Some
of them (mesomorphs) weighed in the vicinity of three hundred
pounds and bench-pressed their own weight with ease. I can remember having Charbonneau's wrists in both my fists, attempting to hold
them still, with hands over the top of my hands trying to add strength
(hands bigger even than mine, and mine are big); there were hands
covering his arms to the shoulder. But he was twisting his arms any
way he wished, as though they were in a sleeve of ball-bearings, so
lubricious was the on-flowing blood. And so plentiful.

He wagged his head from side to side as much as he could and he
kicked his legs as much as he could and he used our strength against
us to make his heart pump faster toward its last pump.

We soon acknowledged that, given where he was in the bed,
despite that we were a veritable uniformed centipede, we simply
could not restrain him with our strength or our weight, much less use
other restraints. It was impossible.

Finally, someone with some common sense suggested that we
attempt to get hands and feet free of headboard and footboard at
once and carry him to the open area of the floor.

This was not easy, but we accomplished it. We lifted him from the
bed, carried him, as he screamed in protest, past the doorframe (this
took more than one try because he managed to brace himself against
it) and laid him on the floor – on the very white and glistening linoleum floor.

Many things about this incident amazed me, certainly the great
strength of a man as slight as Charbonneau. During the times I had
him in jail, he had never seemed truly committed to anything, other

than an on-and-off relationship with this or that woman – there had been several in the time I had known him. But he was clearly committed to suicide. He was committed to his death as he had been committed to nothing in the twenty-five years of his life.

Once we had him on the white linoleum, we managed to get a pair of damnable Australian cuffs on him (Pretrial had to have a try at these newfangled cuffs, which were very difficult to get on and get off). The wounds he had inflicted on his jugular and his carotid seemed not to hurt him at all; yet, although the cuffs were on only just tight enough to restrain him, he complained of the great pain of the cuffs.

Although many of us from Oakalla had dealt with attempted suicides and successful suicides there, here in this new setting we looked to the medical staff to tell us the proper thing to do. Had we been without medical staff – as we were at every moment of crisis I can remember at Oakie – we might have been more effective and relied on our own training and common sense. The medical people simply argued among themselves. Finally it was decided – or someone simply ducked into hospital control and emerged with them – to apply some gauze pads.

It fell to me to steady his head between my knees while others restricted his torso and legs to prevent movement as much as possible, mostly with the use of weight rather than strength. We were being fairly successful. I was steadying his head with my knees and hands when the doctor handed me some pads and told me to apply direct pressure. It is a very strange feeling to have your fingers two knuckles deep in a wound, and stranger still to learn how very hot blood is inside the body.

All the time I was holding George's head, he was staring up into my eyes. Each of us looked at the other as though standing upside-down, with eye contact the only place to look. He was pleading that I let him go. I explained that I couldn't do that for reasons of duty that he knew perfectly well, having been to jail as often as he had. This discussion and direct pressure did not stop his bleeding, nor did it stop me executing my duty to prevent his death. Amid the great confusion, someone had called an ambulance, paramedics, and the trauma team of the Vancouver Fire Department, all of whom went into huddle after they arrived to decide who was going to do what.

This sticks with me: the incredible inkblot-like pool of blood which appeared behind George's head like a black halo, the blood very, very dark violet against the spotless, white linoleum – the darker because it adhered to the smooth surface of the floor and had more surface cohesion of its own and, therefore, was deeper than it might have been otherwise. The floor near the head was not full of droplets or splatters, just one large, dark blot that expanded in high contrast against the white linoleum, its edges very sharply defined. It began to eliminate the shape of his head with its dark hair, and I was left only with his eyes staring into mine, making the same request long after his verbal pleading and his attempts at violent motion had ceased.

He was becoming weak and somewhat faint. He was bundled up by the various uniformed people and taken off to the hospital. A door closed. We were all left standing and sitting and kneeling more or less in the positions that we had been doing what we had been doing in. We were looking blankly at one another and then at ourselves with our three or four different kinds of medical and security uniforms ruined by the copious blood. We were suddenly very aware of the blood as a thing in itself rather than something that related to an emergency, and then as wet memory turning cold, but sufficient to replay again and again in our minds what had just transpired.

I don't know how long we stood there and milled around not saying very much because the actions had said all there was to be said. It was the end of morning shift and there was nothing much to do except wash, change clothes, and go home. As the prison began to put itself back together, someone of high rank, entirely arbitrarily, ordered that we throw away the uniforms that we had been wearing and not attempt to have them dry-cleaned.

Someone asked, "Even the shoes?"

"Affirmative."

I stood at the sink and rinsed off the blood. I rinsed it off my hands, my face; it had splattered on my glasses, in my hair, in my mouth. I had never liked the taste of my own blood when I had cut myself and always marvelled a little at people who sucked on their fingers when they cut them. In the urgency of the situation, I don't believe the taste of the blood registered that day.

It seemed to take a long time to get dressed. Before I could get out of the men's locker-room, someone came in and said we had to report to the boardroom before going home. Someone else pointed out that the overtime was rolling. I finished getting rid of the blood except for the bits around the cuticle and under the nails and went to the board-room. Not everyone who had participated was there; doubtless some had got away early.

S.C.O. Percy Deverell was there conducting what was later to be called a "debriefing." He spoke about what a wonderful job we had done. The incident was discussed and critiqued, but I have no idea whether anyone "unloaded" anything – and "unloading" is the point of debriefing. (If a debriefing is a buffer against trauma, I don't know that it works.)

As the debriefing proceeded, the prison received a call from Van-couver General Hospital, where Charbonneau had been transported. One doctor and most of the medical staff were still in the building. The hospital informed us of good news. We had saved his life with perhaps a two-minute margin. None of us was so ingenuous as to receive this news as due to anything but brute luck.

The hospital informed us of bad news. The prisoner had hepatitis B. But the hospital did not tell us what to do in view of this fact.

People began to group into little clumps and argue about appro-priate action. One clump decided to go off to Vancouver General Hospital and speak to experts there. Another chose to go to St. Paul's Hospital. By this time, I was convinced that no one had any idea what to do about anything.

Our own staff physician said, "Oh, I don't think there's anything to worry about, unless you have a break in the skin; I'm going home and just take a shower." This did not make a whole lot of sense to me, knowing that blood had gone up my nose and into my mouth. If one had a tiny cut, say a paper cut, who would know if there was a break in the skin?

I went to the telephone and called my own doctor. I was suffi-ciently rude to the receptionist, who told me he was busy with a patient, to get her to put him on the phone. I explained to him about the confusion, and he said that the rest of them could do whatever they wanted to do, but I was to do as follows: "Bring your ass out here to Burnaby. I'm going to stab it with a syringe full of gamma globulin." I did. And he did. Then he sent me home.

I stepped under the shower at about 1800 hours. When I came out of the shower I lay across the bed, intending only a nap. I didn't wake until time for work the next morning.

When I arrived, the first thing I heard was that Charbonneau, in the middle of the night, with two maximum guards present, long after the stitches, transfusions, and sedation had all been administered, managed to get his hands sufficiently free to tear at the stitches and set himself haemorrhaging again. This too was thwarted.

The last time I heard of him he had gone off to a federal institution. He never returned to Vancouver Pretrial, but by then he was already convicted. Working in records, I could have pulled him up on the computer at any time and learned his whereabouts. I never did. Something in me was determined that it was none of my business where he had been sent or whether his Corrections Services ID number had been cancelled or reassigned because he was dead.

A couple of months later, when I was visiting a friend in Toronto, we were speaking of a mutual friend who had attempted suicide repeatedly when I pulled this story out of the deck and told it for the first time. When I began, I found I was no longer sitting, but pacing up and down the living room, swallowing frequently and pausing because of nausea, and my eyes kept welling up.

By this time I had been in corrections long enough that I had seen many people as bloody as this person was. I had seen them shot. I had seen them dead lying on bunks and floors in pools of their own blood. I had helped take them down from having ripped themselves to shreds on concertina wire during escape attempts. I'd never had any problem (with the possible exception of my first encounter with a stringer) discussing these events with other guards or nurses or whomever. But I had never talked about Charbonneau.

This was probably the first time in my experience in corrections that I realized that certain occurrences go to places where the intellect cannot pry them out, clean them, and neutralize them. When I trained at the Justice Institute, I not only read *Adaptation Syndrome* by Hans Selye (the world's leading – and, incidentally, Canadian – authority on critical incident stress), I also followed up with more reading from the bibliography. And my years of dealing with emergencies had proved to me that I was mentally prepared (and had been commended for it) for thinking clearly in high-pressure situations and walling off things deleterious to my mental health. And yet, here, three thousand miles from where it had happened, simply giving the barest details of the anecdote, I was losing control of myself. And it had nothing to do with my fondness for this particular inmate. One tends to be fonder of inmates who do not cause trouble than of those who do.

Charbonneau was not special. He was familiar. He was not a problem. I had seen others with whom I had probably more in common take their lives. I had known plenty of writers with whom I had much in common attempt and commit suicide.

I'm not sure to this day why I was unable to control myself in telling that story.

Or looked at another way: why I *was* able to control myself.

I did not burst into tears. I did not throw up on my friend's rug.

And I did finish telling the story.

12

High-Tech Fleas

——————————— • ———————————

*The economic and technological triumphs of the past
few years have not solved as many problems as we
thought they would, and, in fact, have brought us
new problems we did not foresee.*
– Henry Ford II

SHORTLY after Pretrial opened, the Most High of the Most High
happened to step into an elevator when a rookie was doing his
first hour or two of training during one of the busiest periods of the
day. The poor rookie-in-training in Control managed to get the door
of the elevator open and the Most High of the Most High entered. It
happened that the experienced guard beside him, while a very good
Control officer, was a piss-poor teacher and had very little patience
during busy times – especially with those in training who couldn't
monkey-see, monkey-do instantly and remember it forever.

The Most High of the Most High spent fifteen or twenty minutes
in the elevator, pressing and pressing the button. Every now and then
the kid would answer "Control." The Most High would order him to
take him to this or that floor and open the door. The kid would get
him to the floor, then lights would go off all over the place and he
wouldn't remember to open the door.

When finally released at the Control level, the Most High of the
Most High demanded access to Control, ordered the kid into the elevator and trapped him in there for an hour. The Great Presence perhaps felt better after this exercise, but it likely didn't teach the kid
simple procedure: when you hit the button to move an elevator, you

keep your hand on the button; it is a physical reminder that there is someone in there and he is to be let out after you check the landing monitor to determine it is safe to do so.

A couple of incidents indicate the degree of discomfort those of us from Oakie had with the newfangled weapons and electronic security.

"Mister Yates, this is Acting Principal Officer James Larabee. We require your assistance with two gentlemen from Two North. The moment the doors was cracked, they came out like they was at Caesar's Palace and tried to go fifteen rounds. I'm bringin' them up to your loving care until Warden's Court."

"Bring the first one up."

"Comin' up."

I plunked down the phone and turned to my shift back-up in segregation, Raymond Nicholson, who was shining his shoes. It was 0700. I had just arrived, and had yet to put mine on. "Jimmy Larabee is bringing up a couple of scrappers." I checked the board. "Let's put one in seven and the other across the commons in eleven. I don't want a screaming match."

Nicholson nodded, took the flat, and popped the doors manually to check the cells, marching across the common area to the beat of a drummer only he could hear.

Per procedure, Jimmy looked in the glass of Segregation Control before radioing for Central Control to crack the door to Six North. I nodded. Then I went out with Nicholson still in Seg Control. I took custody of the con and Jimmy changed places with Nicholson to oversee the frisking and lock-up of the prisoner.

No one transfers into seg without a skin frisk. Mandatory procedure. I removed the cuffs and requested that the scrapper remove his clothing, which Mr. Nicholson would examine closely item by item.

The kid – taller than either of us and skinny – erupted into invective. "You fucking perverts. I'm not taking off my clothes. Fuck you." I was sleepy and not at all in the mood.

He looked at me and the colour of my hair. "Fuck you, you old prick. I know Tae Kwon-Do." I glanced back at Jimmy and gave him a bored look. Jimmy was expressionless, holding his P.O. clipboard in one hand and the radio and the Seg Control body-alarm in the other. Beside him was the red phone, an emergency hotline straight from Seg Control to Central Control which had a blastingly loud and unique ring. On the wall, not two feet away, was the intercom with its prominent red button. Hit it and Central Control would answer. By radio, by body-alarm, by hotline, Mr. Larabee might launch a Condition Yellow or call for "back-up on the double."

The Segregation Control idea is not bad in that those inside it are completely safe physically. But it's very bad in that it is as soundproof as Central Control. But Central Control has an intercom between elevator lobbies and inside. Seg Control does not (a little more cost-shaving, I guess). The kid was dancing and working himself up and making volumes of white noise out of which all I could hear was "Tae Kwon-Do . . . Old prick . . . Tae Kwon-Do . . . Old prick." His shoulder-length locks were bouncing around as he danced. Finally, he grabbed a stance and started some kind of martial-arts manoeuvre. There was an arborite table nearby and four chairs. On this table we piled clothing after each article had been searched.

I pretended to turn away in disgust from the martial-arts hero, then whirled and grabbed his long hair in both hands and shot him across the arborite table, knocking it over and the four chairs to the winds. Before he could regain his feet, I grabbed his hair again and placed his Adams' apple against the hard, sharp edge of the table. Nicholson had moved off to the side to spectate, as was Nicholson's habit. "Nicholson, get the fucking shoes and pants, you asshole," I growled. Nicholson took his time because the kid was trying to kick his face off, and every time he felt Nicholson messing with his laces he yanked the foot away. Nicholson was on his hands and knees like a mustachioed terrier racing from one foot to the other. The kid was not overly muscular, but his adrenalin was off the top of the scale. He didn't seem to feel the bite of the table. Nicholson was getting nowhere with the shoes and the pants and I was tiring. If he got loose, this idiot was going to grab a chair and destroy the place – us first.

I was looking straight through the glass at Jimmy. He was watching, absolutely transfixed. I began mouthing "Back-up . . . Back-up

. . . Back-up." I could feel my grip slipping on the kid's hair and he was trying to get a solid karate punch at my nuts. He was pounding hell out of my thighs. I was getting nowhere with the attempt to have the delegate from Trinidad read my lips. I tried ESP: "Jimmy, for fuck's sake, hit the alarm and get some people in here. Pick up the fucking red phone [you didn't have to dial it, just picking it up set it off in Central Control]. Squeeze the button on the radio and tell them Condition Yellow." Finally, Jimmy came out of his hypnotic state. I grabbed a tighter hold. Damn, I was getting the shit punched out of my body below the waist, but thankfully not the target (my right thigh and hip were black and blue for two weeks).

I couldn't believe my eyes. With all that emergency shit to hand, Jimmy was so stupefied by the electronic possibilities and dazed by the spectacle through the glass that he reached down and grabbed the *black* phone and began dialling. He listened and hung up. It was busy. This was a bright man but, under pressure, he simply could not bend his mind around the options before him. He dialled again. Then hung up again. I was losing it, and Nicholson had given up on the shoes and was standing off to the side again looking bewildered. Jimmy dialled again, and this time I could see his mouth moving.

"Condition Yellow, Six North! Condition Yellow, Six North!" Decibels leapt from operations seventy to emergency ninety. Wade was security on the opposing unit, the hospital; he was first man in the unit door. He was huge. The two of us put the wildman on the floor and sat on him until the rest of the staff arrived, at which time we manhandled his clothing off. When told to bend over and spread his cheeks, he looked around at the twenty or so screws around him and did so.

My thigh hurt like hell.

I took him by the collar and marched him into his cell. He hadn't said a word since the herd had flooded through the door. I started out the door to lock it.

He yelled, "You old prick . . ." and launched some kind of a round-house Bruce Lee kick at me. Not much talent, this guy. As his leg came around, I grabbed his ankle, and charley-horsed his thigh muscle hard with my right, then dumped him on his bunk on his head.

He was rubbing his thigh muscle and looking, for the first time, a little intimidated.

"Enough with the 'old prick' shit. Can you dig it?"

"Yes – yessir."

I went out and locked him down. I was wiped. I went into Control and sat down to take inventory of my corporal damage. Jimmy was still standing there. I said, "Mister Larabee, kindly hold some staff back and process your other fighter. I'm gonna sit here and lick my wounds."

He did and they did. Jimmy knew exactly – afterward – what he should have done. I didn't bite his ass off for getting me hammered up. We'd worked the Old West together and he had been one of my training officers. And, very important, he was the only person in the branch who collected my books.

With both cons as quiet as the rest of the unit, we settled in for the shift. I did tell Nicholson that as a guard, he was a great used-car salesman.

No more than half an hour after I locked down the Tae Kwon-Do Kid, he was at his window and knocking on the door. I took the flat for the slot where you slide in trays and gimped over to his door and unlocked the steel flap.

"Sir?"

"It's Yates. Read the tit-tag."

"Mr. Yates, I want to apologize. I was really mad as hell but I wasn't mad at you. I had no call to take it out on you . . ."

"Yeah, I know. Apology accepted. You okay?"

"My leg hurts."

"Christ, I hope so. You want the nurse to have a look?"

"No, just a charley horse."

"Walk around in the cell and exercise it. It'll go away."

The kid was so well behaved (he pulled thirty days in seg for fighting and causing a Condition Yellow), I made him the segregation cleaner.

Good kid. Lousy martial artist.

Pretrial is famous for buying any kind of security toy that a salesman with snakeskin underwear and alligator shoes drags through the door and waves under the noses of the Most High.

The bane of our existence was the body-alarm, which we called a beeper. A beeper is a small – slightly larger than your average pager – battery-driven deely-bob that hangs on your belt with your keys and other crap that drags the waist of your pants down to the crack of your ass. Early in my employment at Pretrial, my beeper was inadvertently the cause of a "Condition Brown," a mishap that happened to staff on many occasions thereafter.

Each unit was assigned a beeper. When you came on shift, you picked up your beeper with your keys at Control. Before entering your unit at the beginning of a shift, you did a beeper check. If you were working Five North that day and were in the gym with your cons and happened to whack your beeper against something, the sonofabitch would go off, a light would flash in Control, "Condition Yellow, Five North" would come over at ninety decibels, and every line screw and brass in the building belted for Five North, which was empty. Usually a beeper malfunction was the result of a Condition Brown, which occurs in the latrine.

Like this:

I entered the can in my staff-station, dropped my pants (carefully, so as not to acquire trouser wrinkles and get written up), and struck Rodin's *The Thinker* pose. Suddenly, sitting there on the throne, I felt a tremor like an adolescent earthquake. Then I heard the unmistakable sound of many joint shoes pounding around the elevator lobby. And voices – but I couldn't make out a word.

I completed my mission, composed myself sartorially in the manner befitting a Vancouver Pretrial Services Centre officer (I verified this in the ample mirror) and emerged from the staff washroom. I was going to sit down and make entries in my files, but there seemed to be the sound of a political rally going on in my unit. I looked out the door. The door to my unit was open. Better check it out. There were more line staff and brass on the unit than cons. The cons were looking bewildered. The staff were maintaining paramilitary bearing while dashing in and out of every cell. I joined them to help in the search. I turned to Larry Chambers and asked what was going on.

"Condition Yellow."

If I didn't call a Condition Yellow, who did? There was no closed-circuit TV on the unit. Or so I thought. You learn something every day. Larry asked me whose unit it was.

"Mine." By this time, I had an S.C.O. in my face.

"What's the problem here, Officer Yates?"

"Beats me. The tier's been mellow all shift." Everything had been turned topsy-turvy and the cons were cowering in corners of their rooms. The S.C.O. grabbed his radio. "Control, this is Two."

"I read you, Two."

"Can you confirm that the Condition Yellow came from Five North?"

"The light is on right in front of me."

"Roger, Two out."

"Control out." The radio protocol was very stiff at Pretrial.

With obvious disgust and impatience, the S.C.O. asked whether I had hit the body-alarm button by accident. The button is counter-sunk in the top of the contraption so that if you have large fingers, you have a hell of a time even finding it.

"Not a chance. Haven't had my hand near it since I put it on my belt at the top of the shift."

"If you heard the Condition Yellow and there wasn't a problem on your unit, why didn't you call Control and cancel?"

"Didn't hear it."

"Where were you?"

"As we marines say, I was in the head having a 'hot charlie.'"

"What?"

"In the fucking shitter."

"I see. Is there any chance that the alarm got jarred against the toilet or the floor?"

"Can't rule out the possibility, sir. I'm pretty careful of it even though we were told in training that the only way it could be activated was by hitting the button itself."

"I think we just discovered otherwise," said he with a look that said: Yates, you did it on purpose, you sonofabitch. He then ordered everyone back to his unit and scolded me for using Oakie language in the holy vertical jail.

Sometimes the damned nicad batteries of the body-alarms didn't charge properly. Sometimes they malfunctioned for reasons known to none, as happened to Officer Andy Tyabji. Poor Tyabji was doing his best to shed his image as an Oakie fuck-up. He knew there was *fire this yo-yo* tattooed on his ass. Until this incident, however, everyone at Pretrial was very impressed with his performance. Tyabji had Found It – a religious experience visited upon several Oakies. Pretrial had told Charlie Bessasson: we're going to take your best. Charlie agreed so long as they took his best *and his very worst.* Charlie may have fallen off the brew-truck and broken his leg as a line screw, but he had been around the bureaucratic block so many times as a warden that the *Neues Reich* at Pretrial knew better than to mess with him.

When the room doors to a unit are computered open, the locks turn quietly – unlike the unit entrance doors which ruin your hearing when they're unlocked – and all the doors swing open a few inches. The inhabitant comes out and pushes the door back. This is good news and bad news. This gives the officer a quick view of the contents of each room simply by walking around the unit. Also, if the unit tries to take him hostage, the guard can jump into a room and slam the locking door behind him, and hit his body-alarm. The bad news is that while the officer is off the unit, the cons can slam the door of a con they don't like with the con outside so that he has to ask the screw to crack his drum for him (he, of course, has no idea how it got slammed). Or the cons can slam the door with the target inside his room (he, of course, better not have any idea who slammed the door). An unauthorized slamming of the door can get you several days on lock-up or Warden's Court with time in segregation a distinct possibility.

A con Tyabji had known and liked from Oakie had just come on his unit. The con was baffled by the four-channel radio unit set into the wall. Tyabji went in to show him how it worked.

Bam! Some joker slammed the door of the drum with Tyabji and the con inside. Tyabji had a key for manual locks on his belt, but they don't work from the inside. The con was terrified that he would be blamed. Tyabji was terrified of the brass. The body-alarm is to be used only in "life-threatening" situations. Tyabji and the con go way back and the situation was about as life-threatening as a summer breeze. Tyabji and the con sat on the bunk trying to figure out what to do. The other cons looked through the wire-reinforced glass and pointed and giggled. It was a good-natured prank.

What the hell, the body-alarm was the only way. The screw in the opposing unit was a rookie Tyabji had never seen before and wouldn't have the savvy to glance into Tyabji's unit. Tyabji had the con listen at the base of the door while he listened up higher, then hit the button.

Nothing. He hit it again. Nothing.

McCoy, another ex-Oakie con, showed up at the door and asked at the top of his voice what they were going to do. Tyabji told him what he was trying to do and asked McCoy to see if he could catch the attention of the rookie across the way.

The kid was nowhere to be seen.

They were stuck. If he asked one of the cons to get on the staff-phone or the intercom, it was automatic digger-time for them. They only had their con-phone – which, of course, would not access joint numbers, other units, or staff numbers.

McCoy came back. He knelt at the door. "Boss, will that key fit under the door? I'll get your ass out and nobody will know." McCoy knew the routine and exactly what was going through Tyabji's mind. His contract was good with McCoy and the con in the room. No worries there.

Tyabji and the con struggled to get the big key off the ring. The ring was heavy-duty and wouldn't pry open easily. Finally, they got it off and the key just cleared when Tyabji slid it under the door. McCoy unlocked the door and handed the key back to Tyabji. Tyabji was mad as hell and wanted to know who the joker was. McCoy gave him a knowing look. "We'll handle it." Tyabji had been around the system for more than ten years and McCoy and some of the others on the tier owed him big-time.

Then Tyabji did a very un-C.Y.A. (cover yer ass) thing. He called

Control and asked to do a beeper-check. He could hear the whine of the response unit in Control.

Control: "Works like a damn."

Tyabji: "Bullshit."

Control: "Punch it again."

He did. They said it worked fine.

Tyabji was in the staff-station, which is more central in the building.

"Bullshit. The fucking thing doesn't work when you need it on the unit." He hung up without realizing he had been talking to the fink squad (those who reported faithfully and copiously to the Most High).

Within minutes the tower P.O. was in his face interrogating him. Tyabji, still not seeing the far-reaching disaster he was about to meet, told the P.O. to radio Control for another beeper-check. Then Tyabji took him on the unit and into the cell and handed the P.O. the body-alarm. The P.O. tried with the same result as Tyabji. Then the P.O. tried it from the open common area nearer the centre of the building. There it worked every time. The P.O. went away saying he would report it to maintenance.

Within a half an hour, the P.O. reappeared with a replacement and told Tyabji he was to see the S.C.O. and might want a shop steward present at the audience.

There he was asked whether there had been a life-threatening incident on his unit. No. Did he understand that he would be disciplined for setting off an alarm in the absence of such an incident? (Despite that the High and Almost High could activate an alarm with impunity whenever they felt a "drill" appropriate.)

Yes.

Then why was he setting it off?

Door slammed by a con.

And how did he finally get out to call Control and ask for a beeper-check?

Little did the joker (who meant no real harm and got roundly thumped by McCoy and company for jacking a good staff around) realize he had set in motion a concatenation of events as ineluctable as those of a Greek tragedy. They hung Tyabji's ass out to dry. Attempting to set off alarm. Total breach of key control. And on. And on. He was smart enough to take the shop steward with him, and while he managed to fend off being fired, he took a long, long suspension (corrections suspensions are always without pay, until and unless you appeal and win).

The rest of us were grateful to learn the beepers were defective. We distrusted and despised the damned things. They made it uncomfortable to sit down and we constantly feared we would set the thing off with the fold of a shirt or the side of a chair or a roll of fat. The matter was supposedly taken up in the safety committee, but it went nowhere. Over time, it was discovered that there were several places in the institution where the frequency didn't work. Some of the auxiliary rookies rented pagers and wore them to work. (The switchboard was known to report to the powers when an officer had too many private calls coming in. Now the wife or the girlfriend could page and the guard could call back.) But there were places in the building where neither pager nor beeper worked. And there were all sorts of metal things on the unit that could be dismantled to pry the door open in case the unit really wanted the guard or inmate locked inside a drum. While there were numberless false Condition Yellows (one beeper malfunctioned three times in the same day without anyone touching it), I never knew anyone to activate a beeper intentionally without reason to do so.

The whole Condition Yellow process had tremendous ramifications for staff safety. Bored prison guards will tamper with anything, as will cons, but not with the body-alarms. No one wanted the heat of having to face the wrath of the entire shift in the parking lot after work for having sent them on a very dangerous wild goose-chase. And the words "life-threatening" have very serious implications for a prison guard. The idea of a Condition Yellow, of running through an office-furniture obstacle course to respond to an emergency, is madness. If they were going to use the body-alarm system, then the jail should have been designed much differently.

Anything that modifies the sense of mental well-being of a

maximum-security inmate should be looked at closely, whether it's ventilation, food, sense of security from other inmates, whatever.

The one thing that the experienced maximum staff and the university nerds had in common was terror of these tons and tons of electronic trash. Pretrial was the Tower of Glitches. The elevators glitched. One cell-lock would glitch while the rest worked. Then the doors to the units glitched while the cell-locks worked. The temperature was always haywire because the sick software that controlled the venting seemed impervious to cure. And added to this mess was the way the security requirements had collided with architectural design. It was specified that any possible avenue of escape for prisoners be impeded with thirty-hour bar at spaces of six inches (it would take thirty hours to get through one side with a jeweler's diamond wire saw and then the saw would hit the core, which rotated and stopped saw-efficiency altogether). It was a nightmare for the architect to design around, and when it came to the venting the consequences were disastrous. In winter we had to leave the patio doors open. On certain shifts, this was a violation of security procedure, despite the fact that the patios were securely barred and later the bars were screened over to prevent anyone from below hook-shooting a weapon up to drop through the bars.

As Oakalla was an emblem of the Industrial Age, Pretrial is surely one of the Age of Infotech.

Corrections will become higher- and higher-tech. As will crime.

13

Jail-breakers

—————————————— • ——————————————

The thinner the ice, the more anxious is everyone to
see whether it will bear.
— Josh Billings

JAIL-BREAKERS are troublemakers, not escapees. Not necessarily violent themselves, they delight in driving line staff crazy for the sheer fun of it. They like to disrupt the orderly prison routine, then sit back and watch what happens. Sometimes they are bugs (mentally-ill cons), sometimes not. Generally the jail-breakers do not do what they do with malicious intent. They can't get away with their antics in the general prison population, so they haunt the segregation units.

The greatest jail-breaker of them all was Harold Jones. Harold was a manic-depressive. To Harold, a jail was his habitat and staff and cons were his family; the outside world was completely baffling to him.

Harold was one of the few jail-breakers who, when on his medication, could re-enter the general prison population. He liked to be busy both on and off medication. Give him unlimited supplies of sugary coffee and tobacco and he would keep the living unit or segregation spotless. Every con who had done time in the province knew Harold, and if he was driving everyone crazy on a unit, the cons let the staff know before taking things into their own hands. Harold was a mascot to both staff and inmates. We had all seen him in all of his phases. Now, by the time he was in his late forties, he had spent most of his adult life in jail and had read virtually everything he could lay his hands on. And he had as close to a photographic memory as I have ever seen.

Having spoken of his pleasanter qualities, I now offer the killer of jails in all his glory. When Harold had had enough of the street and longed for Mother Jail, he hurled a brick through a window; or went into an expensive restaurant and gorged himself, defying the waiter to make him pay for the meal; or created a public disturbance after first ascertaining that the police were near. In one case he decided that an Eastern country had offended him and did a dancing weenie-wag for the staff of the consulate when they exited the front door to go home. He knew the Criminal Code of Canada very well, and was always lucid enough to commit crimes that would get him no more than two years less a day.

Once inside and booked in, the nurse and psychiatrist checked his phase. If he was rocketing off the walls, he came straight to segregation for his own safety. As long as I or one of the other Oakies was on shift, Harold could be managed. Standard procedure was to let him bring us up to date on the horrors of the street, give him coffee, give him tobacco, give him plenty of books. Pretrial had the best library in the system and a fulltime librarian. When Harold came in, I made sure that she brought up plenty of academic stuff.

But woe unto the rookie who went by the book with Harold and refused him the extra rations of coffee, tobacco, or books. He would begin his "payback" by banging on the door and saying he needed extra toilet paper because he had diarrhoea. He would promptly plug the toilet and flush it and flush it until the water came out under the door and threatened to flood the entire unit. The rookie would get the water-chase key and turn off the water to his room.

This was only the beginning. Next came the heat/smoke alarm. Tobacco and matches can only be denied when the inmate abuses them. Before setting off the alarm, Harold would hide matches in places you could spend hours searching for and never find. You could strip-search him, change his clothes, and move him to another cell and, sure as hell, he would have matches somewhere you hadn't looked and set off the alarm again.

Remember that cracking a segregation cell always requires tight security procedures and several staff. Harold knew exactly when the jail was busy and it would be the greatest disruption to draw staff away from sending bodies off to court, the movement of meals, doctor's parade, or afternoon visits.

There were no smoke alarms at Oakie. Pretrial was a far safer institution (at least in the beginning) for the segregation inmate. But for Harold in one of his moods, it offered a veritable prankocopoeia of possibilities.

He soon discovered that the alarms could not only be set off but the alarms themselves were made of plastic and were inflammable. If you didn't get in fast enough, the alarm would be no more than a blob of black burnt plastic.

But the property damage was nothing compared to what Harold could do to the mind of the guard who dared frustrate his simple demands. Harold would lie on the floor and begin soliloquies that would include long verbatim passages of Freud, Jung, the Bible (always the King James Version), instructions from the back of Campbell's soup cans (not just the English, but *mode d'emploi* as well) and whole episodes from "The Lone Ranger" and "The Green Hornet." These would come under the door at such a volume that you could scarcely hear when an inmate in another room was yelling some request.

Vancouver has several phone-in radio stations. Often I have heard Harold reproduce an entire show. He was a great impressionist. He would do the voice of the host and all the voices of the callers – under the door. So loud that nothing could be heard. His imagination was limitless. The guard who crossed him was in for flood, fire, and mind-searing babble.

Harold had an outrageous sense of honour. After a day shift of reducing a screw who didn't know him to a mental greasespot, an experienced screw could come to work and make a contract with Harold. If a bargain was struck, Harold would cease the nonsense instantly, take great pride in cleaning up all the mess he had created, and the shift couldn't be smoother. If there was no renewal of the contract with the next shift, it all began again.

A few years back, a guard put a reporter on to Harold and he calculated that over the years, with staff costs (including those police and guards he sent over the brink with stress), Harold had cost the taxpayers more than any other inmate in B.C. history.

Usually you can come to terms with jail-breakers, or zero in on what they most want and beat them at their own game. Sometimes a whole jail full of experience is useless.

This was the case with Jerry Murphy. He was a very athletic and handsome black kid. I first met him at Oakalla where he told me he had boxed Golden Gloves, had a job in North Vancouver, and on and on – and he was in on a bum rap. But, then, almost everyone awaiting trial is innocent. After Jerry had been inside about a week people kept coming off the tier whipped to hell. Jerry would get a guard alone and snitch that this or that jerk was beating hell out of the inmates. He had us all on. We spent all our time moving out the inmates Jerry had "centred out" (tattled on) to heavy tiers, most of them protesting that they hadn't done a damned thing. This guy could have looked God straight in the eye and lied his ass off. Murphy kept this bullshit up until he was king of the tier.

Eventually, he was found out, labelled a "rat," and took a thorough thumping at yard. He promptly signed himself into protective custody. He caused trouble on the P.C. tier as well and eventually wound up in South Wing Obs where Olson and others were kept. It amounts to triple protective custody.

When he came to Pretrial we put him straight on the P.C. unit but he lasted only a couple of hours. Then it was Segregation City. The segregation unit at Pretrial was not at all to his liking. He was a grandstander and there was no audience. He was not a smoker, but he demanded tobacco and matches and received them. He promptly set his cell on fire.

Then he got into some of Harold's tricks. He stuffed his towel in the toilet and flooded the cell and half the unit. He screamed and beat on the door until finally it was necessary to put him in restraints.

Because segregation is potentially so explosive, each evening the

S.C.O. makes rounds with the nurse, interviewing each inmate. Each evening Jerry would tell horrendous tales of being beaten, and denied meals and every other version of "cruel and unusual punishment." When the S.C.O. asked to see marks where he had been beaten, Jerry could never come up with any or he would protest that his skin was dark and they simply couldn't see them. He was examined again and again by medical staff. Each evening he was advised that he could write to Inspection and Standards, the Ombudsman, and others, if he felt unjustly treated.

Jerry ate like a horse and was as healthy as one. Those of us who worked segregation got tired very early on of being accused of not feeding him. People who don't get food lose weight. Jerry was putting on weight. We demanded that the tower P.O. be present when he was handed his meal and the P.O. stood there and watched him eat. And that was the end of that nonsense.

He wrote letter after letter to Inspection and Standards, his member of Parliament, his member of the legislative assembly, and the Ombudsman. There was a blizzard of paper. And the I. and S. guys (who remembered the same stunts from Oakalla) tromped down to hear his complaints, hating the empty nonsense of it all, and interviewed every guard he pointed the finger at. He knew he was tying up a battalion of people and driving them all nuts, but that was the object of the exercise.

When the investigating authorities (who are obliged to investigate any and all complaints) made it clear that they were becoming very impatient with his unsubstantiated accusations, he shifted into another gear.

His next big play was in visits. And it was big. Segregation inmates have the same rights with regard to visits, access to telephones, mail, and other U.N.-guideline privileges, as other inmates. About fifteen minutes after Jerry had been escorted down to the visits area, we had a "Condition Yellow, Visits" on our hands. Jerry was supposedly being visited by his common-law wife and an infant. The visits area was open and packed with families and friends of inmates talking to friends and relatives across tables. Jerry had jumped up, grabbed two glass baby-bottles and smashed them against one another, showering glass and milk all over the child, the woman, and the surrounding area. Civilians and inmates were flattened against the wall not knowing what to expect next. He shouted that if anyone came near he would kill the baby, then he was going to kill the wife, then he was going to kill himself. Visitors and visitees were stunned. But he didn't move toward the child or the wife. The wife grabbed her baby and headed for the wall. He moved away from the table and pointed the glass toward himself. As soon as staff entered the room, he turned the broken bottles toward us. Now he was going to kill us.

Jerry was well over six feet. Bill Corelli, arguably the deadliest guard – and the least flappable I ever met in corrections – is only about five-six or five-eight. Per standard procedure, staff began to fan out so that Jerry would have to keep turning to determine who was going to make a move on him. In my peripheral vision I saw a blur. Like a lightning bolt, Corelli was airborne and nailed him with a karate kick along the left of his jaw. The bottle fell from his left hand. A ton of line screws were instantly on top of him and disarmed the other hand. He was cuffed, back in segregation, and on secure-visits-only status before he knew what had hit him. Some of the guards got glass cuts on knees and elbows, but I don't think Jerry got a scratch.

But his pointing the sharp glass at his own throat had drawn such a gasp from the crowd that it gave Jerry a whole new plan: numberless bogus suicide attempts. He ripped up sheets and sat on his bed waiting for a guard to lift the slide of his window and look in. There he would be with a hangman's noose of braided sheet around his neck, pretending to draw it tight. He would pretend to do himself in with just about anything in the cell: utensils (which were plastic), smashed cups (which were plastic).

Like Harold, Jerry was a nickel-and-dime criminal who loved jail. He may have been a psychopath, but he wasn't a manic-depressive. Jerry simply did what he did because he did it. I had become used to his being in and out of Oakalla and Pretrial like they had revolving doors. And then, Jerry wasn't gracing us with his presence any more. You get used to the periodicity with which certain inmates return. When they have been gone too long, the guards notice and begin asking whether anyone has heard anything about Harold or Jerry.

Heavier criminals get themselves croaked a good deal, but the jail-breakers seem to persist.

One day I was watching a news item about some sort of contro-versy regarding prisoners' rights in Quebec. Suddenly the screen was full of Jerry's face. Ah, the sincerity of the expression. Ah, the with-God-as-my-witness tone of voice. Ah, how familiar.

Mmmmmmm, poor corrections *de la belle province*. With Jerry on their hands, they wouldn't have time to check on the wars with the Aboriginals and Anglos.

14

AIDS

•

The diseases of the present have little in common
with the diseases of the past save that we die of them.
– Agnes Repplier

IN 1985, a new prisoner at Pretrial was classified immediately to the
hospital unit on Six South. He was emaciated and homo-
sexual (and told anyone who would listen that he was). He had sores
on the exposed parts of his skin. His eyes were sunken and the skin
around them very dark. This description in itself gives no absolute
clue. One who mainlines speed (methadrine, dexadrine) has the
same appearance, as do drunks who don't eat because it takes the edge
off the buzz.

Still, this guy really looked sick. One day he would have an appe-
tite and make passes at the younger, weaker hospital inmates. Then
the next day he would stay in bed for most of the day and eat little or
nothing.

One graveyard shift, he hit the emergency button in his room.
When the nurse went in, he wasn't breathing. She administered CPR
and brought him around. He was put in an ambulance and fired off to
the hospital. He was diagnosed as having pneumonia with certain
complications, put on intravenous antibiotics and was back in a
couple of weeks.

Sheena Cornwall, the nurse who gave him mouth-to-mouth, was
under thirty and had a couple of kids. On graveyard the seg officer

(me, in this case) covers both segregation and the hospital on his rounds. She expressed to me fear that she might have caught something from this guy through giving him CPR. I assumed she meant hepatitis B, but they had done blood work on him at the hospital and, while he had once had it, it was not active now. I pointed out that pneumonia is not communicable. And she was up to date on her TB inoculations.

She mentioned AIDS, but neither she nor any of the other medical people seemed to know much about it. The doctors weren't talking about it. The nurses weren't talking about it. I said there must be some kind of test for it. She said she didn't think it was available in British Columbia.

I had to see my own doctor about some routine thing and asked him about it. He brushed it off and said there was virtually no incidence of AIDS in B.C., and they would doubtless come up with a vaccination against it.

Time passed and I didn't think about it much. Then I talked to an infectious-diseases specialist with knowledge of AIDS-monitoring in B.C. He said that there was a conspiracy of silence going on in the medical community about a clear and present danger. A deadly danger. He had fought to get the test for B.C. and lost. I began to interrogate him about exposure in maximum remand. He told me that, given the exposure to addicts and homosexuals in a setting like Pretrial, we were far more at risk than people in health-care settings. In fact, there was probably no higher risk place to be in society than where I worked.

He asked whether we had one-way airways for CPR. No. Were guards at Vancouver Pretrial required to use rubber gloves, masks, or gowns when dealing with emergencies where bodily fluids were present? No.

In short, he scared the hell out of me.

I began to talk about what the specialist had said with the medical and security staff at Vancouver Pretrial. It had been all around us, but no one had put it together. The prison moccasin telegraph is international. First, we found out that guards were dying of AIDS down in the States – and not just in the San Francisco area. So? There are gay guards, there are bisexual guards, there are guards who mainline substances. People are people.

Then another wave of information came that guards who were hard-core, holy-rollin' Christians who had never copulated with anyone except their wives were dying of AIDS. By this time, news of contaminated transfusions was rising to the surface. Maybe guards were dying because of transfusions. No, there was case after case where the guard had had no transfusion. And they had not performed CPR (at this point, no one knew whether AIDS could be transmitted by mouth or not). These cases temporarily comprised a medical mystery.

Meanwhile, the best information was coming out of Europe – especially France and Germany. One well-documented article on AIDS world-wide was calling for the establishment of AIDS *Leperkolonien* (sealed-off colonies for victims of AIDS).

Next came the information from the States that inmates who knew they had AIDS were making little darts, using a matchstick, a pin, and a piece of paper for a feather to make it fly straight – I made them as a kid. The AIDS-infected would jab themselves with the dart and then when a guard passed they would toss it at his pants-leg. Often he wouldn't feel the prick of the point until he turned a certain way and it nicked him. But a nick was enough. The mystery of the deaths of the Christian, monogamous heterosexuals was solved for the most part.

One inmate in the States was caught tossing a dart. The inmate was charged with attempted murder, and they made it stick.

The situation was getting hairy as hell. Line staff were looking all the time for anything resembling a dart or any other implement that could be used to transmit infection.

The United States instituted mandatory AIDS-testing for federal prisoners and it was left up to the individual states to do as they wish with their own institutions.

After all this, there was still no formal acknowledgement in the federal and provincial corrections systems of Canada that there was any risk of contracting AIDS – although there was plenty of ignorance and plenty of argument in the scientific community about the nomenclature of AIDS. We began to pray that there wouldn't be so much as a con spitting in our faces – prison guards wipe a lot of spit off their faces during a career in corrections, including the brass because they preside over Director's Court and the end-users are not always happy with the service.

At first, it was fairly simple. People had AIDS or didn't. Then came the added nuance of human immunodeficiency virus and a new acronym, HIV positive or negative. As these terms came into parlance, a few of us looked them up. But you couldn't assume that the person on the same landing with you had the least idea what you were talking about.

Finally, with one incident, the lid blew on the terror contained just beneath the surface.

It was on a graveyard shift. I was making my rounds in segregation. I stopped at each room, lifted the metal slide, and shone the flashlight through the wire-reinforced glass. I needed to see flesh and breathing rhythms. Because the glass was laminated with the wire, it was very difficult to get the beam of the light to tell you very much. Also the colours of surfaces, such as skin, were distorted, partly because of the glass and partly because of the city-light pollution coming in the window of the cell.

All was more or less well on both the seg side and the hospital side, but I kept going back and raising the slide on the room of one kid. I could see flesh and I could get rhythms of breathing, but there was something wrong. The breathing was too shallow. Given the light, I couldn't make out the tone of his skin and swinging the light back and forth I could make out – intermittently – something shiny on the side of his pillow. It didn't add up. From my Oakalla days, shiny meant wet, and wet meant trouble. But I couldn't pick it up every time I swung the beam. Then I would check again for breathing. He was breathing.

If I set in motion all the procedures for cracking the cell, I was going to catch hell for a bogus call if there was nothing wrong. But "tilt" was flashing on the screen of my intuition.

Lark was the night-shift S.C.O. I called down and said I wanted to crack the cell. He asked whether I had breathing. Yes. He asked whether I saw flesh. Yes. Then why didn't I do my rounds and shut up? Because, for one thing, I thought I was picking up flashes with the light. (Lark was ex-Oakie and the mention of the possibility of something wet in the cell on a graveyard had meaning for him.) Was I sure? No, I wasn't sure but there was only one way to find out. Okay, I was to get the nurse and he would grab back-up and come up. Any graveyard opening of a room required the night-jailer (a real S.C.O. or an "acting"), unit officer, back-up, and nurse.

The nurse had been pulling a lot of graveyards and there had been a rash of incidents. She was fried. Lark came up with radio, stick, and clipboard. With him was O'Bailey, who had a look of deep dread in his eyes. Lark ordered Control to crack the door. I stepped in and turned on the light. The kid was blue. He was breathing, but just barely. Lark stepped in, flattened himself against a wall and stared, fearing what he knew and didn't know about AIDS. There was a very unpleasant and wide stream of mucus streaming from the kid's nose and mouth. His skin was blue and he was getting more cyanotic by the minute.

I walked over to the bed and looked on the far side of the inmate's body. A large and almost full hypodermic was hanging from his left arm. Toward the needle part, blood had backed up into the cylinder, red cloudlets which wouldn't quite mix with the clear stuff. With my right hand I pulled it out of his arm. (Because of the rule for continuity of evidence, once an officer has evidence in his hand, he must hold on to it until it is placed in an evidence bag before a witness, sealed, and he signs over the seal). The inmate had obviously gotten the crank full of dope from a visit and suitcased it (stuck it up his keester); the thought of where the syringe had been did not give me joy. I was holding the evidence up and away from my body. My right hand would be tied up holding the damned thing until we went down to the S.C.O.'s office and sealed it.

The nurse hadn't moved. I asked whether she was going to take vital signs. Then I realized she couldn't move. She was simply making muted screaming sounds. Lark got on the radio to Control telling them to get paramedics, rescue, and the trauma team from the fire department.

The inmate had a towel in the room. I told Lark to grab the towel and dab the mucus away from his nose and mouth. Maybe he could breathe better.

"Take a flying fuck, Yates. I wouldn't go near that cocksucker at gunpoint."

I grabbed the towel with my left hand and tried to clear away his nose and mouth, but the discharge was thick and I didn't make much headway. I must have looked like the Statue of Liberty trying to tie her shoe with one hand.

O'Bailey didn't know what to do. O.B. (as we called him) used to work the West Wing at Oakalla with me. I've seen him flip and fly around the room like a balloon expelling air. Not now, please, not now. The nurse had forgotten to bring her medical bag. O.B. asked if she wanted the medical bag. Continuing her whimpering with her arms crossing her chest, she nodded. "Oxygen?" I asked. She nodded. O.B. was gone like a shot to the hospital unit without a clue where to look for the oxygen equipment or the doctor bag. He was back like a shot asking where they were. Lark took the nurse out in the common area, sat her in a chair, took her keys off her waist, and told O.B. to check the supply closet.

"Lark, we're gonna lose this kid." I was still dabbing ineffectively with one hand and holding the hypo with the other.

"Then he's gone." I had known Lark for years. I had seen him wade into the middle of a rescue situation and perform like a champion. A lot of cons owed their lives to the cool thinking and quick action of Lark. He was lazy, but when there was a problem, he was on top of it.

Tonight he was nuts.

I said, "Fuck the evidence." And moved to lay the syringe on the basin. Lark frowned.

"You know the drill. You let go of it and I'll write you myself."

Suddenly the room was full of the trauma team from the fire department across the street. Christ, they were bigger than guards. The honcho took one look at the syringe I was holding, then reached over and grabbed the con's hair and started slapping him. Another of the team had grabbed a couple of towels and summarily wiped away much of the mess on the con's face. I couldn't believe it when the kid began to groan and grunt and then put his arm up to keep from getting whacked again. The trauma guy sat him on the edge of the bed and told him to take a deep breath. The kid was very groggy but did so. About that time the paramedics arrived with a gurney, put an oxygen-mask on his face, and wheeled him out.

Lark told O.B. to cover for me while I transported the evidence, then radioed for the Three Landing guard to accompany the con to the hospital and stay there for the rest of the shift.

Lark sealed the evidence in the bag and I signed it. He suggested I wash the guy's south end off my hand. I did so. When I returned we checked the visits list. He had had only a lawyer visit. Both of us spent much of the rest of the shift filling out forms and piling up paper.

The hospital called to say that the kid had pneumonia. They also mentioned that the kid said that the heroin in the syringe was supposedly pure. He hadn't been trying to get high. He had been attempting to kill himself.

After a couple of weeks the kid was back in segregation. As I was doing rounds he said: "Somebody told me that a Yates who pulled the needle out of my arm . . . was gonna be on this shift."

"Yeah."

"You Yates?"

"Yup."

"Goddamn it, that fucking horse cost me three thousand bucks. I should have been outa here."

"How about a coffee with double cream and double sugar and we'll call it even?"

"Even."

Lark and I didn't torpedo the nurse for freezing. Lark promised to speak to the head of the hospital and suggest some time off for her or a few visits with the shrink before she returned to work. And we never discussed his refusal to give me a hand. After all, he was supervisory and shouldn't have been in the room at all.

Betty Gerrard and I were sitting in the staff-station talking about AIDS. She had more than ten years in service and was worried. She suggested we have a meeting at the Police Athletic Club. The group which met were all top-grade correctional officers with spotless records. It was useless to invite even principal officers. They went along with policy or else. Privately, they had their worries too, but we line screws were in a better position to set up a squawk. A couple of the P.O.s had indicated they would help grease the way. In our group were gay males, lesbians, straights, marrieds, singles, and all levels of education from grade 12 on up. We scratched out a proposal over Pepsi (several of us were non-drinkers) and beer. I was elected to put it in literate shape and head up the chain of command to the top.

Instantly, John McIntyre, recently promoted P.O., gave me permission to take it to Jim Browning, one of the S.C.O.s. Jim was pleasant and said he would get back to me as soon as he had made an appointment for me with one of the High and Mighty. Within a week I had the appointment.

I entered and was invited to sit down. I handed the Great One a copy of the proposal and produced a pile of materials on the disease in German, French, and English.

Our proposal was quite simply that we be given the use of the copier to reproduce materials for what could loosely be called "A V.P.S.C. AIDS newsletter" – to keep staff who wished to peruse it up to date on research. I really thought I would find a sympathetic audience in this man. He had an M.A. with a science background.

Shuffling through the materials I handed him, he began, "Mr. Yates, we all realize that you are better educated than some of us here. And I can appreciate the quality of the staff who have signed this proposal. The cost is really not a problem. But you see, I feel that we must avoid alarming the staff unduly." I listened to this cock in the ear for a few more minutes, then asked, "Would you take the matter forward to the operations meeting and possibly the safety committee?"

"We've already discussed the matter in ops meeting. What I'm telling you now is our position at the moment. You're welcome to express your concerns to the safety committee through your steward." With that I was dismissed.

That meeting and the stonewall I encountered produced various reactions. I think the gays were the most offended. They had read everything they could and were sensitive about the education pro-grams in San Francisco, which were proving extremely effective. Some of them transferred out. One quit and went back to Ontario. Betty Gerrard transferred to Nanaimo. Another woman applied to the Vancouver city police and was successful, as was one of the single men. For the duration of the time that I was at Pretrial – about three years – there was never any information disseminated about AIDS.

15

Keeping Records

•

The "realistic" view of the world compatible with
bureaucracy redefines knowledge – as techniques
and information.
– Susan Sontag

O NLY AN hour into the shift in records, the holding tank was bursting at the seams. Standing room only. Roscoe Schulz, my partner – we were the Ferrante and Teicher of the book-in keyboards – kept humming the first four notes of Beethoven's BumBumBum-*Bum*. He had been humming it for weeks. I had been threatening him for weeks. I began whistling dissonant to his Bumming, but he didn't notice.

Not the least of the security at Pretrial is that it is tunnelled to the provincial court in one direction and the Vancouver City Police Station in the other. The cons come from the police holding tank to ours via the tunnel. Some are in for classification out to camps, New Haven, and other jails. Some are brought in on immigration holds straight from the docks or the airport. Some are coming back from court convicted but not yet sentenced.

Thus some go upstairs to await their sentence dates. Some go up to our classification officers, thence to transport. Some from the cop-shop are charged and remanded in custody until docket schedules are arranged. Accused are remanded on two grounds:

Primary grounds: Reasonable and probable cause to suspect that they won't show up for trial. F.T.A. (failure to appear) is our most serious crime; it flouts the entire symbolic value of our criminal justice system. Sometimes, this is a person from out of province who has breached the Criminal Code of Canada in British Columbia and is considered legally a "foreigner" (his home is more than one hundred miles outside the jurisdiction where he was apprehended). Much more often, the accused has a history of heavy crimes *and* the unsavoury habit of failing to show up for court.

Secondary grounds: The criminal justice system has reasonable and probable cause to fear that the accused will continue doing what he was allegedly doing or will repeat what he allegedly did.

The result is that there are more bad bad-asses per square inch in maximum remand at Pretrial than in any other federal or provincial institution. I remember once working a unit which held nothing but Murder Ones and four kidnap-torturers.

Back in records, the more the holding tank filled, the louder grew the growling over seats, cigarettes, and anything else they could think of to potshot at one another about. Schulzie and I were calling them out one by one and flying over the keyboard to book them in. But we couldn't keep up. Soon the holding tank was full and we were putting the overflow in other, smaller tanks and attempting to book and watch all the tanks at once.

BumBumBum*Bum*.

A hell of a commotion began in the main holding tank. We could see that the room was filling up with smoke. Schulz and I were over the counter and yelling for back-up from the other end of records and the change-room where some sheriffs were loitering.

We went through the door and began yanking bodies out to be looked after by other staff and found in the middle of the room one con who had chosen this magic moment to set himself afire. The man on fire was wearing provincial-issue greens. More plastic than cotton in them. Each time we attempted to grab his pants and tear them off, the damned burning plastic splattered on us and burned. I found a jacket on the bench. I put it over his legs and choked off the flames. Someone behind me began to dance and scream that the province was going to have to buy him a new jacket. Finally we cuffed the firebug, put him in a tank by himself, and called for the nurse.

The previous day, Schulz and I had heard "Staff up!" from the other end of the records area and had rocketed over in time to see an inmate keeping several officers and sheriffs at bay with a chair. He was just back from court, where he had been handed a sentence he did not receive gladly. He had told the judge and all present to fuck off. He had been a great pain in the ass while he was being escorted back from court; now, with the cuffs off, he was about to prove that actions speak louder than words. While the rest were staying out of range, Schulz and I found a couple of chairs of our own and began walking toward him. No Condition Yellow had been called yet. We walked toward him and began widening the distance between us. This worried him, which was the idea. The unarmed officers waited for their chance. Finally, he took a hell of a swing in Schulz's direction, which offered the opening the young jock types had been waiting for. They tackled him. We got rid of all the chairs and the usual prison dog-pile ensued. The problem was to get the cuffs to the bottom of the pile where the con was presumed to be and get them on him.

It happened that Dave Kennedy, the S.C.O. in charge of records, was off that day. In his stead we had one of the classification officers substituting as boss. Just as the guys toward the bottom were about to cuff the dude, the boss, Matthew Aligizakis, emerged from his office. Guys like him are known in the system as "social workers" – they are the Pollyanna types.

"Just a moment. Just a moment," says Aligizakis, "I want to speak to this man." We located the con's head among the arms and legs. It spoke, telling Aligizakis to fuck off.

"That'll be enough of that," Matthew replied. "Now, let us reason together. If these officers let you up without restraining you, will you settle down so we can discuss your complaint rationally?" Matthew is an educated and genteel human being.

"Sure," wheezed the con, who could barely breathe under several hundred pounds of us.

"Allow him to stand up."

We looked at one another and began extricating ourselves like linemen at an NFL game with a flag down on the play. We stood. The con stood. Matthew was standing there with a triumphant look on his face. At which point the con pasted Matthew in the mush, breaking his glasses and nose and splitting his lip. Matthew went down like a sack of potatoes. We leapt upon the con again, dog-piled him again. And cuffed him again. Control was notified, Condition Yellow was sounded, the con was escorted off to segregation, and we returned to business as usual. Matthew went to Emergency at the nearest hospital and took a few days off to heal his body and his officerly bearing.

Kennedy was easy enough to work for. We knew him from Oakalla records. He had been around for more than twenty years. He did, however, have a war going with the Most High, and they were looking for any excuse to fire him as head of records. This made Kennedy somewhat spooky.

From my keyboard, I called out, "Bob, initial A." I could see a hand waving from one of the small tanks. I approached the tank with the flat. I opened the door and instantly felt I was in full hallucination. The creature inside was a head taller than me, had on black jeans, a blouse so busy it looked like a couple of puppies under a blanket, and fluorescent lipstick. She was seemingly Native in origin – and mad as hell about I know not what. A drag queen.

"Please take a seat over there." I indicated the chair on the opposite side of the monitor.

She muttered something, glowered back at the tank, then sat.

As records work goes, booking-in is not as boring as the change-room (handing out provincial-issue clothing and supplies to new book-ins and street clothing to those going to court), but it's close. First, we make up three files on each inductee: warrant, medical, and progress. Then we question the accused field by field and screen by screen until we have the prescribed information to generate a face-sheet, which includes a graphic representation – photo or digitized video image – of the face.

There are many opportunities to be bored to a stupor in corrections, but those who succumb to the swamp of boredom do not last. Two middle-aged eccentrics, I of mid-forties, Schulz of mid-fifties, who are not bored, must be a little off the wall. Durable corrections people like us are masters of gallows humour, geniuses of foul-mouthed invective, monarchs of the incredible prank. This is the stuff survival is made of.

"BumBumBum*Bum*," Schulz hummed.

I continued politely, professionally filling in fields on the screen. She talked. I tapped the keys. The more I typed the snarkier she became, the louder and more impatient she got. Her voice was beyond description. I wanted her to quieten down. In my peripheral vision to my right, I could see that Schulzie was ignoring his book-in, had turned my way to give the scene his full attention, and had a looks-good-on-ya-Yatesie look on his face. I knew that if I made eye contact with him, I'd be gone, and the nine-foot draggerina would erupt like Mount St. Helen's.

Just what I feared, the S.C.O., Kennedy, had heard the hoopla. Here he came, Mohammed's mountain with epaulettes, pussyfooting up behind me to look over my shoulder. Maintaining my deadpan face, keeping my interrogative voice even, I continued coaxing information from her. Staring, staring at the computer monitor.

"Occupation?"

"Cock . . . sucker!"

I heard laughter being choked off behind me and to my right. It was decision time. Could I or could I not resist? Nope.

With a mind of their own, my fingers keyed in COCKSUCKER.

I heard a groan of horror behind me. If I hit enter, "cocksucker" would go rocketing into the database.

Next field. Without missing a stroke, I inquired, "Are you a Catholic or Protestant cocksucker?"

"Oh, Christ," Kennedy moaned.

Our Lady of the cyanotic lipstick replied, "Atheist cocksucker."

I typed in ATHEIST COCKSUCKER.

Schulz was bent double, immobilized with wheezing giggles. Kennedy was whimpering. He knew this was the last field on the screen and it was time to hit Alt and F4 to plant this info and bring up the final screen. If I sent this to the printer and the top brass got the face-sheet, Kennedy would be dead meat. The dragger was into the put-on by now and was enjoying watching Kennedy and Schulz. I gave her a wink and she cracked up. Schulz cracked up. I cracked up. Kennedy didn't crack up until he saw me surreptitiously move the cursor back up the last two fields and change "cocksucker" to "unemployed" and "atheist cocksucker" to "Protestant." (In our inane system there are only Catholics and Protestants on earth.)

There are some very dangerous people in maximum remand. Some of the inmates are a little suspect as well.

16

Graveyard Shift
in Segregation

•

One man's word is no man's word; we should quietly
hear both sides.
— Johann Wolfgang von Goethe

WHEN I reported for duty, S.C.O. Kennedy was already steamed. A con named Joe MacTavish had turned afternoon shift into yo-yo-ville. He'd snapped out of his skull and Kennedy couldn't send a rookie up to segregation. So Officer Yates got to go.

"He's snapped on what?" I inquired.

"Horse and coke."

"Which, of course, were sent to him by God as a going-away present."

"Lawyer. Lawyer visit," I was told.

The keystone screws had noticed that MacTavish was bouncing off all the walls of the cell and had gone in to skin-frisk the room. Mostly rookies. They had found a balloon of heroin. I couldn't believe the rest: the idiot who had the balloon in his hand was so excited he had put the balloon down on a chair while he was rousting the room. The con had stepped over, grabbed the balloon and swallowed it. They just stood there while he swallowed it instead of stuffing cuffs in his mouth or simply ripping out his larynx.

"Lawyer?" I asked.

"Shoulda seen 'er."

"I've seen this flick before. Why didn't they have the bastard in secure visits?" In secure visits, there's glass between cons and visitors, who talk via telephone.

"No reasonable and probable grounds until now. If he lives, he'll be classified high-risk and have only secure visits."

"Yup. Cow's gone. Might as well close the barn door."

In order to get drugs into the highest-security institution in North America, first you need money. This guy had plenty – enough to retain three of Vancouver's top firms. When you're up for drug conspiracy and hoping to get it pled down to importation or trafficking, you need all the talent you can get, if the evidence is sour. Good sense tells you that a top lawyer is not going to stroll into visits with a balloon, a crank (syringe), and the makings for several lines of nose blow. Nay, nay. Instead, an articling student – preferably a pulchritudinous female – mules the dope. This is a good strategy, because chances are that the visits are being manned by a bashful young guard with the ink not dry on his criminology degree. This young feller is fairly handy at frisking when it comes to dealing with men. But the sight of a curvaceous young thing about his own age toting a briefcase throws a kink into his operations. Chances are very good he'll simply let her through without touching her. In other words, she could be toting a sten-gun in her lingerie. Actually, however, she's probably packing what was ordered in her briefcase: drugs.

There are certain contacts and papers with which prison personnel are not ever to fiddle: letters to and from lawyers, M.L.A.s, the Ombudsman, M.P.s, and so forth. And, because they may contain papers, consensus is that briefcases cannot be frisked. Wrong. The frisker may not read said papers, but he could still frisk the bejesus out of the contents, check for false bottom, whatever. If the student mule were ever caught, the law firm would, of course, know nothing about the transaction. The student would be dismissed with due ceremony. However, briefcases are not frisked. And as long as there are contact visits, the prisons will be full of drugs. This particular evening, MacTavish had had a lawyer visit from something who looked like centrefold material.

I arrived on Six Landing, and Bill Corelli popped the door.

"Hi, Mikey. Wait'll you see this asshole. You'll be on your feet all night." An ex-logger with a glass eye began to tell me at length how it went down. That he personally had the balloon and put it on the chair, then the con picked up the balloon, then the con swallowed the balloon. And now the balloon is in the con's stomach and somehow it isn't his fault that I am going to check the bastard every five minutes all night long, and if the guy dies, it's my problem, not his problem, as he's about to go off shift. Somehow he will make it up to me later just to show that he's a good sport.

I looked over the log to see when the addict was last checked. Ten minutes before. I dialled Control and asked for a beeper-check.

My beeper working okay, I walked out of Segregation Control into the common area of the living unit and strolled from cell to cell, lifting the steel slides that cover the windows and shining the light in to check on each individual. The addict's light was on and through the wire-mesh glass I could see that he was unconscious or semiconscious, but I stood there long enough to determine that his breathing rhythms were more or less normal. I checked the rest of the unit, a count of only about five. I then headed over to Six South, the hospital unit, which is also my responsibility on graveyard.

Not much interesting there. One slash (unsuccessful, full of stitches and asleep). One the shrink thought might slash. One suspected to have AIDS (emaciated and sallow enough). One wet-brain (brain damage through alcoholism). One pacing his drum in a ritual pattern and on his way to Forensic for a psychiatric profile. And, sitting at the desk, Gordon the nurse. By way of avoiding another boo at his manuscript on healing by the laying on of hands, I mentioned to Gordon that I had to hurry back to seg for my five-minute checks. Gordon is a good soul, but now and then he did work himself up into a fervour about healing. It made me shudder a little, intellectually.

At approx 0035, I noted some stirring of MacTavish in cell 12. He seemed to be mumbling, but he'd have to mumble in decibels exceeding *sotto voce* if he wished to be overheard through a 12-gauge steel door. He didn't appear to notice me looking in. I was of two minds about his evident consciousness. On one hand, it meant he hadn't overdosed on the heroin. On the other, I wondered whether movement might cause his stomach acid to be more active and possibly chew through the rubber of the balloon before shift-change at approx 0700.

The phone rang. It was Kennedy the Wise.

"Let's go by the book on this one, Mikey. He has a very unpleasant priors sheet. The uglies he hasn't done personally he's paid to have done. Watch yourself."

I was again counting sleeping bodies (except for the nut-burger who was still pacing) on Six South and talking briefly with Gordon when the noise began on Six North. I ran for the door and hit the button.

"Control."

"Pop Six North, now!"

Wham! And I was through it. The noise was coming from cell 12. I banged up the slide. The sonofabitch had one shoe off and was whacking the plexiglass cover of the light with it, making a hell of a booming sound. He had awakened the other segregation inmates and they were screaming pleasantries. I yelled over the noise for him to cool it, or I'd cuff him to his bunk. He looked at me dreamily and shouted back, "Fuck you, you pig fucking dog."

I liked that. I've been called almost everything by almost everyone, but never "you pig fucking dog." Nice. Original. Has a certain melodic quality. Like saying Edna St. Vincent Millay.

I dropped the slide and ran to Segregation Control to call Kennedy. I thought the balloon had burst. Then I called Gordon and asked him to get over on the double. This is standard operating procedure for cracking a cell on graveyard. You can have more bodies than this, but no fewer. Nurse and boss must attend.

I checked the time and went back to the cell and lifted the slide. I could hear the elevator moving up the tower. The door between Six North and Six South fired and Gordon entered with the medical bag.

MacTavish's eyes were dilated like craters as he pounded on the housing. The bad news about people who are high on heroin is that it sometimes gives them delusions of adequacy. Occasionally, they think they can whip an army of guards. The good news is that their reflexes are screwed. The wild card here was the cocaine.

Enter Dave Kennedy and the back-up.

I must describe the back-up in some detail here because it is pertinent. The back-up was a thing of male beauty. The back-up was the paradigm of what an experienced line screw *doesn't* want to see appear as back-up. Very pretty guards, male or female, who spend much of their lives arranging their looks, are not eager to get into a scrap and damage their work before the mirror. This one was tall. It was French Canadian. It was a body-builder. Key here is that the face was beautiful. Dark hair, deep brown eyes, a perfect pencil-line moustache. Its uniform was flawless, with the correctional-officer star sewn exactly five inches above the cuff on the left sleeve and the near-blinding shine on its shoes. There was not a mark on its meticulously shaven face. It was about twenty-five years old. It was to be married in two weeks. Its name was Jean McSween. It had been hired straight off the street without experience of crime on either side of the word. It was innocence personified. It marched dutifully in the waddling shadow of Kennedy. I made eye contact with Kennedy. He looked heavenward. I made eye contact with Jean McSween and knew in my soul that an Andean condor could fly between his ears without the slightest possibility of touching anything like grey matter.

Control unlocked MacTavish's cell door, which swung toward us, and I entered the cell, moving to my right to allow my back-up entry. The con looked at me dazedly with the expressions on his face changing like masks from anger to amusement to fear. Then the angry look returned. Standing near this guy, I noted how much bigger he was than I. Then I noticed that my peripheral vision wasn't delivering the image of my back-up near and ready. Mr. Perfect had gone.

Then came a surprising change in MacTavish's mood: "Yeah, sure, you want the shoes, you got the shoes. Here. I was just trying to figure out how to turn the light out."

The other cons on the unit stopped bellowing to listen at the cracks of their doors, while Dave explained very formally and diplomatically that he was the boss and, should the disturbance continue, it would be his unhappy duty to instruct his line staff to restrain him, MacTavish. He then asked whether MacTavish felt he could now settle down for the night.

Yes, MacTavish slurred, he was quite certain that he could and was very sorry for any untoward behaviour.

I turned to my left, despite what my peripheral vision had told me, expecting to see my back-up exiting the cell. No McSween. Dave had been speaking from the door, because it is a strict security regulation that the boss not enter a troubled cell. Nurse Gordon had stayed out of sight because he knew he was there as much as a witness as a purveyor of first aid (he is quite good at settling down troubled prisoners when the show of force in the form of uniforms has failed).

We closed the cell and took the shoes to Seg Control. McSween left his post outside of all the action and returned to his landing down on one of the wimp units on Three Landing.

"That's back-up?" I asked Kennedy.

"Well, we have to give these twits on-the-job training, if they're not going to have them spend their first six months in service at Oakie," Dave shrugs. "Them's orders. Send them in on scuffles, cell-extractions, and Condition Yellows."

I had to do my rounds at the hospital, so I headed off. Kennedy was on his way down the tower to his office. It was getting on toward 0500, when you doubt if you can make it through the rest of the shift. You wash your face in cold water, comb your hair, and look forward to the runner who delivers the morning reports to exchange a few words with another half-dead human.

When I got back, MacTavish was still pissing around in his cell, muttering, and conscious enough to make eye contact when I raised the slide. But he said nothing. I presumed that the cocaine was keeping the heroin from allowing him to sleep. I didn't know how long the effects of either drug would last. And he may have had other drugs, already ingested, that we knew nothing about.

Later, as I walked across the unit, I heard noise coming from cell 12. I pushed up the slide. MacTavish was sitting on the bunk with a shattered Melmac cup in his hand, middle finger through the handle, waving the jagged remainder of the cup before him. Having established I was watching, he smiled and began raking the jagged edge across his left forearm between wrist and elbow. He was scratching himself but not drawing blood. I dropped the slide, sprinted into Seg Control, and phoned Kennedy.

"S.C.O."

"Dave, you better haul ass up here. That housedog asshole has stomped a cup and he's trying to slash with it."

"Jesus Christ, Mikey, gimme a break, it's time to go home. Half of morning shift is . . . Aw, fuck, be right up."

I hit the intercom button.

"Control."

"Troubles, Billy, pop Kennedy and the back-up through, and get the nurse over here on the double." I headed back to 12, pulled a notebook out of my ass pocket, made some notes, and lifted the slide. Upon hearing the slide, MacTavish began scraping at his left arm with the cup again.

The door between hospital and segregation fired and Gordon and his medical bag were standing by. Distantly I could hear the doors firing on lower floors and the elevator moving in its tube. Then Kennedy came in with radio and clipboard and Prettyboy McSween dancing behind.

Kennedy lifted the slide.

"The big pig, himself," MacTavish bellowed.

Kennedy dropped the slide. "He's bluffin'. He hasn't given himself any pain, but he can tear himself up with that toy if he gets serious. Pieces of it are all over his bunk. Get in there and take it away from him and the broken pieces and we'll restrain him and dump the problem on morning shift."

"Okay," I said on behalf of me and my back-up.

The lock whirred and the door swung open. As it did, MacTavish turned the sharp cup toward me and started to stand up. I covered the three feet in a single stride before he could reach full height, drove my right shoulder into his chest to knock him back off-balance, took his right wrist with my left hand, and cranked with everything I had, grabbing one ear of his collar as I did so. His ass plunked down on the bunk again and I heard the cup hit the floor. He was screaming obscenities at the top of his voice. I kicked the cup toward the door and looked over my shoulder. I was alone in the cell. My so-called back-up was standing outside the door looking in. What was this, a spectator sport? I began digging pieces of the cup out from under his ass and pitched them with my free hand one by one toward the door.

Good old ex-Oakie Kennedy had reflexively moved to the doorway. In my peripheral vision, I could see him inching into the cell. He was violating procedure, but his radar was telling him something. I'd got as much of the cup out of the bed as I could with the guy rolled to my right, so I shifted my hand to the other ear of his collar and began to roll him the other way. He was resisting. Kennedy tried to ditch his clipboard and radio and give me a hand, but there wasn't enough room. I got MacTavish crosswise on the bunk, face to face, trying to keep all the variables in mind through the bleary end-of-graveyard funk. I couldn't get enough leverage standing sideways to him, so I squared up and inadvertently presented him with a prize target. He went for it. His right foot connected with my left testicle with enough impact that I could see celestial bodies beyond Pluto. My knees, I knew it, were going to go.

All I wanted to do was to hit the floor, assume the foetal position, and scream primally. But I still had his collar in my left grip. I pulled his head toward me and swung. No peace officer with any sense, even in dire circumstances, punches where it will leave marks. My right connected above his ear and back from the face. I held on to the collar. Then I connected with a backswing in the same area on the other side of his head. I had to get his mind off my crotch and get out of the cell. Finally, I felt the right body language and heard the right noises. MacTavish was out of fight. Somewhere in the mêlée I heard Kennedy's voice at the radio: "Condition Yellow, Six North, Condition Yellow, Six North." My right hand was throbbing in concert with my scrotum, and I felt like I was going down again. Kennedy's strong arm was threaded through mine and I was out the door, and in a chair in the common area, where I opened my mouth and screamed in agony. The cell door was slammed.

Nurse Gordon, God bless him, had thrown a gel ice-pack into his medi bag. He handed it to me from a discreet distance. "Here, Mr. Yates, you should go in Segregation Control and apply this right now." Kennedy and Prettyboy McSween helped me there. Gordon stuck his head around the door and observed that my right hand was very swollen and blue and said I should try to give the hand some benefit of the ice-pack as well.

Right.

Things were none too clear nor steady. I made it to my feet and dropped my trousers to my ankles, and eased myself down onto the ice-pack.

Bear in mind that in a Condition Yellow, every line officer in the building responds to the area. All of the night shift and most of morning shift responded to this one. I don't remember hearing their approach. But there I was as around fifty people flooded through Seg Control – half of them female guards – pants around my ankles. Some of the comments as they passed in one door, around me, and out the other door to the common area, I'm told, were hilarious. I was too stunned and sleepy to retain memory of them.

The morning S.C.O. took over from Kennedy to move MacTavish to another cell. Dave asked whether I needed a stretcher. I didn't know. I stood. I seemed to be coming around, except that there was a lot of pressure in my scrotum. British Bob Falkland offered to drive me to St. Paul's Emergency where he explained that he had a wounded officer on his hands who needed attention right away.

Amazingly, the nurse took me immediately into one of the cubicles separated by sheets, told me to get my britches off and get up on the gurney. In my shape, what with the pain and dizziness flicking in and out, this was no small task. I was standing by the gurney trying to figure out whether it would be more difficult to climb Everest when the nurse reappeared with a little two-step device which she placed beside the gurney.

Finally, stretched out on the gurney, I closed my eyes. I could hear Falkland attempting to give the nurse the medical insurance number that we use for prisoners. The sheet was pulled aside and the nurse approached me asking for my insurance number.

"It's in my wallet. There in my pants. Just get it out of my wallet."

"We're not allowed to do that, sir."

"Are you telling me that you want me to get down from here, go over there, get the wallet, and hand you the card?"

"I'm afraid so, sir."

"Why didn't you tell me that before I got up here?" This she didn't answer.

I groaned and whimpered my way off the gurney, down the steps, over to my pants and handed her the card. "Now, if I climb back up there, do you promise to leave me the fuck alone and send me a doctor so I can get out of here?"

"You don't have to be rude, sir," she huffed.

"Lady, would that you had my balls and I your enviable dispassion."

I scaled the heights again and lay with my eyes closed. Suddenly I heard Falkland burst into roaring laughter. No one had said anything. He was still laughing when I heard the rollers on the sheet-track and I opened my eyes to see the curtain closing. Perhaps someone simply peeked in. I started to close my eyes again when I heard papers rustling to my right and low. I turned my head.

The voice was beyond description, a cross between Minnie Mouse and Miss Piggie. So high, I thought she was faking it.

"Hello. I'm Doctor Rumbahl," she squeaked. I'd be amazed if she was an inch over four-feet-six. "So you've experienced a blow to the groin." At this, Falkland lost it again.

Rumball?

"I take it this happened in the line of duty."

"Yes."

"I'll have to examine you."

She asked me to get my gaunchies off and climbed the two steps. Even then, she had to stand on tiptoe and scrunch her chest against my right leg to get at my balls. No worry about an embarrassing erection. This was a sure-fire hard-off.

Then it felt as though she inserted her arm to the elbow up the testicle tube. "Does that hurt?"

"Yaaaaaahhhhhh!" I thought I would be the first human brick-piercing projectile to breach a hospital wall.

"Well, you have internal bleeding," the midget intoned. If I didn't, I certainly did after her probe.

"You'll need to go home and put those on ice. Do you have an ice-bag?"

"No," I gasped.

"Actually, a bag of frozen peas would do just as well." She unhanded my scrotum and climbed down. At that point, my dick had retreated in terror so far, I felt like I had indoor plumbing.

On the way home, I stopped by the store and picked up a couple of bags of frozen peas, one for my nuts and one for the hand, as recommended. I was in the doorway of my apartment when the phone rang. It was Fran Ouellette from the prison.

"Mr. Yates, I just wanted to warn you that the inmate is rattling bombs: Inspection and Standards, ombudsman, lawyers, the whole nine yards. You might get your notes up to date before you go to sleep. The unit officer called and said he had called Rankin, and Rankin is on his way down to counsel his client."

"Thanks."

"Mr. Kennedy has done a detailed incident report. I don't think there's anything to worry about, really."

I was thinking about putting on the answering machine and getting into bed with the peas, but the thought of waking up in a pool of cold water unnerved me. So I sat on the chesterfield for a while with the bags of peas, smoking a cigarette, and jotting a few notes in my government-issue notebook. The phone rang again. The number was unlisted. Everyone who had it knew I was on graveyard and should be asleep. I grabbed it.

"What, for chrissake."

"Yates?" Sounded long distance.

"What?"

"It's Crampton." A "Morningside" producer.

"Toronto?"

"Today's the day."

"For what?"

"Day after the election. Remember? You promised."

I had known Crampton for years. He was executive producer of the old "Vancouver Show" on CKVU, and before that I had been a morning-radio editorialist for him on CBC. I could hear Gzowski in the background yakking to someone about the provincial election. Crampton's idea had been that it would be a great idea to get all these "high-energy" weirdo non-political-scientist types to give their off-the-wall responses to the campaign and the election results. Crampton had put the arm on me months ago about this, and I had agreed in a weak moment and forgotten about it.

"Come on, it'll only take a few minutes. It's live."

What choice did I have?

Gzowski announced, "And now we're going to talk to the poet J. Michael Yates, who wears a belt-buckle with M–I–K–E on it. I didn't believe it until he walked into the studio with it on." Little did he know I was perched on a packet of frozen peas. After we had finished, and I'd hung up, I wanted to laugh hard, but it would have hurt too much.

Bedtime. Piss on the peas. At this point, I had frostbite as well as internal bleeding.

Brrring! I could not believe it was the telephone again. "What, for fuck's sake!" I shouted.

"Mikey. Thought I'd get your machine and have you call back when you woke up." It was Greg Mooney from the joint. "Listen. Rankin [MacTavish's lawyer] just left. You gonna charge MacTavish in outside court? You can make assault peace officer stick. Maybe aggravated assault."

"Haven't thought about it."

Greg proceeded to tell me about Rankin's visit to MacTavish. Harry Rankin is one of the most venerable of West Coast criminal lawyers and a folk-hero to those who love left-leaning millionaires. Dutifully, Harry had trotted down to Pretrial and listened to MacTavish's tale of woe. Afterward, he rushed down to Fran Ouellette, the senior correctional officer who was handling the paper on the incident. Greg, who was in the room during the episode, told it as follows:

Harry: "In all my years as a defence lawyer, never have I seen an inmate take such a beating from a guard."

Fran: "Is that so? Funny, our medical staff didn't find any marks on the man. Did you see any?"

Harry: "Well, he had marks all up and down his left arm where the officers had put the handcuffs on too tight."

Fran: "Funny thing about cuffs, Harry. When you put 'em on too tight, they leave a single mark on the wrist. Goes away in about ten minutes."

Harry: "Well, he had marks and scratches . . ."

Fran: "Harry, the man broke a cup and was raking his arm with it. The only reason staff were in there was to keep him from further self-inflicted scratches."

Harry: "And what is this nonsense that he kicked one of your officers in the groin. The man didn't even have shoes on."

Fran: stands up and comes around the desk in front of Rankin. Bends over and begins untying one shoe: "Harry."

Harry: "Yes?"

Fran: "Tell me if this hurts."

The exchange imploded in laughter. Rankin asked if the officer was going to lay a charge for outside court. Ouellette suggested MacTavish write me a note of apology and ask me not to. Harry said his client was looking at ten, and the judge would probably look at the assault as *de minimis non curat lex* ("the court will not stoop to waste time with trivia.") A cop or a guard getting smacked around a little comes with the turf.

I had no intention of wasting days off sitting in a foetid courtroom, so I didn't charge him in outside court.

MacTavish got forty-five days more segregation time in Director's Court for booting me. Then, when he was sentenced, and went off to federal before the forty-five days were up, laughing at Pretrial, a wag in records called records at Kent penitentiary (the federal institution in the Fraser Valley where he was sent).

"Hi, listen, we've got one sentenced to ten heading your way and he owes us some digger-time."

"No problem. How much?"

"'Bout ninety days."

"He'll do 'em."

PART THREE

New Haven

17

Heaven

•

I don't like to commit myself about heaven and hell –
you see, I have friends in both places.
– Mark Twain

NEW HAVEN Correctional Centre, a minimum-security institution in Burnaby for young-adult offenders, is the Elysium of
corrections in Canada. It is based on the Borstal philosophy, which
was born in England almost a century ago and inaugurated in one
wing of a prison in Borstal, Kent, in 1902. The Borstal concept evolved
into a rehabilitation program for offenders between the ages of sixteen and twenty-one, based on the premise that imprisoning youthful
offenders with older offenders would only teach them more crime.
The program was based on a "definite indeterminate" sentence, in
which the length of sentence depended on how long it took the resi-
dent to complete the Borstal training program to the satisfaction of
the headmaster or director and his board. Tom Courtenay was a
"Borstal lad" in *The Loneliness of the Long Distance Runner*; Brendan
Behan was moved to write of his experience in *Borstal Boy*. The
present president of the Borstal Association of British Columbia is a
graduate of New Haven. Numerous prominent lawyers and other
professionals are graduates of New Haven.

In Canada, the New Haven Act was passed in the B.C. legislature
in 1949, giving the province an indeterminate sentence like that in
England. The mandate of New Haven was to take only first-time

offenders between seventeen and twenty-three. The first twelve inmates in what is now the only British Borstal program on earth were marched over the ridge from Oakalla to New Haven.

The place is quite unlike a prison. The atmosphere is free and relaxed: no fences, no concertina wire, no uniforms. It has been in operation since 1937, although it closed during the war and was re-opened in 1947 by Selwyn Roxborough "Rocky" Smith, probably the most influential man in B.C. corrections this century. After the New Haven Act was passed in 1949, the new Borstal-style program there was a minimum of nine months long – or as long as the director determined was necessary to give the "lad" the tools he needed to cope with life in the community as a good citizen.

However, by the time I arrived at New Haven in December 1987, the indeterminate sentence had been repealed, the Young Offenders Act of British Columbia had raised the age of offenders who came under the Criminal Code of Canada to eighteen, and the minimum time for the program had been reduced to four months. At Oakalla, residents were called "inmates," at Vancouver Pretrial they were "prisoners," at New Haven, they were "trainees."

When you think of New Haven, forget everything that television and movies have ever insinuated into your mind about prisons. There are no guns and no locks. Occasionally we need handcuffs, but we always have a hell of a time finding them. When we do, then we have to find a key.

The guards are not guards but vocational instructors and dormitory supervisors. The Borstal program deals with the total individual. He goes to bed at 2200 each night, lights-out at 2230. He is up at 0600 in the morning. He is required to shower and shave. He is required to shower after work. He is required to shower after mandatory physical training. He is allowed no facial hair. And his hair must be trimmed so that his ears show and the length in the back clears the collar. A contract barber is brought in to give them a professional trim. If the barber isn't coming in for a few days, we use a volunteer to chop the hair to the proper specifications, albeit with a few divots to be ironed out by the professional barber.

Trainees do not wear uniforms. When working in the shops they may use prison greens or overalls of some other colour. It makes sense because the material is cheap and tough. They work in the shops from 0800 in the morning until 1130, with a coffee break. Then lunch break for half an hour. The meals are magnificent. Then back to work until 1500, with another coffee break in the middle.

Between 1500 and 1700 there is time after showers to telephone home or play pool or ping-pong in the large lounge. Or watch the forty-inch TV. Or run around the full-sized track. Or have a game of softball or touch-football or soccer. Or stroll out to the pond and feed the ducks. New Haven raises its own cattle, pigs, chickens, and ducks, as well as vegetables of every variety. The place is virtually self-sufficient.

The point of the Borstal program at New Haven is the opposite of that of Oakalla and Vancouver Pretrial, where the point is to subtract people from society and warehouse them at great cost. New Haven tries to maintain as much contact with the community as possible. A trainee comes in as a "pre-junior." There is a board meeting once a month where each trainee is assessed. He passes from pre-junior to junior to intermediate to senior to senior/temporary absence, at which level he receives passes to go home on weekends, to go on job interviews and take employment, or to go out each morning on educational leave.

During the day, trainees work on vocational crews overseen by vocational instructors: kitchen, farm, wood-shop, metal-shop, clean-up, or on various community projects, sometimes in conjunction with other ministries such as Fisheries or Forestry. Three nights a week trainees attend academic classes. Each trainee is assessed by the teacher and given assignments according to his level of achievement. Many take correspondence courses at the university level. Others attend technical schools.

On afternoon and night shifts the dorm is overseen by dorm supervisors, who are also case managers. The dorm is divided into four teams of ten beds each, and two staff are assigned to each of four teams. Each team has a team captain and an assistant team to the highest office on the campus: a trainee who is senior duty monitor for the month. Each shift has a duty monitor, who chases about with a clipboard taking the count, and who can tell staff where any trainee is at any given time. It is an honour system in which responsibility and accountability are handed in layers to the trainees as they rise through the ranks of the program.

Program is the key word. To many of the young men who come to New Haven, it is the nearest thing to a home they have ever experienced. They receive complete support from peers and staff for their accomplishments, as well as discipline and structure. The approach is holistic. If the kid has low self-esteem because he is skinny, the weight-lifting group takes him in hand and puts him on a program. If he is fat, he is encouraged to look to his diet. If the problem is acne, it is looked after immediately. If a trainee's posture is bad, it is the case manager's job to get the kid to pull his shoulders back, maintain eye contact, and converse standing on his hind feet. Teeth are taken care of. Life-skills are taught, including how to prepare a résumé and how to look for jobs. Physical training is rigorous and mandatory, vocational work is mandatory, and great collective pride is taken in the proper keeping of the grounds.

We get to know the trainees' families, and they get to know ours. I was on duty one night when fellow-staffer Bernie Cox showed up with his two boys. His older boy was a computer nut and dashed off to check out what the cons were doing on the computers. My (then) ten-year-old stepson, Dave, is a chess freak and loved to come down and vanish upstairs to take on all comers at chess. Afterwards they would take Dave into the lounge and teach him to play pool. New Haven graduates stay in touch with staff and bring families back years later to show them the place where their lives were turned around.

On my first visit to New Haven, I was very impressed with what I saw and heard. I'd been forced to go on disability leave from Pretrial because the stress and violence there had brought on symptoms of heart failure, and I was not enjoying hanging around the house. I was looking for an opportunity to get back into corrections in a less stressful environment.

Director Andrew Burns, who was showing me around, walked us out toward the farm area. On the left was a lovely pond with an inlet stream at the upper end, weeping willows around the edges, and geese and ducks on the bank. Burns grabbed a handful of pellets from a metal container and threw them straight down into the water, nowhere near the ducks. I was mystified. He grabbed another fistful and threw it straight down again. I was about to point out that the ducks were over on the right when a rainbow trout that weighed at least ten pounds swirled on the surface below us to eat the pellets. Then at least six more joined in the feeding frenzy. I wanted to work here.

We walked around the grounds some more and discussed what dreams Burns had for expanding the program: the previous director had let the library go to hell. I asked about the possibility of putting together a computer-education program. What about a campus newspaper? He told me that in earlier times there had been one, but it had died. The possibilities were virtually limitless. This would be an opportunity for me to utilize my teaching skills, my criminology studies in case management, and all the life experience I could muster.

18

First Shifts

——————————— • ———————————

Some of us are like wheelbarrows – only useful when
pushed, and very easily upset.
– Jack Herbert

DIRECTOR Andrew Burns had told me that wearing a uniform
was optional. I asked him what his druthers were. He said he
didn't have any, but he was going to have me dead-head a couple of
afternoon shifts just to observe, and I might wear the uniform so that
the trainees would know I was not just another pretty face. Five minutes after walking down the drive and into the dorm, I regretted wearing the goof-suit. I might as well have been wearing a ballerina's tutu.
The staff and cons looked at me like something from outer space. The
instructors wore bits and pieces of uniform as work clothing and
there was one guard who wore a uniform on day and afternoon shifts,
but no one took uniforms seriously.

The staff office is called the bull-pen, for obvious reasons. It has
windows so that staff can see into the lounge, the lobby where the
phones are located, and the upper lobby where the bathroom is
located. I was paired up with an old-timer with a handlebar moustache. He had been there since Christ was a cowboy and my two shifts
were his last before retirement.

I had asked Burns for some program study materials and he'd
handed me a few pages on Borstal philosophy that were written in the
thirties. He assured me that the staff and trainees would point me in

the right direction. Then he said he had one important word of advice for me.

"Yes?"

"Relax."

"Relax?"

"New Haven is so unlike anything you have experienced in corrections, particularly Pretrial, that the only way to get it is to relax and just let yourself float with it."

Al, my handlebar man, was all grunts and monosyllables. A trainee dashed in dressed in rugby pants and T-shirt, and asked him if he could go on another team and get something. Al shook his head. Another asked to go up to the weight-pit. Al nodded. And there was a kid hanging around in the bull-pen with a clipboard. This was the duty monitor. His job was to keep track of where everyone was all the time. His performance would be evaluated at the end of the shift. I would gradually come to find out that everything was evaluated and everything reviewed on board day (the last Wednesday of every month), when it was decided who would be promoted, demoted, or held at the same level.

The trainees came in from the shops and took off their work-boots before going up the few stairs into the teams. Some went up and napped, some hit the track and began doing laps, others were doing chores of various kinds. My God, there were sixty-eight acres for all this traffic to get lost in. These were convicted criminals and I was standing around in a uniform and people were flying off hither and thither. Nobody seemed worried. What the hell would make them come back? I was still a correctional officer and an escape was an escape.

Al grunted that if they were going to be "walk-aways," they usually walked within the first three days. They hadn't had any intake of new trainees for a few days, so not to worry.

He yelled at the duty monitor to get him the senior duty monitor. A tall genteel Native kid entered and Al tossed him the keys off his belt and told him to show me everything.

The kid had lots of presence and breeding, whether acquired at New Haven or at home. Only those with strong leadership qualities made it to senior duty monitor. He told me so much my head spun. First, we entered the lounge where there was a full-sized snooker table, a ping-pong table with room for Olympic-style play, and a forty-inch TV where about half the count were sitting in rows of seats watching MuchMusic. The duty monitor proudly told me that all this top-of-the-line equipment had been bought with profits from projects they had done in the metal, wood, and other shops. They welded, repaired vehicles and repainted them, and made fencing which was sold through local lumber companies. Later they secured big contracts with Canada Post to refinish metal mailboxes and wooden sorting-boxes.

We then went back to have a look at the medical room where doctor's parade was held and the nurse and psychological people held their counselling sessions, and to the dispensary which had two beds and a bathroom with a bathtub.

Up the stairs from the level on which the bull-pen and lounge were located were the teams: Heath, Stanton, Horniman, and Davies – all named after early staff at the institution. The teams played all sorts of tournaments against one another and competed on Saturday clean-up to see which team would be deemed the cleanest.

Each team had ten beds. Around each bed there were chest-high risers which afforded privacy. Each had an ample closet for clothing and books and other personal effects, and a bedside table with a drawer. There was a light above each bed for reading. The teams were very neat. Unlike at Oakalla, there were no walls and ceilings filled with porn shots. Unlike Pretrial, there were no bulletin-boards where family shots could be placed. But as I was to find out on morning shift, during inspection, inside the closets was open-season. Porn books were not allowed in, but the inside of virtually every closet looked like an Oakalla drum – pictures materialized as if by magic. But no one messed with the inside decor of the closets so long as the clothing and effects were neat and the closet was free of dust and tobacco grains. The pictures were traded around as kids trade baseball and hockey cards. When someone was released, he bequeathed his collection to his closest buddies.

The senior duty monitor explained that there was inspection each morning before breakfast, but serious cleaning was done on Saturday, which was more or less white-glove time. As we walked from team to team there were young men reading or dozing, but they had nothing to say to a new uniform.

Even in December, as we walked through the afternoon, New Haven seemed a bubble in time where one could stop and focus without being hounded by distractions. A tree break protected any view of the place from Marine Drive. There were just the buildings and acres and acres of arable land.

Finally the duty monitor asked where I was from. Pretrial and Oakalla. This impressed him, and he asked me a few questions about those places as we left the dorm and headed over toward the shops and gymnasium. Then he found out that I wasn't just visiting New Haven, and wondered which team I was assigned to. I explained I was working the slot vacated by a guard called Bailey, whom I hadn't met. He said it was likely I would be assigned to Heath Team, which was Bailey's team, and he was right. I was primary case manager for five kids and back-up case manager for the other five on the team.

We visited the gymnasium, which has to be the best-equipped in the B.C. corrections system. Bill Boxleitner (who was to become a close friend) oversaw the condition and purchase of sports equipment.

We took a quick look at the barns and tons of farm equipment. There was a small herd of cattle, pigs in their own barn, and a huge chicken-coop, as well as the aforementioned waterfowl. And there were dogs and cats attached to the place and some of the staff brought their dogs in on afternoon and night shifts.

Then the youngster mentioned that we ought to be getting back to the dorm because it was almost supper time, so we picked up the pace and arrived just in time to see the teams getting ready to go up to the main building, the heritage administration building that housed the dining room and kitchen.

When we got back to the dorm, the trainees were bunched up into their teams, waiting. From the porch of the main building the duty monitor blew the whistle. One team went out the door, butting cigarettes before leaving (no smoking between buildings) and walked in an orderly fashion up the hill. I went up the hill with Al to oversee the line (the handling of food in prisons is a very weighty issue). When one team had been served by a squeaky-clean kitchen crew dressed in whites complete with hats, the duty monitor blew his whistle again and the next team came up. The food was delicious and there were seconds. Everything was home-made, including desserts. They sat four to a table, as at a restaurant, and watched their manners. The staff sat at one corner. At the end of the meal, everyone remained seated until the duty monitor asked permission of staff to dismiss them.

First he called "Quiet!" then waited until you could hear a pin drop. Then he looked at Al. Al nodded. He made a few announcements he had written on his clipboard and acknowledged that we had a new staff-member – me – who was doing his first shift at New Haven. I stood.

"Don't let this silly costume fool you. I was trying to hang around incognito." They chuckled politely.

The duty monitor then dismissed them by rank or by whatever order staff said – in the event one table had been boisterous, it would be dismissed last – and everyone filed back down the hill for the evening's organized activities.

On his way down, the duty monitor took down the Canadian flag and carefully folded it with a volunteer's help. Putting up the flag and taking it down was an essential part of a duty monitor's routine. The program was filled with details like this on which they were evaluated. It was the duty monitor's job to keep track of everyone. To stay on tap in case staff had messages for trainees. He was graded on his appearance during the shift.

Mondays, Wednesdays, and Fridays there were academic classes for two hours (and, once I had the computer-education program up and running and two P.C.s installed in the dorm, those participating, if they had their other studies caught up, could remain down in the dorm with me for instruction). On Tuesdays and Thursdays, there was leather club, church groups came in, and there were Alcoholics Anonymous, Narcotics Anonymous, Cocaine Anonymous, and Adult Children of Alcoholics meetings. And every night there was some form of vigorous exercise in the gym for at least thirty minutes. Sometimes aerobics, sometimes calisthenics, or games like basketball or floor-hockey or volleyball. In the summer the playing fields were filled after work and after supper.

Then I was taken up and introduced to the cottagers. These were not trainees. They were any age from twenty-four to their sixties. They could be provincial or federal people in custody. Usually they were white-collar types rather than violent criminals. Some were in for impaired-driving charges, and some for non-payment of child support. They worked on the various crews but were not required to participate in the more structured parts of the program. Quite often they tutored the trainees or ran the laundry. There were only six of them.

The next cottage over was the chapel, which was used when the pastor could get enough together for a service. Each new intake had a session with the chaplain who, like his equivalent at other institutions, handled news of death in the family and "Dear John" letters.

The next cottage was used for the leather club and other crafts and had a piano and a couple of guitars for the musically inclined.

The last cottage was the old segregation unit, no longer used. If an infraction was bad enough to warrant segregation, the trainee was taken up the ridge to Oakalla and pulled his seg time there.

My first shift was "crazy Tuesday," an evening with every kind of twelve-step meeting imaginable. A church band was in to put on a performance in the lounge and it was leather-club night. Bodies were streaming in every direction and volunteers were rushing in and out of the bull-pen asking for keys. Only two staff were running the whole show.

Between 2000 and 2100 that night, I was alone in the office. The farm foreman (each crew had a foreman and an assistant foreman) came in and asked me for a form. He had to tell me which of my keys to use to get into the key-box. Then he had to explain to me that his crew went out and did a final check on the animals, filling out the form for the instructor the next morning. If they didn't report back within a certain time, they were responsible to him.

At around 2100, it was cookies-and-cocoa time. The kitchen crew had organized food and drink for the meeting going on in the main building and those left in the lounge lined up to receive cocoa and cookies at the bull-pen door, which was a Dutch door with a counter for serving. It kept nerds from grabbing more than their share and sprinting away.

At 2200, everyone filed back from his activity, and trainees broke into crews to clean the lounge, telephone lobby, and upper lobby, and the duty monitor, chased staff out of the bull-pen so he could sweep and mop and make coffee for the on-coming night shift. At 2230, it was lights-out. There was an intercom in the bull-pen which would allow us to listen to each team to see if there was any talking or horse-play going on. Then we toured each team to say goodnight.

It was all so amazingly complicated, yet so orderly, without guards standing over everyone demanding that this or that be done. If problems occurred, the staff spoke to the senior duty monitor, who spoke to the proper team captain. If necessary, a parliamentary session was held in the lounge among seniors and those eligible for temporary absence and chaired by the senior duty monitor. If something couldn't be solved, a trainee came to staff as a last resort.

The staff had plenty to do interviewing the kids who made up their case-loads, and writing volumes in their files, taking care to note positive things as well as negative. The place was a veritable paper factory: temporary-absence applications, parole applications, work-release applications, applications for courses, and for tutoring. And most of it had to be done on afternoon shift. The trainees couldn't be kept awake for case-management interviews on graveyard, because loss of sleep might mean loss of a finger in a saw in the wood-shop.

The staff's shift schedule was set up on a sixty-three-day cycle, with as many as seven days in a row on and a maximum of seven days in a row off. It began with three graveyards and four afternoons, then days off; next, four graveyards and three afternoons, then days off; and then would come five day shifts in a row.

The graveyards involved closing down of the grounds, closing the main gate, which was a single bar and simply kept drunks and neckers out but wouldn't keep out anyone sneaking in to make a drug-drop, nor bar the way for anyone walking away or simply sneaking up the

hill for a quickie in a car parked in a lane. We also had to secure the
main building, set the telephones to relay to the dorm, and file reports
which came in on the printer from Oakalla.

Graveyard was a good time for catching up on files. Or writing.
Or, as usual, trying to keep from dozing off (frowned upon). Or
bringing in videos and watching them in the lounge (frowned upon).
Every now and then there was excitement. Perhaps someone would
be caught sneaking in – there were far more problems with people
sneaking in to steal things or drop drugs than with trainees escaping.

We had a faulty silent fire-alarm system which suffered seizures
from time to time. The suited-up firemen would show up at the dorm
door ready for action complaining that the gate was locked. We would
have to go through the long process of calling the alarm company and
fill out incident reports and the pissed-off firemen would disappear
cursing the alarm company.

One graveyard there was a scuffle on a school night in the classroom while I was supervising studies and tutoring. I walked into the
room and the two scrappers jumped apart – without my saying a
word. I pointed out that fighting was a chargeable offence. They nodded. I also said that while punching someone you're angry with in the
head can be a momentarily satisfying experience, having an ex-Oakie,
ex-Pretrial screw break up the fight was an experience they would
remember for a lifetime. They stared with wide eyes, then nodded. I
said that if they were prepared to kiss and hug and become betrothed
then the incident had never happened. They nodded. Good. I
returned to the other room. The scuffle never happened, and there
was no more friction between them. Truly I was in heaven. The place
was a prison guard's dream.

Only once did a look or a shout fail to stop such nonsense. Both
kids were "iffy" placements at New Haven. They had done maximum
juvie time at Willingdon Youth Detention Centre and were a little
sub-New Haven standard. One of them had barricaded himself
behind a door of one of the teams after taking something belonging
to the other. The young ape from whom he had taken the object was
shouldering the door and the noise brought me over the top of my
desk, out the bull-pen door, up the stairs, and around the corner. Any

other trainee would have backed away instantly at the sight of me, but this nitwit saw me and kept shouldering the door. I grabbed him by the back of the neck and clamped, then walked him toward the bull-pen. Trainees were rushing out of the teams to watch. In front of the others, I could see that the thought of attempting to deck me crossed his mind, but he thought better of it.

I kept hold of the neck until we got into the office, then tossed him into a chair for a chat. I closed the door and began to talk to him. I happened to glance over at my partner, who seemed stunned. It took a couple of hours to get the two trainees sorted out, and afterward I asked my partner, Sorensen, why he had been looking at me.

"I've been here for five years and that's the only time I've seen a staff-member get violent with a trainee," he said.

Violent? Grabbing an inmate to whom you have given a direct order to cease destroying the place is violence? I shook my head. "Well, in my placc, what would you have done? Kissed his ass and let him destroy the door and frame?"

"I probably would have yelled for you."

"Check."

I didn't even charge them. In three years I laid only two charges at New Haven, compared with five on my first shift at Pretrial.

No one liked day shift. The day man was the go-fer. He drove vehicles to pick up supplies for the shops, and for the bursar who made up canteens. The good news was that because of the location of New Haven at the bottom of a ridge, they couldn't radio the cars and make the day even crazier. You left with a list of errands in the morning and a list in the afternoon. Quite often you had to pick up new intake at Oakalla, pick up payroll, or go as far as Pretrial on some errand.

As soon as I was settled in, I was determined to jazz up day shift and make it fun. The dress code didn't allow blue jeans or runners. I began by buying a pair of black leather runners and strode into the office and pointed out that these were walking shoes, as I didn't run. Then I bought bizarre fluorescent belts and gaudy shirts and ties. My crowning achievement in dress came one morning when I walked in for breakfast and one of the cottagers looked at me and said, "Christ, you look like a test pattern for an Afghani TV station."

The philosophy of New Haven calls for maximum contact with the community. I rarely left the campus on day shift without one or more trainees to assist me on the errands. If it was a money transaction, I gave him the cash, he made the purchase, and it was his responsibility to deal with the merchant and present the bursar with proper receipts and change. Often they would accompany me to Oakalla where there would be some seven-foot rookie at the gate armed to the teeth with .38 and radio and looking like he had a poker up his ass.

Dressed like a nightmare, I would motion him close to the window of the vehicle and say "I'm Yates of New Haven, president of the gay, grey guards. We've received your application for membership and it's being processed. You have the gay part right, but the grey is a problem. However, for a few hundred dollars we have a product called Portuguese formula. It's not Grecian, but it's close."

Needless to say, I was waved through in short order where I would go into Main Gaol and cause more havoc with my attire – particularly in records, where Derek Van was in charge and would go along with anything. We would embrace before Mounties, sheriffs, guards, and cons and he would have me model my outfit – to the absolute macho horror of all. It was wonderful.

At New Haven the day man comes in at 0700, organizes his schedule for the day with the principal officer, and gets the keys to a vehicle sufficient to the tasks at hand. One day I had a hospital run – two young fellows to take down to Vancouver General Hospital, where they were going to have their wisdom teeth extracted.

They were two very interesting kids. One was a tall, skinny white (a wigwam-burner in Native parlance) named Jones, who was affable, as well as hyper and yappy. The other was a short Native (wagon-burner) named Oliver from the Mount Currie Reserve. This reserve is notorious for its vitriol against whites. In times past, when you drove through the reserve, there were aerosol-paint signs that read "THIS IS MT. CURRIE, WHITE-EYES, WATCH YOUR ASS." "THIS IS INDIAN

TERRITORY. ANYBODY WHO FUCKS WITH ANYTHING ON THIS RESERVE WILL BE SHOT." The Indians who come to jail from Mount Currie are a tough lot.

Natives do extremely well at New Haven, and few escape. I don't know why. It may have something to do with the fact that the New Haven atmosphere simply does not support ghettoing. The Native kids do not hang out with Native kids nor the whites with whites. A group going off to the weight-room may include a black, an East Indian, an Asian of some sort, a Native, and a couple of nondescript Anglos or Celts. This happens in spite of the fact that we do not attempt any sort of quota system based on ethnic background on the teams in the dorm – an open bed is an open bed; but we could wind up with half a team of ten being of Asian extraction and they still wouldn't clump up and yammer in Cantonese.

Having been worried about the human penchant for racism most of my life and having been fed that same media pap about racism as everyone else, I was really curious to see how the prison race gangs put it all together. It was during my last days at Pretrial and the New Haven years that the so-called Asian gangs began their ascendancy. At New Haven, we had first the honcho of the Red Eagles (Chinese), then the boss of the Lotus gang (Chinese, Japanese, and white). And several members of these gangs and others. They may well have connections with the triads, but I have seen a number of red-haired and freckled members of Asian gangs. And Natives. And East Indians.

It is possible that prisons in the United States have a more profound sense of race than in Canada, but I doubt it. The chicanos I have had in prison have shown no interest in ganging up with other Hispanics. If I have five blacks in a unit, one or two might be American (but from different cultures in different states, with little in common), another might be from Trinidad, one from Haiti, and so on. The black from Trinidad would probably find more in common with a Hispanic from Colombia, which is a Catholic country, or a Tahitian with an Algerian so they can pass the hours France-bashing.

In short, the racial issue in Canadian prisons is a non-issue. Bear in mind that before the Natives had Europeans with whom to war, they warred against each other. Their traditions are different from band to band, let alone from nation to nation, as are their languages.

One time I had among my cases a Colombian drug lordlet who spoke no English. I teamed him with a black Brazilian who had both Portuguese and Spanish as well as English. But as soon as the Colombian had enough English to associate with other cons of his colour and station, he abandoned the poor Brazilian, who was simply in on an immigration hold. This is the only instance of racism I can remember.

I never did – at any of the three institutions – find the racial families I had expected.

The Indian trainee from Mount Currie, Oliver, had character – not because he was Indian, but because he was Oliver. He stood straight, short though he was. The constant expression on his face would frighten a charging rhino, so rocky and inscrutable it appeared. Everyone knew not to fuck with Oliver.

On the other hand, Oliver never looked for trouble. He never heavied others. He did his own time. He did his own program of work, school, P.T., hygiene, and month by month was promoted from pre-junior to junior to intermediate to senior and, finally, senior/temporary absence. Oliver had served as assistant team captain and team captain. He had served as senior duty monitor: the trainee chief executive officer. And he had done all this without kissing any ass, without ever being assigned extra-duty hours for screwing up, and certainly without ever being charged under the *Correctional Centre Rules and Regulations* for a major infraction. He was his own man. There were skills to be learned at New Haven and he filled his tool-box. Quiet as he was, he even joined Toastmasters. The experience didn't turn him into Almighty Voice or Daniel Webster, but he held his own and placed in the final standings.

Usually on the way to the hospital I'd take a fairly circuitous route, hitting all the main places where women could be seen. It doesn't very much matter whether they're nurses or office workers or whoever; the kids love to see girls. Never mind the fact that their girlfriends are in every Sunday to visit them and they get off campus frequently. Never mind that we have lots of women on staff and they see them every day. It's the principle of the thing. The trainees like to pretend they're in jail and never see women.

So this time I drove Jones and Oliver through the Metrotown complex and they took note of the gorgeous ladies there, and we drove down Kingsway and saw many a lovely standing at a bus stop. Then we drove into the Vancouver General Hospital area, where there were thousands of nurses wearing tight-fitting uniforms one could almost see through.

I was not very talented at day shift because I never knew when to go to bed; I'd be lucky if I got four hours' sleep before I drove an hour to work. Once I got to the hospital or dental office or wherever, I would try to find a comfortable chair that wouldn't destroy my gimpy back, and nod off.

Not only would I nod off, I'd sit in a position so that when I did nod off, I'd snore. When I fall asleep and snore, it scares the hell out of me and I awaken as though I'm under siege. This always gave the trainees a giggle, and they'd move a little farther away from me, as if they didn't know me. Then I'd set about dozing off again.

At the hospital with Jones and Oliver, I found the chair I was looking for and sat down. And nod off I did. And snore I did. And wake up.

Jones went into hysterics. But Oliver, ever in control of his emotions, his dignity, his pride, managed only a *sourire*. Because he was cool and he was tough.

I dropped my chin to my chest again and had another shot at diving into doze. Before I could, a voice was whispering into my right ear.

Jones (*sotto voce*): "Hey, Mr. Yates, would you mind if we rode the elevators?"

I (normal tone): "The elevators? Your appointments are right here on this floor, right around the corner there. The nurse is coming for you in due time."

Jones: "Yeah, we know where we're supposed to go. We just . . . uh . . . want to ride the elevators, if you don't mind."

I (whispering now): "Why?"

I looked over at the elevators. This part of Vancouver General is heritage-quality. The elevators had the old brass-handled manual doors that you yank open and try not to get your head smacked by while you reach through and grab the handle of the inside hinged web-work door, which must also be opened and closed manually before the contraption will go up or down. When you get in, the damned thing lurches and seems to move an inch an hour.

Finally Jones said, "Well, it's not really for me. It's Oliver."

I whispered back: "Why doesn't Oliver ask?"

"He's embarrassed."

"Why?"

"He's never been on an elevator."

This woke me up instantly. My God, how little we know about the experiences of one another, about backgrounds, about the people we meet and deal with. Mount Currie is located less than one hundred miles from Vancouver, with jet-set Whistler between the two places. Oliver had been in our program for maybe six months. At age twenty-one, he had never been anywhere on this planet where he could ride an elevator.

I said: "By all means, ride the elevators."

The two of them stood with dignity and walked to the elevators – not too fast. Oliver looked at the door system as if it were a contraption of the devil (which indeed it was), but Jones stepped in front of Oliver and handled the doors like a professional elevator operator. Before the doors could damage their manhood, they jumped in.

I didn't time how long they were gone. I was far too amazed to doze again. Then I heard the sound of the elevator door.

The white kid had a smile on his face as though he had just performed a miracle and Oliver was doing his best to be cool. But his eyes were as big as any other kid's on earth who had just had his first roller-coaster ride. This was a complete revelation to him, a kid who had scampered up and down mountains all his life and probably faced down grizzlies, but had never been in an elevator.

Oliver continued to do well in the program and was finally allowed to go out on job search. One day around Christmas I was striding through the Metrotown mall, hell-bent on getting somewhere quickly, when I felt a tug on the tail of my shirt. It was little

Oliver. He had on his street clothes: rugby pants, an AC/DC T-shirt, and a jacket brought in by the Salvation Army. He also wore the biggest grin on his face I have ever seen.

"Man, Mr. Yates, this is really somethin', isn't it? This is really fuckin' somethin'."

The mall was tarted up for the season. It had multiple levels and elevators made of glass and all manner of gauche glitter. Jaded as I was, this was a mall like any other mall to me. And it was a Christmas like any other Christmas – mostly a mess.

I stopped in my tracks and looked around. Remembering the elevators, I saw what to Oliver must have been like Henry James's image of Paris: "a jewel which is at once all surface and all depth." And I put my arm around the kid's shoulder and said, "Goddammit, Oliver, it really is somethin'."

We stood there looking high up at the upper levels and down at the lower levels, where people streamed though their shopping. Oliver added quickly, "I'm on my job search. I just thought I'd take a short-cut through the mall, it's more direct."

"Perfectly reasonable to me. There are some construction sites around here that look like they could use a skookum dude. Might give 'em a try."

"Yeah."

We went our separate ways down the marble hallways. When I looked over my shoulder, I caught Oliver looking back at me.

"Really somethin', man!" I shouted.

"Really somethin'!" he said. And it was.

19

Education at New Haven

———————————— • ————————————

He who opens a school door, closes a prison.
– Victor Hugo

THE KIDS felt involved and proprietary about my new computer-education program because the computers and software were purchased with money from a contract with Canada Post for the refurbishment of their equipment. The boss and I made up a computer shopping-list and then went to the software outlets as a team. As a professional Scot, Burns was determined to get the best deal possible. I did the talking and wheeling and dealing while he stood there and looked directorial and signed whatever needed to be signed, leaving his card with the merchant. We did our best to give the impression that if they gave us a hell of a deal on the software package, the entire British Columbia bureaucracy would stampede through their doors. What a team. We should have been ashamed of some of the deals we pulled off. We weren't. They virtually paid us to take the software out of the stores and load it on the computers: résumé programs, several word-processing programs, grammar checkers, typing tutors, programs to make banners and signs. We loved these forays.

As soon as the computer program was in full swing, instantly the whole place took on a new look. Computer-generated signs were posted everywhere. And we had a new office: that of the computer monitor. Team captains could make signs having to do with team cleanliness, work-crews, and so forth, under his watchful eye and assistance. Many of the kids learned skills through the program that opened up new, legal career-paths for them, earning them terrific incomes. Norman Huntington was the most successful.

Norman and Abbie Matharoo were booked in together as co-accused. Matharoo was a particularly dark and skinny East Indian; Norman Huntington was a particularly light and skinny WASP. Just looking at their teeth, clothing, and skin, you assumed that these were two sidekicks from good families. Then from listening to how well-spoken both were, it was clear that both were as well-educated as you could get by age twenty.

When I looked at their files, I couldn't believe it. These ninnies had been nabbed on robbery thirteen times – mostly Ma and Pa grocery stores – with a pocket knife. On each and every charge, the Crown had to prove theft and assault beyond a reasonable doubt. And if they had been nailed on thirteen, how many more had they gotten away with? Lots.

And why would two well-bred young men go on a robbery spree? Their only explanation was that they were bored and tried it once and got away with it and so kept doing it. I don't think they knew the exact number of robberies they had done in a period of a couple of months. They could have gotten fourteen years on each count. They didn't because they had never hurt anyone. And neither one had any previous record.

Abbot Matharoo was hyper and yappy but remained aloof during the time he was at New Haven. He did just enough vocational work to get by. He had a couple of years of post-secondary work and so was allowed just to read under the supervision of the teacher. Staff didn't pay much attention to him. There wasn't a hell of a lot the program could do for him other than get him in physical shape. He was determined to be above the rest of it all.

I told Matharoo he'd better get his act together or he'd never make parole. He had all his paperwork in on time, but I was sure they would dork him on the first try given the seriousness of the charges. I'll be damned if he didn't go in and fast-mouth his way into parole. We never heard from him again.

Norman Huntington was another story. He was as quiet and composed as Matharoo was loud and jittery. Unlike Matharoo, he jumped into the program and took what he could from it. He had grade 12 and a year of university, but he had never touched a computer before coming to New Haven. I started him out doing simple menu-driven tasks like making signs. It was love at first touch. He was gone on computers. He moved into word processors, databases, spreadsheets, and when he wasn't working on the computers, he was reading about them. Burns and I brought in a computer-assisted design (CAD) program for him. CAD programs are about as tough as computer programs get. He was on top of it in no time, and Burns had Huntington designing, to precise scale, all sorts of buildings, including new shops and changes to existing buildings.

Huntington became computer monitor and held every other office New Haven offered, including senior duty monitor. He was so busy he decided not to go for parole but take two-thirds of sentence and walk out without probation. He was as good a role model as ever came through New Haven. And he was a natural teacher. Whether he was explaining the responsibilities of a duty monitor to a new intermediate or explaining the difference between base and extended RAM, he was patient and clear in his presentation.

Eventually, it was time to go. He had a lovely girlfriend who had a job and had arranged accommodation for the two of them. He was enrolled in Douglas College to take drafting and he had a job lined up as a clerk in an engineering firm.

Norman stayed in close touch. He and his girlfriend would drop by of an evening to see the staff and trainees and sometimes come for dinner. He often telephoned to tell me about the fancy computer equipment and plotters they had at the engineering office. He knew it would make my mouth water. I countered by asking whether he got to play with the toys, knowing he didn't, and I could hear him grinding his teeth over the phone.

One evening shift, on a crazy Tuesday, he called with an impish tone. I was going out of my mind with people running in and out of the office, screaming questions, horseplaying outside the office, and the religious troops were queuing up to ask for keys to the chapel, consultation rooms, whatever.

"Norman, go on, but make it quick, it's Tuesday, man."

"Right, okay. I just have to know how much you make?"

"I dunno. Last time I heard, we were the lowest-paid prison guards in Canada, including Newfoundland. Somewhere between eleven and fifteen bucks an hour. Then there's shift differential. A few more cents per hour on afternoon shift and a few more for graveyard. Some years there's a lot of overtime, some years not. Depends on the call-board. There are a lot of variables."

I was nodding at one kid who had weight-lifting gloves on to give him permission to go to the weight-pit. Shaking my head at another kid who was playing air guitar because he wanted to go up to the chapel and practise. "The Christians are using the chapel. You can, however, go up there and quote John Lennon that the Beatles were bigger than Jesus and come back and report what their reaction was." He shook his head. He wasn't going for it. He trotted back to the lounge to play pool. Back to the phone.

"Yeah, Norman, where were we?"

"How much would you say you make a year? I've been figuring. Around twenty-five thousand."

"Yeah, fine, twenty to twenty-five thousand. Is this research for a class? I thought you were doing drafting, not criminology."

"Just listen. I got a raise."

"That's nice, Norman, you're a good boy. Now, I'm busier than a one-legged man in an ass-kickin' contest, you dingleberry. Get off the phone and let me go completely crazy."

"Mr. Yates, Mr. Yates, listen, I got promoted."

"What?"

"I was doing my clerk stuff and walked through the computer room with all the big drum plotters and consoles. One of the big part-ners in the firm had a CAD program up but was having trouble mak-ing a part he was designing for a big hydraulic piece of equipment pivot on its axis, and then he wanted to zoom it. I was going to shut up and keep about my business but I didn't. I said, 'Excuse me,' and asked if I could help. The guy barely knew I worked there. He asked if I was familiar with the program. I said yeah. He got up and told me to sit down. He told me what he wanted. I did it. Then he gave me the size he wanted me to zoom it. Then he gave me some other co-ordinates and I finished up the drawing for him and sent it off to the plotter."

"You're a good boy, Charlie Brown."

"Uncle Mikey, shut up. I'm just getting to the good part."

"Okay."

"He went in his office and got me the specs on a couple of other projects. They were easy, man. I banged 'em out and dropped them on his desk. And the next part is really unbelievable. He looked at the drawings and then took them and dragged the other partners into the boardroom for a meeting. After a while, they asked me to come in. They told me they were giving me a raise, and promoting me to draftsman and they would pay for all further schooling I might need to stay abreast of computers and CAD programs."

"Hey, congratulations, man. How much did you get in total with those robberies. Five hundred bucks, you said?"

"Yeah, but get this. Not counting benefits, I'm making sixty-five-thousand bucks a year as of today. Lisa and I are going to buy an apartment . . . Mr. Yates, are you there? Not too shabby for a twenty-one-year-old kid, eh?"

"Is this for real?"

"For real. I'm no good at bullshit." This was true. He couldn't even tell a joke without cracking up before the punch-line.

"Well, good on ya, Norman."

"Yeah." The kid was so full of joy he could hardly talk.

"I just want you to know I'll be thinking about this for a long time. Like the rest of my life."

To my everlasting surprise, ping-pong became as useful an educa-tional tool as our shiny new computers were. At most jails, staff supervise programs, but they don't actually join the cons in such

things as sports. At New Haven we played on the floor-hockey and
baseball teams and got involved in pool and ping-pong. After dinner
one night, one of the kids came in and got the ping-pong paddles and
balls. "Why don't you come on out and play a game with me?" he
asked. "I'll really make you look bad."

"Are you the best player on the campus?"

"No, but I'm pretty good."

"I only play the best of the best."

"Carver Zilber is about the best."

"Tell him that if he wants to graduate downward to second-best,
I'll take him on."

I had watched the kids playing ping-pong and hadn't noticed
much talent. They all loved the grand slam that usually went straight
up in the air, smirched the ball, or missed the other side of the table by
a country mile.

I liked the Zilber kid. He was about six-feet-five and had a hell of a
reach. He was Native and had been adopted by whites up in Pember-
ton. I kept insisting that with a name like that, he was Jewish, not
Indian.

"Bullshit, I'm a chug."

"What do you think I am."

"You're a wigwam-burner."

"Wrong, I'm two flavours of wagon-burner plus nigrescence
[African] plus a bunch of Missouri Valley Irish," I declared. He held
his skin by mine to show he was darker. Actually, I was a little darker
because I had been out in the sun. "You see, you were misclassified.
They should have made you do time on a kibbutz in Israel with your
own people."

"Yeah, we could play Jews and Indians."

After I made my ping-pong challenge, Carver appeared at the
door of the bull-pen and gave me the eye with a big grin. "I hear you
think you can play ping-pong," he said.

"I'm the Muhammad Ali of ping-pong, only prettier."

"Give me a break."

"That's what you'll be saying if you play ping-pong with me." In my undergrad years, I had been singles and doubles champion, but I didn't tell him that just then.

"Let's go."

Carver served me a fast ball with lots of overhead spin. I undercut it and lobbed it high back to him, knowing that he would sucker in and slam it with everything he had. I was right. It hit his side of the table before it whacked into the net. I smiled. He wound up with the same serve, with the same result. At the end of his service, it was 5–zip, mine. I gave him two serves with opposite spins and he couldn't return either one.

"I believe that's a skunk, Carver."

"It's a fucking fluke. Change sides."

I could hear the kids who had been watching telling those playing pool and watching television, "Hey, Mr. Yates just skunked Carver."

"Bullshit! That fat old grey-haired fart?"

"Yeah, I was watching."

By the time I had skunked Carver three games in a row, we had the whole dorm gathered around the table watching. He began to get the hang of what I was doing to him, and managed to return a few balls gingerly, but never enough for a rally. He had never seen a real defensive game before. Mostly, they simply played by slamming the ball from one side to the other and whoever could keep it on the table won. But Carver had a dynamite reach and a deadly offensive game that was very narrow in scope. After ten games, we were both drenched with sweat and Carver slammed his paddle down on the table. He hadn't gotten closer than 5–21. "Fuck, I couldn't beat you if I had a federal sentence," he moaned.

I walked over to his side of the table. "Let us look at this rationally. When I was your age, I was really pretty good, and you have great potential. I'm thirty years older than you are. Now, it makes sense that if you just pay attention, you'll learn how to kick my ass, but you have to broaden your game. I'll never give you a game. That would be insulting. You'll have to win any game you get from me."

"I've played a lot of ping-pong, but you do stuff I've never seen before."

"Tomorrow night, we'll play again. In the meantime, take it just a step at a time. First, when you lock onto the ball with your eyes, you zen the ball. Concentrate on it so hard that you almost become the ball. Never mind who's watching the game. Block them out. Get into a trance. Your body will do the rest. And don't blow off energy by screaming and swearing when you lose a point. You fuck up your attention. Next, as you follow the ball with your eyes, pay attention to the contact it makes with my paddle. I've been killing you with undercut. The only thing that will cancel undercut is undercut. You do a mirror-image of what I do and eventually you'll wear me down because you have energy and reflexes on your side."

"I don't know."

"Think it over and we'll see tomorrow night."

Another kid stepped up and said, "Play me, Mr. Yates."

"Can you beat Carver?"

"No."

"When you can beat Carver, I'll play you."

Those ten games launched an interest in ping-pong that no one at New Haven had seen before. The line-up for the table was long. When I came on duty the next night, Carver was waiting for me at the dorm door. "Do I get another shot at you tonight?"

"Yeah, we better play. I'm so damned stiff and creaky from last night, I need the exercise."

"I'll take advantage of that."

"Don't count on it."

"After last night, I won't."

We played another ten games and Carver began to practise what I told him rather than try to win the games. His scores were marginally better than the previous night and I only skunked him once.

"How long do you think it will take? That's twenty games."

"Depends on how much time you put in playing with the others and practising what I said. You have to get to the point that you don't beat your chest when you get a point by fluke. The only ones which really count are the ones you get by skill when your concentration, strength, and co-ordination all come together. And the point of the game must become the hypnotic sound and dance of a great ping-pong rally. It doesn't matter who wins at all, just that it has been a great game. To win is nothing."

Carver chewed on that for a while. Then I had about a week of days off.

In time, Carver began to get the spiritual side of it. Carver would apologize for a flukey point and we complimented one another on great returns. I noticed that when he played others, he carried the same etiquette into his game with them. It caught on. If someone slammed a ball wildly into the wall in anger, five or six trainees would tell him he was a horse's ass.

Game by game, Carver's scores crept up. Then he would get as much as a five-point lead or more and I would advance on the table and change the game completely by shortening it to a fast no-spin game and the lead would disappear. One card at a time, I showed him my whole hand.

Hot weather came and we took the table outside and played in the sun. The director and the probation officer would sometimes watch with other trainees as Carver got closer and closer. Eighty games came and went before we were finally getting to deuce scores. On the eighty-first game, we must have gone seven or eight adds into deuce when Carver won with a dramatic slam that I got my paddle on but dropped just short of the net.

We were both bagged. I went around the table and shook his hand. "You see? Didn't I tell you it would happen?"

He nodded. Out of breath. "Yeah, but like you said also, it's no big deal. You were right."

From that point on, we played fantastic high-level ping-pong. We would trade games one night, and the next night one of us would be slightly off and the other would take the best six or seven out of ten.

And all the time that I was playing Carver, he was bringing along the talents of other trainees. By the time he was released, he had brought along a kid named Bartlett to the point where we were all three playing at about the same level. When I brought in expensive five-ply paddles from home, we played only with those. And I never backed away from playing only the best of the players.

Recreational ping-pong reached far more trainees than the

computer-education program did, and had more far-reaching implications for their lives. In the end, these kids had learned a lot about
skill-development, and about winning strategies that they could
apply to any aspect of their lives and any goals they chose to reach for.
They learned, often for the first time, that with correct application,
rather than physical force, they could achieve just about anything
they wanted.

20

Hoods in the Woods

———————— • ————————

The most beautiful experience we can have is the
mysterious. It is the fundamental emotion which
stands at the cradle of true art and true science.
– Albert Einstein

IN THE good old days the staff at New Haven were paid to take the
trainees climbing, boating, and on various other activities. But by
the time I arrived, money for such things was no longer available.
There was a time when members of the Borstal Society volunteers,
getting a bit long in the tooth now, volunteered to take the kids here
and there, but in my time the most active volunteer was Bill Boxleitner. On his own time he organized such things as outings to
hockey games for up-country kids who would likely never have an
opportunity to get to a pro hockey game. By and by it dawned on me,
while talking to one of my shift partners who was a climber and had
been there for twenty years and remembered the good old days, that
there had to be a way to get a hiking program together. But he wasn't
going to do anything on his own time, not after having worked there
during the better days of being paid to do it.

I worked up support among staff for the nifty new idea I had of a
hiking program. I bounced it off Bill Boxleitner before taking a run at
the director. I even went so far as to choose the first hike: Wedgemont,
a local glacier north of Whistler Village, near Mounts Wedge and
Rethel. I collected a bunch of text and maps about the place and, with
materials in hand, I charged in to have a go at Andrew Burns. It would

mean taking only those who were senior/temporary absence because I would have to be doing this on my time and they would have to be on leave, an important technicality. Otherwise I'd have to be paid, and there was no budget for such stuff. And it would have been over-time to boot.

"I like it," Burns said. "And I think Luke Burton will like it. I'll take this material and present it to Luke and see where we go from here." Burton was our district director and New Haven was the pride of his kingdom.

The hike I had selected was high – up to about nine thousand feet, to the very toe of the glacier, so we had to wait until the snow was off the trail. That meant late July or early August. That allowed plenty of lead time to put together equipment, select the trainees, and get everything approved.

It was the beginning of a wild odyssey of paperwork. Burton's first response was that the project was creative and we should start prepa-rations while he chased clearance from Victoria. As soon as I men-tioned it to the other staff – especially Boxleitner, Meg Trumble from the Borstal Society, and Bob O'Callum, who had recently transferred in from the Oakalla hospital – and the trainees, there was all-around enthusiasm. The trainees began to calculate who was likely to gradu-ate to senior/T.A. by the time of the hike, which was targeted for early August. We had a couple of months. When Dave Sorensen, the P.O. who had been there for almost thirty years, heard of the hiking idea, he was sure that there were some old wooden-frame back-packs gath-ering dust somewhere on the campus. Eventually we found a pile of parts of packs high up on the third floor in a room off the museum and personal-effects rooms. The trainees and I began to work on them and we wound up with five complete packs.

In the beginning, it was expected that the mandarins of correc-tions policy in Victoria would check their manuals of standards and operations and appropriate legislation and come back with a simple go or no. The idea had been pronounced "creative" by the district director. From a bureaucratic point of view, it was sound because it required no money to speak of. The kitchen would provide food, which it would have to do in any case. If we had one restaurant meal on the way back from the hike, it would be at the expense of the trainee participants, who would withdraw ten or fifteen bucks from their accounts as they would with any temporary absence. It was close enough – just above Whistler – that we could do the hike as a day-hike. We would travel in an institution vehicle, thus covering everyone on government insurance. And, since I would be doing it on my own time, it would not involve staff costs, nor set a dangerous budgetary precedent.

There were clear regulations for juvenile programs like Outward Bound, with guidelines for qualifications of staff, and so forth. Likewise for simple outings like bike rides through Stanley Park. But Victoria went nuts because what I proposed had attributes of Outward Bound activities and attributes of other outings, but the proposal was neither, and I hadn't all the formal certificates required for Outward Bound instruction.

Numerous questions came back through Burton and Burns. How many hours would be required? Did I have a certificate in survival first aid? It began to look as if it wasn't going to go. The probation officer, John George, was one of those people who is a wind-sock; he guessed the direction of the power and jumped on the bandwagon. And his attitude was rapidly changing from enthusiastic to I-don't-think-it-will-happen. He had mysteriously begun to hear the wrong kinds of noises and started to pour cold water on the project. Burns said we should continue to plan until a final decision came in from Victoria.

Unfortunately, Burns was going to be away on holidays at the time of the hike. Then Burns was gone, the time was nearing, and there was still no decision, only more questions from Burton, who came in once a day to sign releases and do other paperwork of Burns's, and John George, who had assumed other of Burns's duties.

Were there any plans to climb in any areas where there was no clearly marked trail? No. This was a provincially designated and maintained trail which was well described and mapped and photographed, in documents that each of us would have. Did I have a topographical map? Yes. Compass? Yes. Altimeter? Yes. First aid kit? Burns had gotten a fancy fanny-pack first-aid kit before he left.

Silence. Frowns from John George. Finally, one day I came in on
shift and George intoned, "Mr. Burton has some serious questions
about your proposed hike."

"Where is he?"

"At the district office."

"You have the number?"

"You're going to call him at district office?"

"If you give me the number." I jumped on the phone and asked
Luke Burton how it looked.

"They haven't said a final yes."

"How would you call it?"

"Continue with your preparations. Just one last question. Have
you hiked this trail yourself?"

"No, I specifically chose a trail I hadn't hiked so that my level of
anticipation and adventure would be consonant with that of the
trainees. I think this an important element. I have checked with the
Federation of Mountain Clubs of B.C. to make sure that all bridges
and parts of the trail are passable. No rock-slides or wash-outs."

"Right, sounds good to me. I agree with your sense of spirit of the
thing. I'll have something definite for you no later than tomorrow."

When I got down to the dorm, I found the five eligible trainees
standing around the door looking down in the mouth. They said that
George had told them the hike was pretty well off.

"I'll tell you when the hike is off. I've been fighting this paper war
for all this time and I just spoke to District Director Burton, and he's
in our corner. He said to continue preparing. Give me the checklist
and a report on what things we still need." They brightened up and I
later ripped a strip off George and told him to keep his mouth shut. I
was dealing with Burton directly.

One kid was just getting over mild pneumonia and had to be
checked by the doc. Another was a physically lazy sort and I was surprised that he wanted to go along. Victoria had decided that one
supervisor to five trainees maximum was the acceptable ratio, and we
thought that was reasonable. I had tried to find another staff-member
who was free to go, but it wasn't to be. Those who would be willing to

go had shifts the day of the hike. For later hikes I would find both staff
and civilian volunteers.

The next day, Luke Burton drove over personally to tell me it was a
go – with a look in his eye that told me Victoria had been diffident
and would be looking at the results of this hike very closely.

The sick kid wasn't allowed to go and the lazy one bailed out. The
three remaining had been pumping weights and running the track for
a couple of months. I spent the next day with them going over the
equipment. They had organized everything. Davey was foreman of
the metal-shop and had gone over the Suburban from bumper to
bumper. Rafferty had co-ordinated the food with the kitchen. And
Anatoly had laid out all the equipment in the dispensary. We would
be up at about 0330 and leave the campus at around five. That would
put us at the trailhead easily by daylight.

There were a few final decisions about clothing and other inciden-
tals. Anatoly and Rafferty had been home and brought back their
expensive cameras because I promised to bring a tripod and cable and
give them some pointers. In a previous incarnation I had made a living as a photographer and was packing my two ancient Nikons.

They didn't have hiking-boots, but they had agreed to wear two
pairs of socks (the outside pair wool), per good mountaineering protocol, and we were all going to wear moleskin patches on our feet's
"hot spots." Mountaineers look to their feet above all.

Anatoly decided he would wear runners instead of boots. The four
of us had a huddle about this. Said I: "Now, when we leave here
tomorrow, aside from the joint vehicle and food, you guys are really
on your own. You're on T.A. and I'm on a day off. Technically, we're
just four guys going on a day's expedition. What you wear and what
you do is up to you. We have no idea what we're going to encounter in
the terrain. The work-boots you guys decided to wear have shanks
and steel toes. Probably better protection than my boots. If you were
leading the rest of us on a pilot project that might have important
implications for all outings to come, what would you advise the
trainees?"

"Boots. I hate 'em, but I'll wear 'em," said Anatoly.

Thus we reasoned together about all details. They hit their beds early, fearing they might be not be able to sleep for their excitement, and I headed up the hill to my apartment, scarcely believing that the whole thing had finally come together. I spent the next several hours pacing up and down from bed to TV set worrying about what would go wrong, what we had forgotten.

The kitchen crew got up early and threw something together for breakfast for us. They had the packs loaded. We stowed them in the Suburban and hit the road.

I had brought along a portable recorder so that each of us could record his impressions on the trail and later write an article for the New Haven paper. Tape-recorders were contraband at New Haven. I had also brought a handful of rock-and-roll tapes we could sing along with. They kept switching tapes and describing the view of the Squamish highway on tape. In Squamish we stopped for a quick fix of junk food, then rolled on northward, past Whistler Village (where we planned to have some hot food and check out the jet-set young ladies after we came off the mountain), and coaxed the old Suburban farther and farther up the log road. The clearance of the vehicle was good, but it didn't have four-wheel drive, so we pulled off finally and donned packs and boots.

The dawn sky looked indecisive. It wasn't supposed to rain, but when you get above five thousand feet, you enter white-out country. Cloud can drop on you in a matter of a couple of seconds, the fog so thick you can't see your feet.

The trail was steep and rough and surprisingly varied. I always hike with a ski-pole and had brought one along for each of them. I thought it would be a war to get them to use them as walking-sticks, but they tacitly agreed to humour me. I might just know something they didn't. After a couple of hours on the trail, it turned into root city. When you step on a wet root, your foot slides suddenly sideward, and it can be quite treacherous unless you have something to steady yourself. After about an hour over the roots, we hit an old rock-slide. I slipped and banged my camera against a rock and jammed the lens-cap. It wouldn't come off. Davey was the mechanic and Anatoly the electronic whiz. Between them, they finally unjammed it so that I could use the wide angle.

When we got to about seven thousand feet, we were walking through wisps of white-out and the sky was not visible. This gave me some pause, but we kept going because it didn't seriously affect visibility of the trail.

On the lower parts of the trail, I had hit a pace and wouldn't budge from it. The kids whimpered and complained that it was much too slow. I had been hiking a good deal that summer and was in good shape. I tried to explain to them that all exercise is training-specific, and while their running and weight-lifting didn't hinder them, they still hadn't been walking trails. Rafferty and Anatoly insisted on charging ahead. We agreed on a buddy system. You keep your partner on visual, and they all had to stay within earshot. They flew ahead and then waited for Davey and me to catch up and razzed us. I insisted that they drink more water than they wanted and lectured about water and hypothermia and heat prostration. By the time we were on the final approach to the lip of the lake and sight of the glacier, they were listening to every suggestion I made. And there was no more razzing. We were far above tree-line and the approach was a lichen-covered scree slope. Good place to rest and have a drink and a bite to eat. Scree meant big steps up from boulder to boulder, and everything was wet from the fog condensation.

We had heard a Swiss couple coming up behind us comparing our Coast Mountains to the Alps and deciding that the Alps were much superior. You could hear voices clear as a bell half a mile behind. The kids kept asking me what the Swiss were saying and I had been translating. The kids were honked off by the foreigners who didn't show proper respect for this grandeur. I told them to hang on and let them pass and just watch me. When they came by, the Swiss couple switched to English, "Hello. We're from Switzerland, visiting."

"*Ja, ich weiss. Schöne Landschaft, nicht?*" I replied.

They were visibly embarrassed. The kids loved it. "What'd you say, Mr. Yates?"

"I said 'Yes, I know. Nice landscape, eh?'"

"Right on. Do all the tourist assholes think that nobody in this country speaks anything but English?"

"Seemingly . . . Probably part of the Ugly American syndrome."

The redeeming aspect of the scree slope was the wildlife. When the first marmot whistled, Rafferty thought one of us was a ventriloquist. I pointed out the varmint and it was telephoto time. Then I saw a rock rabbit, a pica. And then there were picas and marmots all over the place and we were all burning film like crazy. Anatoly decided he would make slow advance on a marmot. The whistling sound they make is what the village of Whistler is named after. Some of them are as big as badgers and wolverines. We stood quietly while Anatoly stalked one marmot with his Nikon. I couldn't believe how close he got. On two or three shots with a normal lens he filled the frame. It took him half an hour to get that close. By that time, it was final-ascent time. Rafferty and Anatoly scrambled for the top almost in a dead heat, but Anatoly was the more nimble and he vanished over the top first. Rafferty popped over a couple of minutes later.

Davey was glad enough to hang back and proceed at my pace. He was the skinniest of the bunch, but also the heaviest smoker. Good kid. He was in jail as a victim of his own metabolism. The doctor had given him some medication and he had no way of knowing it wouldn't mix with the beers given him by his fiancée's father. Before he came down, he had stolen a police car and there had been a high-speed chase with bullets flying all over hell. He was lucky to find himself alive and in jail in Dawson Creek. Davey had no prior record of any kind, unlike Rafferty, who had the distinction of breaking and entering the home of a famous Canadian movie star for booze and finding all sorts of amazing and unexpected items, and Anatoly, who also had a long juvie record before entering the adult system. I'll always remember Davey saying to me with a big grin as we started up the last hundred yards of near vertical scree, "Guess we've pretty well got her beat now, eh, Mr. Yates?"

"Roughly twenty-five per cent, I'd say," I said traversing my way up.

"I mean we're almost there."

"Yup." I stopped and looked at him puffing up behind me with a disbelieving look on his face. Then I looked up at the hovering white-out and hoped we'd get a good look at the glacier before it hit us.

We were now exposed to the wind that was whipping around the col. When we were perhaps half-way up I heard a noise and looked up. There was Rafferty's upper body and head looking over the edge shouting something urgently, but I couldn't make out a goddamn word. Then he was beckoning us up furiously. What raced through my head as we sped recklessly up was every possible disaster. I thought perhaps I had misread the topographic map. It was supposed to flatten out at lake level on top. In my mind's eye, I saw Anatoly hit the top and instantly drop off a cliff . . . and Rafferty had stopped just short . . . The closer we got to Rafferty the harder the wind blew in our ears. Then we fired over the top. And there was the turquoise lake from which the stream we had crossed and followed all day flowed. And the refuge hut and even an outhouse. And, in the distance, the Swiss couple heading back toward us. I was standing beside Rafferty who was pointing at the lake and glacier (Anatoly was booting down the trail toward the Swiss). "Ah, fuck, Mr. Yates, isn't that the best, the most beautiful fucking glacier in the whole fucking world . . ." He was jumping up and down and slapping his thigh, sweat rolling down his forehead from his hairline and into his eyes.

"Do you mean to tell me that you almost gave Davey and me heart attacks just to get us up here, where we were coming anyway, to see your glacier?"

"Well, isn't it the most beautiful glacier?"

"You said you've seen a glacier before."

"Pictures."

"Yeah, a great looking piece of ice." We started toward it. Anatoly was booting toward a trail along the left side of the lake toward the toe. I cupped my hands and whistled as hard as I could. He turned around. "Stay away from that trail to the ice. Wait for us." He stopped near the hut and waited. The Swiss nodded as they beetled back toward the ridge. We caught up with Anatoly. When we caught up, I unslung my pack and reminded them, "What did we tell Burton about the flight plan? We said no technical climb. Glacier climbing requires crampons, different boots, ice-axes, and jumars. We eyeball the glacier. We don't step foot on it."

"Aw . . . just at the edge?"

"Nope, I did that once on Helm, but at least I had an ice-axe. It was foolhardy. I slipped once, but I arrested with the axe. I was lucky to get off with my old ass still alive.

"We just shoot pictures this time. If this hike goes well, maybe we can get a guide to rope us up and take us across a glacier on some later trip." They all dumped their packs. And we began to dig into the huge lunches that Stan Watson, the kitchen program instructor, had prepared for us: sandwiches, all kinds of fruit, even macaroni salad in plastic containers held together with strong rubber bands. We had been packing a hell of a lot of weight. Stan must have given us ten pounds of food each.

We ate and relaxed and rested and shot pictures. But before we could finish lunch, the white-out dropped on us.

"What now, Mr. Yates?"

"Let's go have a look at the cabin." It was a tin chalet. Rugged as hell. Enough floor space for ten or twelve people to sleep on the combined footage of the loft and main floor. We could get through the night here if the white-out didn't lift. But when we looked out the door, it was already lifting, and we heard voices in the distance. We looked around the cabin. A couple of very athletic and very gay hikers were headed toward us. These kids were not very enthusiastic about homo folks. They were already looking at one another.

The two were very pleasant, but much preoccupied with one another and getting their gear inside in the loft. They were definitely staying for the night.

We went back outside and continued with lunch. The white-out returned and was fogging up my glasses. I could just imagine a night in the refuge cabin with the cons and the couple. I could hear Rafferty saying to Davey, "I didn't know gearboxes climbed mountains." I could see the headline: OLD POET-GUARD DIES REFEREEING FIGHT BETWEEN CONVICTS AND GAYS AT 9000 FEET. They were all about the same age, early twenties.

The white-out got thicker and the kids had that "What now?"

look. I had told them that white-outs can last a few minutes or keep you on a mountain for a couple of days. I sure as hell didn't highlight the possibility of white-out when putting together the proposal for Victoria. We would be fine for the night in any case.

Then the white-out blew off as quickly as it had dropped. It still hovered overhead. I cleaned my glasses and suggested we all fill our water-bottles in the lake. Because of the fog we couldn't see the very tops of the spectacular spires of volcanic rock around the lake, nor could we see the very top of the glacier, but we still got some superb photographs.

The gays had vanished into the refuge cabin and were arranging the loft to their liking. In it was a log-book for visitors. We had all entered our names and the date. Anatoly had stayed in for several minutes. We got on his case about what he was doing.

"Writing a note to my girlfriend telling her how I really feel."

"Is she going to helicopter in to check it out?" Rafferty asked, and we needled him to hurry up. The white-out was looking nasty again. I was making odds on whether we could make it the couple of hundred yards to the ridge before it dropped.

Just about that time, two cowboys from Alberta popped up at the rim and started down the trail. They made it before the white-out dropped again. They had huge back-packs with sleeping bags and inflatable mats and were climbing in western shirts and blue jeans. They, too, were going to overnight. They hadn't climbed in cowboy-boots, but they were cowboy and redneck from head to toe otherwise. They put down their packs and "howdyed" the hell out of us, and Anatoly was laughing so hard he had to walk down to the edge of the lake near the glacier. Then he called us. We were all choking back laughter and jumped at the opportunity to get away from the Albertans who hadn't yet discovered the surprise in the cabin.

Mercifully, the white-out lifted again and we could see the rim. I suggested we grab our packs and go for the gusto. We hit the trail just as the cowboys were gathering up their gear to go in the cabin. We hot-footed it to the rim and started down the steep scree. Skeins of white-out were hanging here and there. By the time we got by the big rock-slide, I figured we were in the clear.

Back down on the protected trail, it was windless.

Our conversation rocketed from one topic to another. Anatoly had the idea that he could take a nine-volt battery and get massive voltage from it and then return the voltage to the battery, which would recharge it. It would be a limitless source of energy.

"Anatoly, do you know what you'd have if you made it work?"

"Perpetual-motion machine," Rafferty jumped in.

"Right."

We were back down on the rooty part of the trail. I was just ahead of Rafferty, who was bringing up the rear. I stepped on a root and invented several new balletic airborne routines before finally landing squarely on the expensive fanny-pack first-aid kit. Instantly the kids were warning me to watch it. "You got us in here; now you have to get us out." We had already made a plan that if something happened to me, one would stay with me and the other two would take the keys and go for help.

The condensation of the white-out was falling in huge drops from the boughs of the trees. Davey went down, then went down again while getting up. Anatoly was in the lead; he went for a skate and then fell.

Never have I lectured on as many subjects as I did that day. Rafferty had a million questions about photochemistry and journalism. Davey wanted to know why if he stopped smoking, he would have better wind. Anatoly's mind was always whirling. He was writing a novel longer than *War and Peace* that we were serializing in the newspaper. They wanted to know about the lichens hanging from the trees, and that led to my childhood and the Spanish moss hanging from the cypress in the swamps in South Carolina, and that led to Tony Joe White, which led to a general discussion of music ranging from Metallica to Bach. I had to keep sending down the bucket into the well of memory to remember the name of every alpine flower we encountered: Indian paintbrush, foxglove, cow parsley, pearly everlasting. It was endless and exhilarating and the talk helped because Davey and the others were beginning to see what I meant about climbing up being only twenty-five per cent of the hike. They were leaning on their ski-poles heavily and trying to lower themselves down step by step without bending an ankle. Then they began to complain out loud and asked why I wasn't complaining.

"I'm tired and sore too, but I do this all the time. Rafferty, what happens every time you bump up another ten pounds on the bench-press and try to break through a plateau?"

"I'm a little sore the next day."

"But not sore enough to make you give up pumping iron?"

"Naw."

"Remember that tomorrow."

The last couple of miles on the trail were hilarious. It was getting pretty dark. The three of them would beetle ahead of me and out of sight. I'd come down the trail and they'd be lying on their backs, resting on their packs. I'd walk past them and they would jump up, charge on ahead, and then lie down again.

It was a short drive from the trailhead to Whistler, no more than five miles. Anatoly and Davey were dead asleep when we arrived for the hot meal.

We had been fourteen hours on the mountain. I called the joint to let afternoon shift know we were okay and headed home. Davey and Anatoly couldn't get out to eat. Rafferty and I found a pizza place and got a big one and some pop. They were bagged.

By the time we got back to New Haven, they were all asleep. We had been a total of twenty-two hours away from the campus. They dragged their asses to their bunks in the dorm and slept with their clothes on, leaving me to unload the gear and stow it back in the dispensary. Then I drove up the hill to bed myself.

Anatoly stayed in bed for a day and a half. Davey booked off work for half a day. Rafferty went to work, but when I came down in the afternoon he hobbled over to me.

"Damn, Mr. Yates, aren't you sore?"

"Yes, but not as sore as you are. You did things with your muscles and ligaments yesterday that you don't customarily do. You just have to get some blood to the places you exercised. Go up to the main building and go up the stairs two at a time and come down the stairs two at a time. Do that twenty or thirty times and tell me how you feel."

This was a revelation. He felt a lot better after he'd tried the stairs and trotted off to persuade Davey and Anatoly they should do the same.

When all the film was developed, we had a magnificent album for New Haven, which Burns sprung for, as well as duplicate prints. There were many other hikes with plenty of adventures and silliness and great memories, but none was as memorable as the day Uncle Mikey's Hoods in the Woods was born. I still write to two of the three kids who were with me that day, and see them from time to time.

21

Tales of
Coitus Interruptus

•

The impromptu forms of sex in prison are to the accepted sexual forms what guerilla warfare is to formal warfare.
– Commissioner Horst Schmidt

IN THE summer, the farm crew needed extra manpower. They used numerous trainees, cottagers, and, later, even the intermittent inmates. Farm-crew duties included all grounds-keeping, as well as care of the livestock, planting and harvesting, care of the greenhouse, and the running of all kinds of back-hoes, Cats, tractors, and tractor-related equipment.

Working on the farm crew successfully for a long period conferred status on an inmate. It meant that he could be trusted to work without close supervision. The instructor couldn't be everywhere at once with sixty-eight acres to supervise. The trainee could be off by himself with his shirt off, enjoying the sun, and he could also be the designated mule to pick up a drug-drop or a bottle of booze and stash it for the crew who came out after dark to lock up and check on sick animals or the feed supply.

If the farm instructor had any special instructions, he would leave them with afternoon-shift staff to pass on to the foreman or to oversee themselves. There were certain areas that were out of bounds for trainees in general, unless by special permission, and other areas that were out of bounds on visits days.

One crazy Tuesday, when the self-help support groups and

religious types inundated the place, we had the usual groups in during the evening, with traffic heading in every direction. In the middle of it all, around 2030 hours, the two farmers designated by their foreman to do evening check came in to get the clipboard and form and keys.

They waited to do so until the bull-pen was filled with people jumping around and asking questions, and the kitchen crew was attempting to set up coffee and cookies. I was a bit amazed that these two nitwits had made it to the farm crew. Both had been walking on the edge of disaster since they entered the program. Each of the two, Jantzen and Hardy, had received "hours" (extra duties) and been confined to rack (his bed area in his team) for being out of bounds (in another team or any place designated out of bounds), but had done nothing to get them into serious trouble.

There was something about their manner that started the stopwatch in my head. It usually took about twenty minutes to do the farm-check rounds, unless an animal had to be medicated (which might add ten minutes). Intermittently over the next hour, while finding temporary-absence and parole applications, helping to fill them out, dashing next door to bail one of the kids out of a computer problem, and stepping to the door of the lounge to threaten the herd with mayhem if they didn't turn down MuchMusic, there was something nagging at my consciousness. Finally, I looked up to my right to see if the farm-check clipboard was back. Nope.

I called the duty monitor in to see if Jantzen and Hardy had reported back to him. Nope. I called in the farm foreman to see if he had seen them. Nope. And he offered to dash out to the farm to check on them. I thanked him anyway and said I would handle it.

I told Mike Schwarz, my partner, that I was taking a walk to do a little farming in the dark. I grabbed a flashlight and both radios and handed one to Mike. Just outside the door, I did a radio-check and started by looking around the main building, sticking to the shadows. Then I passed the pond and entered the farm area.

The big barn door was wide open and all the lights were on. I stuck my head inside. Nothing. No noise. Without turning on the flashlight, I passed the chicken shed and pig shed. It was a bright moonlit night. There was a little glassed-in alcove at the end of the connected buildings. I eased up to the window and looked in.

Suddenly I was looking at the back of the head of Hardy. Then I looked down. A young woman was on her knees in front of him applying oral relief. She looked up and saw my outline. Coitus inter-ruptus. Hardy looked down and saw her looking up. He turned around and saw me and burst into tears. She, on the other hand, got up and composed herself very nonchalantly. As I stepped around the corner to the door, I hit the radio: "Portable One to Portable Two, I need you out here on the double."

"Roger." Mike Schwarz was athletic as hell and could run like a deer.

I walked into the barn and addressed the interloper, "You're under arrest, young lady. Both of you come with me."

I yelled for Jantzen to come out. Not a sound. Then, as Schwarz flew around the farm gate, Jantzen came out of the barn door. Schwarz asked him what he was doing in there. He bumbled and stumbled around. Mike had good instincts. He told Jantzen to come over and stand with Hardy and the girl. I'd take the three of them back to the main building, while Schwarz looked around some more. I walked them down to the P.O.'s office. The P.O. had been listening to all the action on his radio.

I had the two cons and the girl up in his office and we had been there for about ten minutes when Schwarz showed up with a tall girl who was still pulling bits of hay from her sweater. Schwarz headed up into the loft for a look. There was a lot of hay up there, but he was sure there was someone under there somewhere. He finally had to pick up a pitchfork and threaten to jab it into every square inch of hay in the loft to get her to come burrowing out.

Schwarz took the boys into the P.O. while I questioned the girls. As she emptied her purse, one girl sheepishly withdrew a condom. I told her that in spite of the various illegal things that she and her friend had done that night, the carrying of the condom showed that her sex education hadn't been entirely wasted, and praised her for it. Both girls were under-age, one from a group-home and the other living at home.

Hardy continued to boo-hoo throughout the proceedings to the complete disgust of staff and the other three culprits. Then the girls were taken home by the horsemen who, like the rest of us, could hardly maintain an official mien in view of a situation wherein two young women would break into prison for an assignation with two idiots who presumed they could be missing from the count indefinitely without being missed.

Tweedle-dumb and Tweedle-dumber were charged, internal court was held, and they were transported over the hill to the Oakie segregation unit (after stops at records and the hospital). On the way over, I told them to write to the director and apologize and ask that their sentence be shortened. After about three days, he sprang them early, and they returned to be razzed by the other trainees for lousy planning. Both were fired from the farm crew. Come board day, neither was promoted, and they lost remission time. As far as anyone knows, neither attempted to import female company again. Like everyone else, they waited until they reached senior/temporary absence, at which time they could go home and screw themselves cross-eyed, and come back bow-legged.

Because contact visits occurred weekly at New Haven and security was minimal, it was not unusual for trainees to attempt conjugal visits in unlikely circumstances. One graduate came back for a visit to his alma mater with his wife and his teenage son, in order to show the boy where he was conceived: behind the New Haven gymnasium, an area definitely out of bounds. It was probably the quickest place to get to when kissing and groping got out of hand. It was a blind spot to any of the administrative areas.

We tried to make all visits pleasant and thus didn't intrude with guardly presence too obviously. We would amble from picnic table to picnic table outside on visits day, meeting parents and uncles and babies, and eventually work our way around to the back of the gym to take a quick peek.

We had a tiny Moslem East Indian with us for a while. Allah must have had a serious grudge against this dude. He was as round as he was tall. He couldn't get anything right. If a trainee said boo to him, he would burst into tears and materialize in the bull-pen to tattle and whimper. We would have to settle him down and tell him that in jail you don't come to staff with everybody watching and fink on people, because this gets you labelled and you wind up with knots on your head faster than you can rub them; then we'd talk to the team captain and get him to lean on the team not to crowd the guy. The East Indian was too fat to play sports. He was a hypochondriac and asthmatic, and so lazy he was fired from one work-crew after the other.

His wife came in on a visit one day wearing traditional dress, with trousers and a shirt cut at the sides. She must have been eight months pregnant, and he looked pregnant, too. He was wearing rugby pants with an elastic waist and no fly. Later the P.O. just happened to go for a stroll around the back of the gym where he found this ninny attempting the near-impossible with his wife. Given their morphologies, it would have taken a week and required assistance. But it did give us the final ammo to ship him to the Oakie hospital to do the rest of his time. It was protective custody for the lame of brain and limb.

Rob Richie was tall, skinny, bright, but generally nondescript. He had been involved up-country in drug trafficking on a small scale and had had a few scrapes with the law. In a small town, it is difficult to get away with something like dealing dope indefinitely. Then came one scrape too many involving more dope than the RCMP and the local judge could live with, and he got solidly busted. He cooled his heels in Kamloops for about a month until we had a bunk for him, and then he was New Haven-bound.

The kid was quiet and easy to get along with, but he was one of those who ranges from the middle ground to the background of the human landscape. He did all right as a pre-junior, except that he was first posted to the kitchen crew. He didn't take well to working in a confined space. So he was moved to the farm crew where his work reports improved almost immediately. He flourished on the farm crew. He moved up through the ranks in the general program and moved up from farmer to assistant farm foreman to farm foreman.

In time, his parents came down from the Peace River country for a visit and brought along his fiancée. They came in the middle of the week and a special visit had to be arranged. It was the policy of the institution to maximize contact with the community. Some of the trainees had relatives who worked on Sundays and had to visit in the middle of the week. Unless the policy was abused, New Haven was always flexible enough to accommodate.

His parents were very pleasant blue-collar people who were distressed that their son was in the pokey, but glad to see that he was part of a program like New Haven. He took the three of them on the grand tour, lingering long at the various farm projects.

Rob never seemed to prefer one project to another. He was as happy to run the machinery as he was to work in the chicken-house, handle the cattle, or tend the pigs. He was foreman during the time that we had the great chicken debate. One of the farm crew had seen a program on free-range chickens and other animals versus those kept in enclosures for the duration of their lives. The whole campus chose sides and the debate was on. New Haven sells eggs and the money goes into the Inmate Welfare Fund. If they couldn't find the eggs, they couldn't sell them. In the end, the farmers and instructor decided on a compromise measure: to allow some of the chickens to range while the rest remained in the coop.

Rob never made senior duty monitor because he simply hadn't the presence for it, but he did make assistant team captain and team captain of Stanton team, as well as farm foreman. When he reached senior/T.A., he went up-country for Christmas and New Year. However, in temporary absences to come, he went to the Dick Bell Irving halfway-house and spent his time getting to know Vancouver. He wrote to his girlfriend often, but never seemed to miss female company. Several of the kids from Vancouver offered to fix him up with dates, but he declined.

He decided he liked Vancouver. On job-search T.A., he found a job with a commercial flower outfit not far from New Haven. They liked him and sent back good reports. And the job had opportunities for promotion.

So he built his parole plan around the job, enrolling in the B.C.

Institute of Technology to upgrade his business knowledge. He had an uncle in Burnaby who would underwrite his efforts. When he stepped into his parole hearing, he had crossed every *t* and dotted every *i* of the elements they were looking for. His folks came down, his fiancée came down, his local uncle was present, he had a line on an apartment and could stay with his uncle until he could move in, and he had names of counsellors and registrars to whom he had talked at B.C.I.T. In short, he blew them away with his presentation and won parole on his first roll of the dice.

And Rob Richie was out the door. He stayed in touch by phone and he kept in touch with one or two of the local kids who dropped back to visit from time to time and called to catch up on New Haven gossip. He obtained permission from the director to come back to New Haven to attend Narcotics Anonymous meetings. The job was going well. The fiancée had moved in with him and found employment. Everything was going his way.

One afternoon shift, my partner was Mort Vedder, who was an auxiliary, a teacher in North Vancouver who was running for alderman for the fourth time. The kids and I had been whacking away on the computer designing a questionnaire for his campaign for most of the shift. It had been good practice for them. And fun for us all. But my ass had turned to stone and my neck and shoulders were stiff and numb. I needed a walk. It was about 2200 and the graveyard shift would be there in another half-hour. I strolled out toward the farm, which had been locked down by the new foreman and his crew a couple of hours earlier. It was a warm summer night and it smelled great. But as I passed the pond, the "hint of pig," to use Lawrence Durrell's phrase, was stronger than usual. I paused at the pond and leaned on the fence looking at the pattern of moonlight upon the water, filtered through the weeping willows. It had been a very satisfying shift. I reflected on the big return we got on any effort invested in the program at New Haven.

I would have turned back at the gate to the farm, but I noticed that the light was on in the pig barn. I could tell because the door, which should have been locked, appeared to be slightly ajar.

If someone were going to break into the barns, this would be the perfect hour, between the time of the farm-crew lock-up and the first patrol of graveyard. We had had equipment stolen before. Most recently, a number of air-compression tools from the wood-shop had been lifted.

I tiptoed up to the door. The lock had not been japped. It had been unlocked. The key was still in the lock. I quietly pulled the key out and slipped it into my pocket. Whoever was in there wasn't going anywhere. I was blocking the door.

I eased the door open and looked in. The six or eight pigs picked up on my presence and began to squoink and snort but they were used to humans and didn't kick up much of a fuss. The door was at one corner of the enclosure. As I peered through the dim light toward the opposite corner, I discerned a human form with its back to me. It had a shirt on, the shirt-tail out, and the jeans were bagged in the back and at the knees as though the belt had been loosened and the fly opened. The legs were slightly bowed to keep the pants from dropping to his ankles.

I thought I could determine some backward and forward movement and thought maybe it was one of our trainees who had imported his girlfriend and was getting it on standing up in the pig barn, of all places.

During my prison career, when I have surprised someone doing something he shouldn't in a place which was off limits, I had a terrible habit of yelling "Hey!" at about a hundred and fifty decibels. It not only scares the hell out of whoever is doing whatever, it usually rattles me that such a noise came from inside me.

I opened my mouth and out flew the almighty "Hey!"

Goddamn, I wish I hadn't done that.

I suddenly had six or eight airborne big pigs pirouetting in the air, squealing their heads off and ramming the boards of the enclosure, threatening to destroy it. I was hanging onto the door trying to keep from being killed by a porcine juggernaut and inwardly cursing myself for stirring them up. A cattle stampede is nothing compared to a pig frenzy. I kept glancing over at the figure which seemed to be hitching up its clothing and reaching forward. In front of him was a pig which he had tied to the corner post loosely. I say loosely because it seemed to take no time for him to slip the short length of rope off the pig and post and toss it off into the darkness of the barn. The pig joined the others leaping and rushing and roaring around the enclosure. I was motioning to the person I still couldn't recognize to come toward me and attempting to dodge and shush the pigs at the same time. I knew you said "Soooooooey" when you wanted to call them, but I had no idea what sort of noise to make to assure them they were not under siege. The kid was up on the boards out of harm's way.

Finally, he began to ease his way around the edge toward me, squishing through the dung and straw. As he entered the light, I saw it was Rob Richie. Finally he crawled over the pen and was beside me. I turned out the light and closed the door and locked it.

"Where'd you get the key?"

"Had it made on T.A." I remembered that the farm-key had disappeared some months earlier and we had to use the P.O. keys until we could get another made and then the missing key turned up again.

"Do you have any idea how much trouble you're in?"

He nodded.

"For a pig? Gawdalmightydamn, you fucking nitwit!" Now that I hadn't been killed by rampaging porkers, I could feel hysterical laughter coming on. The sight of all that flying, wheeling, squealing bacon came back to me and I was gone. I sat down on the bench outside the pig barn, put my head between my knees and roared until I didn't have a molecule of breath left to laugh with.

Out of the corner of my eye, I saw the little bastard tuck the last bit of his shirt in his pants, pivot and sprint up the trail toward the Southview part of the property. I brought the radio up to my face, but exploded into laughter again. I plunked the radio down on the bench and reached in my pocket for my chewing tobacco. I opened it, but feared I would begin to laugh again, swallow a great glob and begin to hiccup wildly. I stuck it back in my pocket.

All the way back to the dorm, my mind was full of likely scenarios. In courtrooms where the kid is charged with bestiality or about to be breached on his parole and is appealing the breach, I could see myself being asked, "Officer Yates, can you identify the pig? Did you actually see penetration? Were there any other witnesses?"

Just about that time, the ministry had closed Pine Ridge Camp because of cutbacks and were threatening us. Burns and Gosse were doing battle at all levels to keep the institution open. I wasn't going to jinx them. Anyway, by the time I got back to the dorm to grab all my gear and drive home, I was still too convulsed to talk to anyone. Some of the kids accused me of walking out to the farm and smoking wacky tobacky, and it must have looked that way. I dropped the radio in its charging nook, walked out the door, and drove up the hill.

22

Board Day

•

We are all just prisoners here of our own device . . .
The last thing I remember I was running for the door.
I had to find passage back to the place I'd been before.
– The Eagles

THERE is no better illustration of the commitment on the part of staff and trainees to the program at New Haven than board day, which is the last Wednesday of every month. This day is the pivot of the entire program, and it pulls together all parts of the New Haven tradition. Up from the bull-pen to the board came the duty-monitor slips for the month, neatly punched and threaded on a clipboard, as well as the extra-duties book (the record of all extra-hours assigned, confinements to rack, and other minor penalties). The handmade wooden lock-box containing all the trainee progress-log files resided upstairs during office hours and travelled down to the dorm for afternoon and graveyard shifts. On board day, it was usually in the administrative offices before breakfast.

Doing an imitation of Robin Williams in *Good Morning Vietnam,* as day man one board day, I whipped through the teams screaming, "Good morning, New Haven! Arise and go now . . . Those words are from Yeats, the lesser poet. Today is board day. First I'm going up to the meeting and sink all of you, and then I'm going to stay after shift and boo and hiss."

"Oh yeah, Mr. Yates, you just want to hang around for the steak dinner and banana cream pie."

On board day, getting them out of bed, cleaned up, inspected, and well-behaved at breakfast and lunch were no problem. For the trainees, from the standpoint of work, board day was like any other day, except everybody was "lookin' good." They knew their instructors would be going up to present their evaluations of the trainee and to defend them.

By nine, Colleen, the office manager, would have organized the boardroom and rounded up the board members: director, probation officer or senior correctional officer, sometimes a principal officer shows up, the day man (who is the day-shift dorm supervisor), and any other line staff who cares to drop in. All input was welcome.

About a week before board meeting, the board reports were distributed to staff in envelopes with the case manager's name on each. One whole side of the legal-size form inside was filled with boxes and there was a generous space at the bottom for lengthy comment by the case manager. The flip side of the sheet had room for comment by back-up case manager and comments by all other dorm staff. Each staff-member was required to comment on the progress of every trainee monthly. Comments varied from the glowing to the critical. With ten comments by line staff, it was easy for board-members to spot a mere personality conflict in a negative remark, as opposed to a constructive remark pointing up some deficiency.

In addition to the monthly board-report summary remarks, the board reviewed each progress-log from the date of the last board meeting, and earlier when necessary.

The sheets were rated in the categories of dependability, self-confidence, self-discipline, co-operation with staff, co-operation with peers, respect for authority, sportsmanship, cleanliness of the living area, setting and carrying through example and leadership.

If the trainee rates below average in four categories, he is not promoted. And this is the portion filled out monthly by the case manager only. If the trainee has been charged or has fallen behind in work or academics, he will begin losing days of remission – as many as six for his dorm behaviour, six for his vocational work, and three for his school work. With enough negative comment by staff other than case manager, he can be held back or demoted despite an average or above-average report from the case manager.

The pre-juniors are considered first. Pre-juniors are those who are admitted between board meetings. Ordinarily the board automatically passes them on to the junior level at the next meeting unless they have destroyed the place and utterly blown the program. Usually this would indicate that they are not suitable for an honour-system program and the likelihood they would be sent elsewhere is high.

Then come the juniors. It is assumed they have had their period of adjustment and know the program sufficiently that they can be judged by junior criteria. At each level the microscope is stronger and expectations higher.

At the intermediate level, the trainees work closely with the senior duty-monitor, who arranges his schedule of duty monitors for morning and afternoon shifts for the whole month. Intermediate is a make-or-break level. When a kid makes it from intermediate to senior, you can notice the change in his sense of responsibility. The seniors and senior T.A.s carry the heaviest burden of role model.

It is great to watch them come into full bloom at this level. They know they're getting close to T.A. and the whole world is going to trust them to go on social temporary absence, job-search, then work release and educational T.A. And they've earned every step of the way.

After the board members have sifted through the reports (it takes some time to read all the comments from so many staff about forty trainees), one instructor after the other is sent in to present his evaluation of his crew.

By this time, everyone is well-focussed. When the instructor enters and delivers his evaluation, the atmosphere changes somewhat. The kids at work are very visible to everyone, including the director, who moves around the campus in a non-spying way and gets to know the trainees, as does the probation officer. The instructor controls as many days of remission as the dorm staff, but his crew is being judged by only one observer.

We had one instructor for a time who didn't make the transition from working in maximum to the open setting of New Haven very well. To say the least, he didn't bring out the best in his crews. In one case, we had a black kid with a long juvie record who had worked his ass off in all parts of the program. It was extra hard for him, because he hadn't fully decided whether the attention garnered from doing well in the program was preferable to the attention that came with minor rebellion.

Often, in the midst of debate among dorm staff, instructor, and probation officer, it was necessary for the director to step in and referee and render a deciding vote when the forces seemed divided. The problematic instructor wanted to dock the boy three days of remission for not doing enough work. Before the rest of us could jump the instructor, the director was in his face: "I've watched that kid down there working like a dog; he's into body-building and loves physical work." The instructor protested and then everyone jumped into the fray. The boy didn't lose his days of remission. But this meeting, like many board meetings, went well past noon and had to be finished up after lunch.

On board days, the kids get off work at three. They quickly shower and set out the chairs in the main lounge of the dorm in an auditorium arrangement and bring in a lectern. The director enters with the board reports. Silence falls over the showered, shaved, and clean-clothed trainees, and over whatever staff have elected to sit in. The director begins with a recounting of the history and purpose of the board meeting and the read-back. This takes about ten minutes.

Then, as his name is called, each trainee rises and stands while every word on the board report is read aloud before all and every officer who has written each comment identified. As each report is concluded, it is announced whether the trainee has been promoted, held back, or demoted. Each trainee who is promoted is resoundingly and sincerely applauded. For those who are held back or demoted, there is silence, but no derision.

Following the read-back comes an especially elegant steak dinner with a sense of a century of tried-and-true tradition still in the air. The trainees congratulate one another and the seniors begin to plan what they will do on their first temporary absences. Into the evening, the new senior duty monitor is appointed, as are the new team captains and assistant team captains, and work begins on putting together a fair plan for the various crews who will be responsible each night for cleaning the lounge and upper lobby, duties for the teams, and so on. The computer monitor assists them in typing up the various lists on the word processors. All the organizational problems are theirs to solve, and by the time they leave New Haven, they are well on their way to organizational wizardry.

A kid named Davey was coming up for parole soon. His institutional record was flawless. He had participated in and excelled at every New Haven program that came down the pike, including the maiden voyage of Hoods in the Woods. Inasmuch as the beef was fairly heavy – no matter how well a parole applicant has prepared, there is always the wild card of "intent of sentence." At this point, when all "roots in the community" and institutional-record criteria have been satisfied, then the process becomes quasi-mystical. The discretion of the parole board in interpreting intent of sentence is essentially unlimited.

When I came back on graveyard after a few days of annual leave, it was the Sunday before the Tuesday of Davey's appearance before the board. I checked over his application for parole. It had been filled out by a probation officer who was part burn-out, part malingerer, and part simply perverse. An essential ingredient of the institutional record is the institutional record summary, which is to be filled out by the case manager, or by the back-up case manager if the C.M. is not on shift cycle. Anderson hadn't lied about Davey's record, but he had couched the report in such flaccid and tepid language that it was sure to torpedo him. However, it was too late to redo the summary. The papers had already been processed. I needed to pull one out of the hat. Tuesday was two days away and I had two graveyards to pull.

I told Davey to put me on the appearance-list for the day of the parole hearing. I'm sure that between Monday and Tuesday the probation officer ripped through all the manuals looking for some regulation to prevent my appearance. This just wasn't done. On the other hand, there was nothing inscribed by the gods to prevent my doing so.

There was, however, one problem. The applicants lined up in order of appearance in the boardroom of the heritage main building, and it was impossible to know how long each hearing would take. I was scheduled for graveyard shift the night before. Davey would have to eyeball the progress of the queue, then call and wake me up in time to get a coat and tie on and get to New Haven. I had a graveyard on each side of parole day.

Tuesday came. At seven I headed up the hill to bed. Damn I was tired. I had just plunged over the edge into alpha sleep when the phone rang. "Mr. Yates, It's Davey. Matharoo is in there now and I'm next. All my folks are down from Prince George. It should be at least an hour before you need to be here. Is that enough time?"

"Yeah . . . fine." I was dead. Somehow I made it out of the shower without drowning, shaved, and got my best bib 'n' tucker on.

I dozed in the hall while waiting. Once I got inside, the three-person parole panel gawked at me. It was rather awkward. I assumed that it must be my red-eyed appearance. Maybe the collar of my sports coat was up. Possibly I had grannyed instead of Windsored my tie. I apologized. It did nothing to alleviate the tense atmosphere. All four of us in the room were writhing and nothing was happening.

Finally, a grey-haired gent introduced the panel and explained that they were a little taken aback. It was the first time they had ever seen a guard appear at a parole hearing.

"Normally, I wouldn't be here," I admitted. "The appearance of the case manager would be redundant to his written summary of the trainee's institutional record. I am here because I have just returned from holidays and the summary was written in my absence, and not to my satisfaction. The text you have before you doesn't accurately reflect this young man's experience at New Haven." I listed the number of foreman positions he had held, his work as senior duty monitor, his drug- and alcohol-program attendance, and his demeanour on the hike. Although still half-asleep, it seemed to me that I was holding forth like the silver-tongued devil I am. They were all nodding like ornaments in the back window of a car. And I don't think they were listening to a word I said.

When I paused, they began firing questions at me about me. Was I typical of New Haven staff? Yes, I thought so. Would other guards in similar circumstances appear before them? The best of them would, without a second thought. On and on they went into my background, what institutions I had worked at before New Haven and how on earth had I made the transition from Oakie and Pretrial to New Haven.

I had no inkling I would be such a novelty. If they didn't parole Davey after this interrogation and loss of sleep, I was going to flip. I went home to bed. He was paroled, but he had another week to serve. He said that when he went into the meeting after me they were still astonished that I had made an appearance and began asking him questions he couldn't answer. After he went back to Prince George Davey called me a couple of times, but he was very busy in a heavy-duty mechanic-apprentice program.

During the ten years I had been a guard, I had never been to charm school or any other do put on by the Ministry of Attorney-General. So when Director Burns asked me whether I'd like to attend a forthcoming corrections conference, I thought it was a joke. But Burns didn't seem to be joking. He wasn't.

When I got to the conference, I must say I was very impressed. They had people there who talked about financial planning for wage-slaves. They had workshops on day care for shift-workers. It was so well put together that I had to make deals with others to take notes when workshop schedules conflicted. I went expecting to be disappointed and came away with the feeling that I had just attended the best conference of my life.

The first and last sessions were plenaries. The conference kicked off with a motivational speaker and wrapped up with three speakers from the media. On the last day, at the last session, there was a panel of media types from radio, television, and the *Vancouver Sun*.

Chuck Foote, the principal officer who did my evaluations, later told Burns: "During the conference, I was beginning to think that

Yates was sick. Then when the rest of us were standing at the back of the room at the media thing and Yates sat alone in the front row, I knew the shit was about to hit the fan."

My experience in corrections had given me a very different view of media than I had had when I worked in the field. Countless times I and others had called journalists to persuade them to do stories on interesting programs we had cooked up. Nothing. Many of these people I knew in my writing capacity, others were people I had known or who had worked for me when I was a CBC executive. I couldn't budge them even by calling in favours they owed me. They showed up only to report escapes, riots, or allegations of "excessive force" by staff.

The maximum units (especially remand) accepted this relationship fairly stoically. However, the juvenile sentenced units and adult-program units like New Haven needed media mileage, because they require a constantly renewed volunteer base. When you come up with a good program, adult or juvie, the kids jump aboard and suddenly energy and logistical support are in short supply. Thanks to the paucity of media support, our volunteer base at New Haven was comprised chiefly of line staff blowing their days and hours off work. Those of us who used our time off had no regrets about what we were doing.

It was the obdurate spirit of the media that created the adversarial nature of the corrections–media relationship. At that final session, the room crackled with "fear and loathing" on both sides. Gordon Hoag, who introduced the media panellists and had some prefatory remarks, could scarcely contain his own rage. He was director of Willingdon Youth Detention Centre (the juvenile counterpart to Oakalla), and the mayor of White Rock to boot.

For thirty or forty minutes, the panellists held forth on journalistic ethics. There was so much news to cover that they simply couldn't be everywhere all at once, nor could they cover a great many of the stories in which they were personally interested. The kid from the *Sun* was obviously embarrassed by the radio and television idiots. I felt particularly testy about the television reporter. The last major riot at Oakalla involved the escape of thirteen industrial-strength inmates. All but one had been apprehended. This television reporter made B.C. corrections look like Bozo City by making contact with the last hold-out and filing a report each night showing the inmate yammering into the camera. The reporter claimed source privilege and refused to tell police, corrections, or anyone else the whereabouts of the escapee.

Principles aside, and the image of law enforcement aside, the inmate had a long history of violent crime and this jerk journalist was putting the public at serious risk. This kamikaze pilot was taking his life in his hands just by showing up at the conference. He was about as welcome as the rapper Ice-T at a police convention following release of his "Cop Killer" number.

When the panellists finally finished and the floor was open for questions, no one went to the microphone. Hundreds of line officers from all over the province just sat or stood there, arms crossed, silent and sullen. I rose to speak with no idea where to begin, but begin I did. Before I said a word there was scattered applause from the back of the room.

"Gentlemen, I have been in media, as a reporter, in production, as an ad rep, as an executive, and on air, longer than any of you up there – with the possible exception of the man from the talk station. I won two International Broadcasting Awards for my radio work. And I didn't win them for misrepresenting and outright lying as you have just done before us.

"Your representation of the face of media today makes me ashamed that I ever had anything to do with media. You speak of journalistic ethics as though you could afford any. Why don't you have the stones to say that riots and escapes sell newspapers and win ratings? Prison programs that work, that save the taxpayer millions of dollars in the long term, just aren't what the public wants to read, see on television, or hear debated on talk radio.

"You aren't ethical, you're moral cowards. Right here. Right now. Cowardice is associated with the colour yellow, as in Hearst-Pulitzer yellow journalism. As in tabloid print-journalism. As in tabloid television.

"You stand there in your arrogance as though you don't dance to the tune of program directors and story editors and city editors, all of whom are being crowded by your sales department, circulation, and latest ratings.

"You do your utmost to depict inmates and line staff within a stereotypical adversarial relationship; it plays better to the public. Common sense would tell anyone that this is not accurate if inmates and guards are to live under the same roof for years on end. But then you're not in the common-sense business. You're not even in the news business. You're in the bad-news business.

"There isn't a person in this room who will argue with me when I tell you that a great shift is one in which no one has tried to kill himself or someone else, and in which there have been no injuries. But then that's not what you're looking for.

"When you have the opportunity to interview inmates, you catalyze their complaints about staff and conditions. When you interview prison personnel – and this is rare – you carefully cut the tape or edit the interview so that we emerge as the knuckle-dragging assholes you have made the public come to expect."

(As I spoke it was getting crazier and crazier behind me, with screws calling out: "Fucking A, Yatesie . . . Nail that TV asshole's nuts to the floor.")

"The institutions for which we work are a part of society and belong to the public. They are built and maintained by the taxpayers. The taxpayer has a perfect right to a tour of what he owns, to question staff, to question those inmates who waive protection of their confidentiality. Were it not for your perpetuation of taboos, I think the public would come through and have a look for themselves. Most certainly, they can't look to you for accuracy. And that, gentlemen, is unfortunate for us, for you, and definitely for those who bear the financial burden of maintaining the criminal justice system."

I stood to leave and noted that those behind me had the doors open and were filing out. The deputy minister and other Victoria brass were present. The D.M. rushed up onto the stage and grabbed the microphone: "Well, we certainly don't want to leave the impression that the Corrections branch considers the media the enemy."

That was the last I heard as he continued speaking to an empty hall. Outside, a friend from Pretrial praised my speech and added that my ass was probably grass – a possibility that was just dawning on me. But back at New Haven, there were many smiles from the brass, and not one word of reproach.

Postscript

———————— • ————————

There are guards who are more pleasant to be
around than others. There are inmates on the unit
who are friendly, others aren't. In other words,
people are people. How is this different from the
street? There are neighbours you like and neighbours
you don't, in jail and out of jail. I've done a lot of
time . . . People are people.
– John, a seasoned inmate, Vancouver Pretrial,
CFOX interview, 1984

IN MANY WAYS, it seems fitting that I completed this segment of my memoirs at this time. Issues of crime and what to do about them surround us in all media, especially in television programs like "Cops," "Unsolved Mysteries," "Law and Order," "L.A. Law," and "NYPD Blue."

If the percentage of the population apprehended in criminal activity were proportional to the percentage of media time and space devoted to crime, half the people of the planet would be behind bars. Or would they?

There are new directions in crime and punishment being tried, especially in the United States. Most of these new directions have to do with warehousing people in different ways, outside prison, including electronic monitoring (the convict sits at home with an electronic ankle-bracelet that alerts his custodians should he fail to report when specified or move outside specified boundaries). They have very little

311

to do with offering them skills that might lead to options other than crime.

Sooner or later we must ask Corrections to catch up to the rest of the criminal justice system. And, given the rising crime rate, Corrections had certainly better come up with some good ideas in a hurry.

The present trend in Corrections is to supplant the well-trained, experienced line officer with formidably secure architecture and sophisticated technology. But, in my experience, there is no substitute for staff, for jail-wisdom, for experience. Not computers (although they can greatly assist). Not fancy alloy bars.

In a frenzy of short-term accounting, provincial and federal governments are paring down the human component of the corrections system. This is the wrong road. Warehousing people in high-tech structures with vapid environments not only hardens the core of the still-changeable criminal, but burdens the taxpayer with long-term social costs. Both law-breaker and law-abider lose.

There are very serious responsibilities attendant upon not killing criminals. I think these have been very poorly defined and even more poorly shouldered.

Until recently in the history of civilization, we have killed criminals, not detained them and made them a burden on the citizenry after their conviction. They have already been a burden to the economy at the gateway of the criminal justice system by committing the crime, and a burden to the victim and the insurance company for their violation of person and property. If the state does not kill lawbreakers, then rehabilitation must be pursued, scientifically and imaginatively.

Programs such as New Haven indicate the better road, despite the fact that there will always be a few cons who are not amenable to any stripe of rehabilitation nor crazy enough to be routed to psychiatric institutions. "Dangerous offenders" may well have to go to ultra-secure prisons, but there is no way to proceed with the rest of the convicted populace (since we no longer exile or kill them) but *to presume them amenable to rehabilitation until proven otherwise.* I have watched carefully and thought about this for a long time.

This book has involved three groups of people: People in custody.

People not in custody. And guards who are neither in custody nor free of it.

Those who happen not to be in prison at the moment tend to think of themselves as free. Those who were locked behind bars early in their lives and have become "institutionalized" feel free only when in jail. These people have no talent or disposition for filing tax returns, remembering Aunt Flossie's birthday, obeying the speed limit, or attending the P.T.A. Being told by people like me when to rise, when to eat, when to change their clothes, suits them just fine. Just as it's hard for people on the outside to understand how anyone can love being in prison, the "institutionalized" cannot understand how anyone can love mowing the lawn, joining the Rotary Club, or running for office.

The line screw shuttles daily between these two worlds. We belong to the population in custody incompletely and we belong to everyday citizenry only incompletely. I'm not sure we ever know exactly who we are, but in our best moments we have some sense of being "very special people." We know that very few people can do what we do at all, let alone do it well. It is a high-wire act worthy of the Flying Wallendas.

Early in our careers as line officers, we are admonished to "leave it at the gate." I've yet to meet a prison guard who can leave it at the gate successfully. We're told to find someone we can talk to, who will help us "offload" the stress. Then we're told that it's against the law to speak to a civilian (your spouse, your best friend) about an incident or a case. The guards we might speak to likely were there at our side during the very incident we need to offload.

When I went to work at Oakalla, I knew nothing about correctional systems. I was, in fact, not aware that anyone (other than a few philosophers like Jeremy Bentham, who is revered by the literati as a weirdo) had spent much time thinking about *time* as a way to repay society for having broken the law. As young as this concept is in the history of ideas, it is something that the twentieth century has taken for granted.

The most ignorant of citizens is wed to the assumption that because someone has been caught breaking the very relative thing called the law (and the law is what it says it is at a given time and in a given place), he or she must pay the price of loss of humanity – all rights and privileges – by being locked in jail, where only inhuman things happen. This symbolizes his or her loss of humanity. Who, before reading this book, would believe me if I said this or that man, who has murdered more than one person, is my most dependable worker on the tier? Most people prefer to think that one illegal act colours all further acts. And that's nonsense. There are all manner of people who do something criminal in a moment of passion or desperation. Then there are psychotics who wind up in jail simply because they've contravened some statute of the Criminal Code; we watch them carefully and send them to Forensic for a psychiatric profile. And the man who gets drugged or drunk and commits an atrocity returns to his status as human being when his mind has washed free of the chemicals. When he relates to the world of prison as a human being, the prison relates to him in coin.

Those outside prisons seem to take for granted the impressions of prison life they read and see in the media. And so they consider people who work the line in the criminal justice system (including police, judges, and counsels) to be something less than fully human in a kind of filth-by-association paradigm. Prison staff resent this stigma, which is constantly re-energized by the media. This has made prison staff wary and uncommunicative. And this stance, in turn, has made the media even more certain that prisons have much to hide.

Until this cycle of mistrust, skewed as it is on both sides, is corrected, the stereotypes and taboos will persist, and understanding between taxpayer, inmate, media, and prison staff will remain unlikely.

As I hope *Line Screw* has shown, the reason that line staff and inmates have a working relationship is precisely because jail-wise inmates empathize with the problems of guards and jail-wise guards appreciate the world as seen from the vantage of inmates. Rookie inmates and rookie guards may upset the balance of the unit for a time, but their ignorance is taken into account by the jail-wise line.

After more than a decade of thinking about the line, I conclude that those who comprise it – inmates and guards – do their respective jobs rather well. I can't say the same for middle- and top-management public servants, who are at the mercy of political winds.

I further conclude that one who has spent as much time in jail as I have must possess an abiding love of prisons. Let me put it this way: the only career I pursued for a longer period than my career in corrections was teaching at university. On the best day at university, when my lecture was brilliant and my students were being enlightened beyond our wildest collective expectations, I was participating in the *ornamental.* On the worst day in prison, when everything was going wrong, I was participating in the *essential.*

To work the line is to be involved in the essential, the critical, the line between living and not living. Line cops, line screws, trauma-team members – all of us live on the line between life and death; we do this for a living. And some of us grow addicted to the work. After going to work at New Haven it took my body months to shed its expectation of a daily adrenalin rush. We have been called danger-junkies and various other disparaging terms. We don't get too excited; we know the value of the work we do, as do the cons, and, occasionally, the administration, when it remembers the line.

I wouldn't trade the prison segment of the line for any other segment. A prison is a magnificent living organism with a better balance of energy and form than most parts of society. The inmate code is as legitimate and respected a set of human mores as any code of conduct ever confected by Emily Post or Amy Vanderbilt.

Prison society – behaviour between guard and guard, inmate and inmate, guard and inmate – is perhaps the most accelerated dimension of human culture in the sense that most chemical reactions are speeded up by increased pressure, temperature, surface area, agitation. The law takes inmates and guards and places them in a container and applies as much pressure, temperature, and agitation as the system can deliver. The higher the population count, the greater the surface area that reacts to such pressure. Each change that comes from on high, if not gradually introduced, produces a reaction in the form of riot, sit-down, and so on. There is no time in prison for long-held grudges or back-biting. If there are problems, the explosion happens immediately. The resolution occurs immediately.

To get explicit: In my opinion there is not one well-managed correctional institution in North America. Not one. If ever the concept of shared-governance should apply, it is in corrections. Presently, because the public fear the stereotype of prisoners and won't penetrate the taboo of prison and examine what they own and maintain, prisons continue to be places where empires within empires are born. In this climate, any sort of inhumanity can occur.

This book, as you know by now, is not an exposé. There are no hidden brutalities or graft in the Canadian system to expose, that I know of. But our system is rife with opportunities for exploitation in many forms unless and until the public looks seriously at what we do with criminals.